Politics and Society in Scotland

Politics and Society in Scotland

Second Edition

Alice Brown

David McCrone

and

Lindsay Paterson

MACMILLAN

First edition 1996
Reprinted twice
Second edition

Published by
MACMILLAN PRESS LTD
Houndmills, Basingstoke, Hampshire RG21 6XS
and London
Companies and representatives throughout the world

ISBN 0-333-74708-9

A catalogue record for this book is available from the British Library.

This book is printed on paper suitable for recycling and made from fully managed and sustained forest sources.

Copy-edited and typeset by Povey–Edmondson
Tavistock and Rochdale, England

10 9 8 7 6 5 4 3 2 1
07 06 05 04 03 02 01 00 99 98

Printed and bound in Great Britain by
Creative Print and Design Wales, Ebbw Vale

Contents

List of Tables

Preface to the Second Edition

The electoral events of 1997 necessitate a revision of the edition that first appeared as recently as 1996. The return of a Labour Government for the first time in 18 years would, on its own, have made a difference to Scottish politics. But added to that were two unprecedented further massive shifts: the Conservative Party lost all its seats in Scotland at the general election for the first time ever, and in September the Scottish electorate overwhelmingly endorsed in a referendum not only the principle of a parliament for Scotland but also its capacity to alter the basic rate of income tax by a small amount. The prospects for politics and policy in Scotland were therefore transformed.

This new edition deals thoroughly with the changes. Chapters 7 and 9 have been revised to take into account survey data on the 1997 election. Chapter 5 has been completely rewritten to deal with the new prospects for policy-making. And Chapter 8 discusses the developments affecting women following a general election in which the proportion of MPs who are female rose to an all-time high (although still only 17 per cent). All the chapters have been revised to some extent to take account of the new situation and prospects.

Yet for all that the book remains true to its original intention of taking not only the point of view of political science but also those of sociology and history. According to these perspectives, the events of 1997 were less unexpected than a day-to-day journalistic commentary might suppose. What happened would not have surprised anyone who had read the first edition because the events were the culmination of trends that had been developing for half a century or more. This message was not fashionable when we first wrote it in 1995, still in the aftermath of the Conservatives' surprising victory in 1992. Its caution may be equally unwelcome now, as the country starts out on a new constitutional future. Of course a Scottish Parliament and the electoral destruction of the Conservatives matter. But many features of Scottish society and politics will continue to be shaped by the same forces that have been at work for many decades. The book is as much about these as it is about the undoubtedly important events that have occurred since it first appeared.

Why a new book on Scottish politics?

The time is ripe for a new textbook on Scottish politics and government. Since the mid-1950s Scotland has diverged considerably from England in its patterns of political behaviour. The weakness of the Conservatives north of the border is complemented by a discourse of nationalism used not only by the Scottish National Party (SNP), but also by the Scottish Labour Party and the Scottish Liberal Democrats. The emergence of a distinctive political agenda in Scotland is, however, poorly understood. On the one hand it is often treated merely as a negative reaction to Conservative hegemony in England. On the other, it is seen as an abstruse and idiosyncratic legacy of former statehood with very few lessons for other societies. This book takes issue with both viewpoints. It argues that Scotland has had a high degree of civil autonomy within the post-1707 British and later UK state, and that a political process emerged through which conflict with Westminster is managed and negotiated. Towards the end of the twentieth century the compromise between Scottish civil society and the UK state is being renegotiated so that a Parliament with control over most domestic affairs will be re-established in Edinburgh after almost 300 years. It is impossible to say whether this will ultimately lead to full formal independence in the twenty-first century as Nationalists hope and Unionists fear.

The book also takes issue with the view that Scotland is a special case. The UK developed as a unitary state but containing considerable national diversity within it. It is becoming clear that (as Daniel Bell, the American sociologist, pointed out) the nation-state is too small for the big problems of life, and too big for the small ones. In states like the UK the contradictions between unitary state structures and internal national diversity have become most apparent. The conventional nation-state no longer has the capacity to control in any meaningful way its economic, political and cultural sovereignty. We will argue that the Scottish case should be seen as an exemplar, even a forerunner, for new political arrangements in which shared and limited autonomy between different levels of government – Scottish, British and European – become more common. In this regard Scotland has to be seen as a marker for the future, not a deviant case.

This book provides an up-to-date review of Scotland's politics in the widest sense. It provides a historical overview of the relationship between politics and civil society in Scotland since 1707 (Chapters 1 and 2); analysis of its constitutional position within the UK and its system of policy-making (Chapters 3 and 5); an account of the development of its economy within political constraints (Chapter 4); a description and analysis of patterns of party political and electoral change (Chapters 6 and 7); a discussion of the changing role of women in Scottish politics, both formal and informal (Chapter 8); and an examination of the relationship between culture, identity and ethnicity (Chapter 9). Conclusions – for Scotland and for other nations too – are drawn in Chapter 10.

Three ways of looking at politics

Thus the book draws on a variety of academic disciplines, looking beyond the institutions of politics to their base and origins in the wider society. The institutions and the events of politics do have their proper place in the book, of course, and this political science approach is our first way of looking at politics. Before we can consider explanations of events, we have to know what is going on in the first place and who is taking part. A large part of the book is concerned with events, agencies and people. Chapter 6, for example, looks at the political parties in Scotland: they have a dynamic of their own which has to be discussed separately from any assessment of their popular support. The outcomes of politics matter, if only because the victors get access to power. So Chapter 1 is primarily concerned with who won, and only secondarily with explaining why. Another way of putting this point about the importance of events is that the explanation of the politics of the 1990s may partly be a matter of what is going on in society in general, but it is also strongly influenced by what happened in politics at earlier points in time. Margaret Thatcher's victories, and Scottish political reactions to these, are as much a given fact of 1990s politics as is, say, the changing social-class composition of Scottish society.

However, in this book the institutions and events of current politics are set in a social and historical context: our second and third ways of looking at politics. We aim to provide an explanation of Scottish politics in the context of Scottish society and the way in which that has changed over time. Thus the current debates about the role of women cannot be understood if we look only at events within the political domain. Certainly the arguments about how to get more women into elected office are most obvious and vociferous among politicians and political activists, but the pressures to which they are responding come from deeper changes in the position of women in Scottish society, which are sometimes only tenuously related to political action. These topics are covered throughout the book, but especially in Chapter 8.

Another current example is in the European dimension. The politics of this in Scotland now has many aspects, from the SNP's policy of 'independence in Europe' through the Labour and Liberal Democrat proposals for direct representation of a Scottish Parliament in the UK delegation to the Council of Ministers, to the Conservative Party's view that Scotland's European interests are best served by a combination of a Scottish Office base in Brussels and the occasional participation of Scottish Office Ministers in the UK delegation. But these political debates can be understood only if we look also at the growing economic importance of the European Union (EU) in Scotland (Chapter 4), and the cultural changes which have brought a European identity into Scottish life as 'Britishness' has declined (Chapter 9). This growing European dimension to Scottish politics is dealt with at many places throughout the book.

Furthermore, if events and society both matter, then our third discipline is unavoidable: history. This is not a history book. It is primarily concerned with Scottish politics as it is now. But when is 'now'? Is it since the 1997 general election when the Conservative Parliamentary representation was wiped out in Scotland? Or is it since 1979, when the referendum on a Scottish assembly failed to deliver one, and when Margaret Thatcher came to power? It cannot be that either, because why Thatcher won, why Scotland did not support her, and why devolution did not command widespread enthusiastic support are crucial questions for understanding what happened in Scottish politics in the early 1980s; and answering these questions involves going right back to the type of welfare state that was established in Scotland from the 1930s onwards. History, then, comes into this book as a way of explaining the present.

So the book is an attempt to explain Scottish politics using a variety of academic approaches, and paying attention to debates about the nature of late twentieth-century politics in general. Scottish politics are not only interesting in their own right; they also have lessons for small nations throughout Europe and beyond. And, in a world of supra-national government and limited sovereignty, all nations are now 'small', and so the Scottish experience is potentially relevant to everyone.

ALICE BROWN
DAVID MCCRONE
LINDSAY PATERSON

Acknowledgements

This book is a collaborative work to which each author contributed equally: the order of names on the title page reflects only the alphabet. We are grateful to Paula Surridge for help in understanding the statistical variables in the Scottish Election Study (used extensively in Chapters 7 and 9). The responsibility for interpreting it is entirely our own. We are grateful also to Professor John Fairley for commenting on a draft of the book, to John Hughes for permission to use Tables 4.1 and 4.5 and to Professor James Kellas and Oxford University Press for permission to use Table 6.1.

List of Abbreviations

CBI	Confederation of British Industry
CP	Communist Party
DORA	Defence of the Realm Act
EOC	Equal Opportunities Commission
ET	Employment Training
EU	European Union
FRG	Federal Republic of Germany
GDP	Gross domestic product
HIDB	Highlands and Islands Development Board
ILP	Independent Labour Party
ITBs	Industrial Training Boards
LECs	Local Enterprise Companies
LRC	Labour Representation Committee
MEPs	Members of the European Parliament
MSC	Manpower Services Commission
MSPs	Members of the Scottish Parliament
NPS	National Party of Scotland
PR	Proportional representation
SCOW	Scottish Convention of Women
SDA	Scottish Development Agency
SDF	Social Democratic Federation
SED	Scotch/Scottish Education Department
SES 92	*Scottish Election Survey*, 1992
SES 97	*Scottish Election Survey*, 1997
SHRA	Scottish Home Rule Association
SLP	Scottish Labour Party
SNL	Scots National League
SNP	Scottish National Party
STUC	Scottish Trade Union Congress
STV	Single transferable vote
SWRC	Scottish Workers' Representation Committee
TC	Training Commission
VAT	Value added tax

Chronology

1965   Formation of Highlands and Islands Development Board

1965   Scottish Unionist Party changes name to Scottish Conservative and Unionist Party

1967   By-election: Winnie Ewing wins Hamilton for SNP from Labour

1969   Wheatley Commission on Local Government Reform

1973   Formation of Manpower Services Commision

1973   Kilbrandon Commission on the Constitution: recommends elected Scottish assembly

1974   General election (February): Labour (40 seats); Conservatives (21 seats); Liberal Democrats (3 seats); SNP (7 seats)

1974   General election (October): Labour (41 seats); Conservatives (16 seats); Liberal Democrats (3 seats); SNP (11 seats)

1975   Formation of Scottish Development Agency

1975   Local government reorganisation

1979   Referendum on Labour Government's scheme of Scottish devolution: in a turnout of 64 per cent , 52 per cent vote yes to a Scottish Assembly.

1979   General election: Labour (44 seats); Conservatives (22 seats); Liberal Democrats (3 seats); SNP (2 seats). Conservatives, led by Margaret Thatcher, win power at UK level

1980s

1983   General election: Labour (41 seats); Conservatives (21 seats); Liberal Democrats (8 seats); SNP (2 seats)

1986   Formation of Standing Commission on the Scottish Economy

1987   General election: Labour (50 seats); Conservatives (10 seats); Liberal Democrats (9 seats); SNP (3 seats)

1988   Third Claim of Right: call for a Scottish parliament, and assertion of the sovereignty of the people of Scotland

1988   By-election: Jim Sillars wins Govan for the SNP from Labour

1989   Scottish Constitutional Convention established, as recommended in the Claim of Right

1989   Establishment of Scottish Enterprise and Highlands and Islands Enterprise

1989   Poll Tax introduced in Scotland

1990s

1990   Margaret Thatcher resigns as Prime Minister, replaced by John Major

1992   General election: Labour (49 seats); Conservatives (11 seats); Liberal Democrats (9 seats); SNP (3 seats)

1992   Government begins 'Taking Stock' exercise

1992   European Summit (Edinburgh, December) marked by Democracy March

1993   Scottish Constitutional Commission set up for one year

1993   Formation of Scottish Labour Women's Caucus

1994   Labour Party changes its name to Scottish Labour Party

1994   Death of John Smith, leader of the Labour Party

1994   Monklands East By-election – Helen Liddell holds the seat for Labour (June) against strong challenge from SNP

1994   Report of the Scottish Constitutional Commission to the Scottish Constitutional Convention

1994   Local government etc. (Scotland) Bill receives Royal Assent (November) – formation of 32 all-purpose local authorities fully operational in April 1996

1995   First meeting of the Scottish Civic Assembly (March)

1995   First elections for the new shadow local authorities (April)

1995   By-election: Roseanna Cunningham wins Perth and Kinross for SNP from Conservatives (May)

1995   Appointment of Michael Forsyth as Secretary of State for Scotland (July)

1995   30 November: St Andrews Day. The Scottish Constitutional Convention announces its plans – *Scotland's Parliament, Scotland's Right*

1996   The new councils, 29 mainland and three island, take up office in April

1996   The 250th anniversary of the Battle of Culloden in April

1996   Tony Blair announces (Edinburgh, June) a referendum on the tax-raising element of a Scottish Parliament.

1996   The Stone of Destiny is returned to Edinburgh Castle in November

1997   General election (May): Conservative Party loses all its seats in Scotland; Labour (56 seats), Liberal Democrats (10 seats) and SNP (6 seats)

1997   The new Labour Government publishes its White Paper *Scotland's Parliament* in July

1997   In the September Referendum, in a turnout of 60 per cent, 74 per cent vote Yes to a Scottish Parliament and 63 per cent vote Yes to its having tax-varying powers

1997   The Scotland Bill is published in December, and laid before the Westminster Parliament.

1

Scottish Politics, 1707–1997

The purpose of this chapter is to trace the emergence of Scottish politics as it is currently understood. There are four sections, dealing with the eighteenth century, the nineteenth century, the growth of the welfare state in the twentieth century, and the campaigning for a Scottish Parliament since the 1960s. Although the main part of the chapter deals with the period since 1945, and especially the last 30 years or so, the roots of these recent developments lie far back in the early nineteenth century or before. This chapter is not a substitute for the many good histories of Scottish politics in the eighteenth and nineteenth centuries, but our intention is to take from these the events, processes and ways of thinking that had the most long-lasting effects. Several of the topics in this chapter are expanded in later chapters: for example, party politics in Chapter 6, and the role of women in politics in Chapter 8.

Many histories of Scotland have focused on three key national institutions as forming the basis of Scottish autonomy – the church, the legal system, and the education system. Our view is broader. Certainly this 'holy trinity' matters a great deal. Until the end of the nineteenth century, the autonomy of the church guaranteed the autonomy of other areas of social life, because the church ran many other institutions directly, as will be discussed in detail in this chapter and in Chapter 3. The main religious tradition was Presbyterian Protestantism, Scotland having gone through a more thorough version of the sixteenth-century Reformation than almost any other country in Europe. According to Presbyterianism, the government of the church was (in theory at least) under the democratic control of the male members of the local congregation; in particular, there were no bishops. This tradition was dominated by the Church of Scotland until the mid-nineteenth century, when it split in two, but that schism if anything strengthened the hold of Presbyterianism on Scottish religion. Other Scottish Christian denominations were independent too – most notably Roman Catholicism and the Scottish part of the Anglican Communion, the Episcopal Church.

The separate legal system has always forced London Governments to pay some attention to Scotland, if only to ensure that legislation was correctly drafted to fit in with Scots law. Scots law is based on the Roman law of continental Europe rather than the case law of the English system: Scots lawyers like to think of the law as being based on first principles as much as on legal precedent. In practice, though, Scots law has absorbed a great deal of the English style, and so what matters politically is that the institutions of Scots law have remained independent – the courts, the legal training and the professional associations of lawyers.

And a different educational tradition has ensured that people in Scotland have undergone a distinct pattern of socialisation. In the eighteenth and nineteenth centuries, the structure of parish schools offered opportunities for access to literacy and to universities which were more open to diverse social groups – girls and the skilled working class, for example – than in most other European counties, and were far more open than the English system. Because the Scottish universities were autonomous and had their own styles of teaching and learning, the Scots professions of the nineteenth century – people who gained their initial education in these institutions – were distinctively Scottish in their outlook and intellectual style. As one historian has put it, these people exhibited 'a willingness to make connections between diverse subjects, an interest in general theories, and a tendency to make use of systematic classifications and abstract categories' (Anderson, 1983, p. 31).

The parish schools were founded by the churches, but were taken over by the state in the twentieth century. But the autonomy of the education system from the central British state remained, evolving a continued distinctiveness of curriculum, examinations, teaching methods and social mix. Education has become one of the badges of Scottish identity, and attempts to interfere with it by English politicians have always been met with national hostility. In recent years, that has meant that Scotland resisted many of the educational reforms of the 1979–97 Conservative Government. This resistance forced these policies to be severely modified, and so the distinctiveness of Scottish education has been strengthened in the last twenty years.

But around these three institutions has grown a plethora of other bodies and practices which have become important in their own right in preserving and developing Scottish autonomy – for example, local government, industry, commerce, the Scottish Office, cultural institutions and the media. In the nineteenth century, for example, Scottish business and commerce were self-confident, self-financing and proud to be considered leaders in the British Empire. In the twentieth century, the Scottish Office – the Scottish branch of the UK central state – has taken over the administration of most areas of domestic policy, frequently thereby being able to modify policies which have been devised in London. And the media is ranked by some commentators alongside the original holy trinity as a bulwark of Scottish identity: nine out of every ten newspapers bought on weekdays in Scotland are produced in Scotland for a specifically Scottish market (and seven or eight out of ten on Sundays). This has both reflected a different social and political agenda in Scotland, and also helped to create it.

In Chapters 2 and 3, we provide some theoretical ideas through which to understand this wider concept of 'civil society'. In this chapter we trace how it evolved.

Scotland in the eighteenth century: integration and autonomy

Three key events shaped eighteenth-century Scottish politics: the Union of 1707, the defeat of the Jacobite rising of 1745 and the British wars against France. These events and their consequences laid the basis for a politics that is recognisable to us today.

The Union marked the end of the Scottish Parliament, as it voted to dissolve itself into the new Parliament of Great Britain. The debate about the meaning of the Union is endless. But two points are important for our purposes here: that it took place, thus removing the legislature from Scotland, and that it left Scottish civil society more or less intact. Civil society is discussed more fully in Chapter 2, but for present purposes it can be thought of as all those institutions that lie between the individual and the state. In Scotland, as we will see, these were autonomous, and had roots stretching back to before the Union. Parliament in London kept out because on the whole it was not interested, unless there was a threat to the peace and security of Britain as a whole.

Indeed it was such a threat that led to the second key event, the defeat of the Jacobites. The Jacobites were not merely a colourful and romantic episode (the view that holds in Scotland today), or a simple rebellion on the northern border (the view that probably most English people have if they have one at all); it was the British instance of a Europe-wide civil war between Catholicism and Protestantism. The revolutions of 1688–90 – peaceful in England, less so in Scotland, and bloody in Ireland – had secured the British monarchy for the Protestant cause, displacing the Catholic King James VIII. There were recurrent attempts in the first half of the eighteenth century to restore him, most of them supported by the Pope and by one or other of the continental Catholic powers, notably France and Spain. So when the 1745 rising was thoroughly and ruthlessly crushed in 1746, a half century of potential instability was at an end.

What was at stake here was not merely the religion of the monarch: it was the preservation of the limited but real liberties which the 1690 settlement had secured. Two and a half centuries later, with the accretion of a century and a half of religious sectarianism, it is difficult to imagine just how stark the choice was. The values that became free trade, representative democracy and pluralism were, on the whole, the preserve of the Protestant nations of Europe, amongst which Scotland was proud to count itself. And, though by the nineteenth century Catholics in Scotland were persecuted and the object of contempt, the eighteenth-century Catholic church and its political allies in Europe were in fact threatening and despotic.

So the defeat of Jacobitism ensured that the British state would continue along the path on which it had been embarking at least since the Union: the free market in trade, Protestantism in religion and rationalism in social thought. All three of these were influential in the Scottish politics of the late eighteenth century, as we will see.

In defeating the Jacobites, the state was also striking a blow against their sometime sponsors, France. But from the middle of the eighteenth century, too, there was a series of wars directly against France. These started when that country was ruled by its *ancien régime*, and so the British role could be understood as a defence of liberty. After 1789 the liberty that was being defended was counterposed in British propaganda to the revolutionary terror of republican France. Either way, though, what mattered in Scotland was the unprecedented popularity which these wars gave to being British. A new patriotism was invented, one that fitted well with the rival national identity of Scotland because Britishness was so firmly grounded in Protestantism. To secure their Scottishness, it was believed, the Scots had to be British, because otherwise the central element of that Scottishness – their religion – would be endangered.

While these foreign affairs were helping to secure Scottish politics into a British framework, the politics of Scottish civil society followed a course that was probably not much different from the direction that would have been followed had Scotland retained a Parliament. Linking Scotland with London was the system of elite politics around the Scottish 'manager', the man entrusted by the British Government to coordinate the views of Scottish MPs, and to channel Scottish concerns to London, somewhat like the role of the Secretary of State for Scotland now. The most influential of these managers was Henry Dundas (later Viscount Melville), whose term of office lasted more or less unbroken from the 1760s until after the end of the century. But if his role was like the twentieth-century Secretary of State, it differed because of the absence of party politics in the modern sense, and because bribery and nepotism were accepted parts of political life. As a result, Dundas dispensed enormous amounts of patronage – appointments to public posts in Scotland, but later also in India where he acquired influence too – in return for the support of Scottish MPs. It has to be added that some late twentieth-century commentators suggest cynically that the patronage is not really different from that exercised by the Secretary of State now.

These elite activities had an impact on Scottish society through this patronage. But what mattered in shaping the lives of Scots was the self-governing local state: the independent Scottish Presbyterian church, the autonomous system of local government (burghs representing merchants and other professionals for urban areas and meetings of county landowners in the rural districts), and the separate Scottish legal system. These ran everything that nowadays we would call social policy although, of course, the extent of government involvement was far less than in the twentieth century. The church, through the parish, governed the elementary schools and administered relief for the poor. The burghs regulated and promoted trade. The prominent landowners of the county saw to the upkeep of roads and bridges. They had few regular dealings even with the administration in Edinburgh, far less with distant London. The main contact with London was when the central government needed to raise special taxes for military purposes (a contact that served to emphasise that the London link was about foreign affairs only).

This system of Scottish government was given ideological shape by the emerging ideas of rationality. It was believed that following reason in politics would produce a well-regulated society. It was also believed that reason was what made a polity civilised, and that the best guarantor of the rule of reason was the Protestant religion. Because England was regarded as the fount of reason and a bulwark of Protestantism, emulating that country became the major preoccupation of Scottish politicians, whether local or national. In their admiration for England, they were following a widespread European fashion, but they were also helping to shape it through the writings of the intellectuals of the Scottish Enlightenment: people such as the philosopher David Hume, the economist Adam Smith, the sociologist Adam Ferguson and the historian William Robertson. It should be added to this, though, that the people we now remember as the leaders of the Scottish Enlightenment – Hume and Smith, for example – were not the most politically influential at the time, partly because the very radicalism of their ideas (especially on religion) estranged them from the Scottish political elite. The main influence of Smith came later, in nineteenth-century Liberalism, and in some respects it was not until the twentieth century that Hume's stature as a philosopher was secured.

At the same time, however, these people were also Scottish nationalists. They defended Scottish culture where it did not threaten the link with England, but that veneration for the Union was itself based on the more fundamental beliefs in reason. So it was not Englishness that was preferred to Scottishness, it was reason; and England was merely the means to that. The Scottishness that could be indulged in was sometimes political or religious (for example, Scottish control of its church, or of its legal system). But the criterion that was invoked to decide what features of distinctive Scottish politics should be retained was whether distinctiveness would best permit the freedom of the Scots to pursue their own private concerns. For many matters, the model that seemed best able to achieve that was English or (as the new state evolved) British, and the old Scottish model retained its association with what was seen to be the unfree condition of the pre-Union era. The Scottishness that could be safely developed was precisely those areas of life that were not political, such as the family, language or folk song.

So eighteenth-century politics bequeathed four main things to the politics of the nineteenth and twentieth centuries:

- a belief that political problems are amenable to rational solutions;
- a tendency to regard England as the fount of rational thought;
- the resultant view that the Union was the best way of defending Scottish political freedom, especially from enemies beyond Britain, many of whom were hostile to the Protestant religion;
- a consigning of Scottish culture to the realm of the private and therefore the non-political.

The reformed politics of the nineteenth century

This system of elite politics coupled with local self-government was placed under great strain in the first few decades of the nineteenth century. The essence of the conflict was a perception by the Whigs that the old system was dominated by the Tories. The Whigs were broadly the representatives of the emerging middle classes in the industrialising towns and cities, and they presented themselves as the true heirs of eighteenth-century rationalism. Their leaders, such as Henry Cockburn and Francis Jeffrey, believed that they were in the vanguard of rationalist and liberal thought for the whole of the civilised world.

There were two long-lasting political outcomes of this agitation. The first was the extension of the franchise in 1832–3, both for elections to the Parliament in London, and for the governing councils of the burghs and counties. Although this still left an electorate made up of only about 8 per cent of adult males, it nevertheless represented a vast democratisation compared to what had gone before, expanding the electorate by more than twelve-fold to 65 000. The result was that the Whigs – soon to be re-formed as the Liberal Party – dominated Scottish politics for almost the whole of the rest of the nineteenth century, aided by further extensions of the franchise in 1868 and 1885 (see Table 1.1).

The second major political change around this time was the split of the Church of Scotland in 1843. This Disruption was in protest

Table 1.1 *Votes and seats in Scotland, general elections, 1832–1997*

Year	Percentage of vote, no. of seats in parentheses					Turnout (%)	Number of seats uncontested	Total number of seats
	Labour	Conservative	Liberal	SNP	Other			
1832		21.0 (10)	79.0 (43)			85.0	15	53
1835		37.2 (15)	62.8 (38)			70.9	23	53
1837		46.0 (20)	54.0 (33)			68.0	22	53
1841		38.3 (22)	60.8 (31)		0.9	62.2	29	53
1847		18.3 (20)	81.7 (33)			51.1	37	53
1852		27.4 (20)	72.6 (33)			45.5	33	53
1857		15.3 (14)	84.7 (39)			66.3	38	53
1859		33.6 (13)	66.4 (40)			65.6	45	53
1865		14.6 (11)	85.4 (42)			70.7	37	53
Extension of franchise to all male householders and tenants								
1868		17.5 (7)	82.5 (51)			74.1	26	58
1874		31.6 (18)	68.4 (40)			70.9	22	58
1880		29.9 (6)	70.1 (52)			80.0	12	58
Extension of franchise to all male occupiers								
1885		34.3 (8)	53.3 (51)		12.4 (11)	82.0	5	70
1886		46.4 (27)	53.6 (43)			72.3	9	70
1892		44.4 (19)	53.9 (51)		1.7	78.3	0	70
1895		47.4 (31)	51.7 (39)		0.9	76.3	5	70
1900		49.0 (36)	50.2 (34)		0.8	75.3	3	70
1906	2.3 (2)	38.2 (10)	56.4 (58)		3.1	80.9	1	70
1910 (Jan).	5.1 (2)	39.6 (9)	54.2 (58)		1.1 (1)	84.7	0	70
1910 (Dec).	3.6 (3)	42.6 (9)	53.6 (58)		0.2	81.8	12	70

Extension of franchise to all men over 21, most women over 30

Year								
1918	22.9 (6)	32.8 (30)	19.1 (25) coalition		10.2 (2)	55.1	8	71
			15.0 (8) non-coalition					
1922	32.2 (29)	25.1 (13)	17.7 (12) Nat. Lib.		3.5 (2)	70.4	3	71
			21.5 (15) Lib.					
1923	35.9 (34)	31.6 (14)	28.4 (22)		4.1 (1)	67.9	4	71
1924	41.1 (26)	40.7 (36)	16.6 (8)		1.6 (1)	75.1	3	71

Extension of franchise to all women over 21

Year								
1929	42.3 (36)	35.9 (20)	18.1 (13)	0.2	3.5 (2)	73.5	0	71
1931	32.6 (7)	49.5 (48)	13.5 (15)	1.0	4.4 (1)	77.4	8	71
1935	36.8 (20)	42.0 (35)	6.7 (3)	1.1	1.8 (2)	72.6	1	71
	5.0 (4) ILP							
1945	47.6 (37)	41.1 (27)	6.7 (7) Nat. Lib.	1.2	3.3 (4)	69.0	0	71
	1.8 (3) ILP		5.0					
1950	46.2 (37)	44.8 (32)	6.6 (2)	0.4	1.6	80.9	0	71
1951	47.9 (35)	48.6 (35)	2.7 (1)	0.3	0.5	81.2	0	71
1955	46.7 (34)	50.1 (36)	1.9 (1)	0.5	0.8	75.1	0	71
1959	46.7 (38)	47.2 (31)	4.1 (1)	0.5	1.2	78.1	0	71
1964	48.7 (43)	40.6 (24)	7.6 (4)	2.4	0.7	77.6	0	71
1966	49.9 (46)	37.7 (20)	6.8 (5)	5.0	0.6	76.0	0	71
1970	44.5 (44)	38.0 (23)	5.5 (3)	11.4	0.6	74.1	0	71
1974 (Feb).	36.6 (41)	32.9 (21)	8.0 (3)	21.9 (7)	0.6	79.0	0	71
1974 (Oct).	36.3 (41)	24.7 (16)	8.3 (3)	30.4 (11)	0.3	74.8	0	71
1979	41.5 (44)	31.4 (22)	9.0 (3)	17.3 (2)	0.8	76.8	0	71
1983	35.1 (41)	28.4 (21)	24.5 (8)	11.7 (2)	0.3	72.7	0	72
1987	42.4 (50)	24.0 (10)	19.2 (9)	14.0 (3)	0.3	74.3	0	72
1992	39.0 (49)	25.6 (11)	13.1 (9)	21.5 (3)	0.8	75.4	0	72
1997	45.6 (56)	17.5 (0)	13.0 (10)	22.1 (6)	1.9	71.3	0	72

Note: ILP = Independent Labour Party (MPs joined Labour, 1947); Scottish Universities seat (abolished 1948) excluded.
Source: McCrone (1992), pp. 148–9.

against the influence which landlords could exercise over the appointment of ministers, something which offended against the nominally democratic base of Presbyterian church government. Some 40 per cent of the members left to form a new Free Church, which then set about building up a parallel system of churches, schools and poor relief. The protest was again led by the liberal middle class. The effect of the Disruption was to restrict the influence which either church could have on politics. For the rest of the century, although the dominant tone of politics remained firmly Protestant, the governing structures became mainly secular. Because it encouraged this secularisation, the Disruption was fundamentally important to the development of Scottish politics.

These political activities were led by elites, and benefited only them directly. But there was popular pressure too. Politics extended to the mass of the population. Agitation for parliamentary reform, or against the landlord influence in the church, was widespread among people who could not have expected to benefit directly (for example, working-class men, or women of any class). Popular politics also could be found in riots against bread shortages or against conscription into the militia, and indeed it was riots of that sort which provided the reason why the mass of the people did care about elite politics. A working-class person might not be able to look forward to being enfranchised, but would want the vote to be given to those elite social groups which would be most likely to look after working-class interests and respond to working-class political agitation. In most of Scotland, although more so in the urban than in the rural areas, the era had passed when Tory landlords were expected to do that.

The political system that emerged from the reforms and the accompanying turbulence was liberalism. Scottish liberalism shared key tenets with the liberal programmes of progressive politicians throughout Europe and North America. Central to it was a belief in free trade, and free markets more generally. The role of government was, in that sphere, to remove impediments to the smooth operation of the industrial economy. These attitudes were inherited from the rationalism of the eighteenth century, as was the accompanying belief in free speech and the right of individual citizens to be free of political interference in their private lives.

At the same time, though, Scottish liberalism developed a strongly paternalistic strand, influenced by the Protestant belief that those who had risen to the top of society had a duty to help those who were less well-off. In practice, this paternalism could be interpreted as anything between a fairly ruthless belief in self-help and something approaching a twentieth-century view that the state – or at least the local state – had a duty to intervene to compensate for the harmful effects of the free market.

Thus the Scottish middle class had a view of themselves as natural rulers, helping to free the rest of Scottish society from political oppression and material want. As the century progressed, they extended this vision beyond Britain to the Empire. Just as in the eighteenth century the Scots were happy to leave foreign affairs to a British realm, so now the Empire was seen as the arena in which the Union had had its greatest achievements. The plentiful supply of graduates from the Scottish universities travelled throughout the world as administrators of the Empire, even reserving special parts of it almost to themselves (for example the territories that are now north-west India and Malawi). They believed that they had a mission to spread Scottish liberalism and Scottish Protestantism, and that only the Union could have given them the political influence to do that. All the evidence is, moreover, that the mass of the Scottish population shared this enthusiasm for Empire: the Union was almost never seriously questioned at any time before the 1880s, and even then (as is discussed below) the questioning was about reform, not separation. Scottish trade – the basis of the flourishing heavy industry that became Scotland's staple – Scottish culture and Scottish identity had become intimately tied to the Empire and therefore to England.

The political identity that then flourished in Scotland has been described as unionist nationalism. On the one hand, Scotland had to be in the Union to realise its true potential as a nation: thus to be a true nationalist it was necessary to be a unionist. On the other hand, to be a true unionist it was necessary to be a nationalist because, in the absence of Scottish nationalist assertion, the Union would degenerate into an English takeover of Scotland. Scotland had to remind England (and itself) repeatedly that it was a partner in the Union, and that it retained the ultimate right to secede. The constitutional implications of this strange amalgam of nationalism and unionism are discussed further in Chapter 3.

However, if the Empire preoccupied Scottish MPs, the politics that directly affected Scottish people remained local. This is, indeed, the realm in which the Presbyterian paternalism could have its most profound impact, despite the decline in the direct influence of the church. The new system of local government was made up of an amalgam of elected councils and appointed boards. The boards oversaw a whole range of the emerging state involvement in social policy: the poor law, the elementary schools, the regulation of public health, the maintenance and development of transport, the setting of public morals through the police and prison systems, and the development of the Highlands and Islands.

If this was state involvement, however, it was emphatically local, and it was in that way that the principle of public involvement could be reconciled with liberal scepticism about the state. Local government could be thought of as like a branch of philanthropy, a partnership in which the burgeoning voluntary philanthropical societies had as important a role to play as the more formal structures. These societies also gave an active and influential role to middle-class women, thus bringing women into the governing of Scottish social policy for the first time. Women were also involved to a limited extent in the elected local state too, the local franchise being somewhat wider than for Parliamentary elections by the end of the century.

Nineteenth-century Scottish politics left a legacy that helped shape the politics of the twentieth century:

- the rhetoric of liberalism, applied to a widening range of social groups as the franchise was widened;
- an enthusiasm for the British Empire, as offering unrivalled opportunities for trade and for cultural influence, meaning then largely religious mission;
- a growing belief, founded in Protestant paternalism, that the state had a duty to intervene in society to regulate morality and to mitigate the bad effects of the free market.

The growth of the central state

Localism remained strong in twentieth-century Scottish politics, but this came increasingly into tension with the power of the central state. The key fact about this process, however, is that it was fought out largely within a Scottish realm, because Scotland developed its own version of the central state in the Scottish Office.

The origin of that body is in the creation in 1885 of the post of Scottish Secretary, in response to nationalist campaigning for Scottish matters to be given more attention by Westminster. There would have been no need for this if Westminster politics had remained confined to Imperial matters. The Scottish concerns – which spread across the spectrum of politics – arose because the central government was taking a growing role in social policy.

The Scottish Office has grown ever since. Its main period of expansion was between 1920 and 1940, when it took over the activities of the Scottish boards that had been inherited from the nineteenth century. In that period the Scottish Office became the defender of Scotland's national interest, equally under Labour or Conservative Governments. In a period when the main social questions had to do with the decline of heavy industry and the building up of the welfare state, the crucial political questions were about the distribution of state-sponsored resources. The Scottish Secretary, elevated to a Secretary of State with Cabinet rank in 1926, lobbied for greater public spending, special legislation, and generally for Scotland to be allowed to get on with developing her own welfare state free of interference (but also with access to the superior resources of the UK as a whole).

It was of the nature of this lobbying that much of it took place behind closed doors. It was not the public politics of a formally federal state, such as Canada, where the provincial premiers could come back from Ottawa waving their achievements in front of their electorates. But the Scottish politics were nonetheless distinctive for all that, and indeed may well have been all the more idiosyncratic because so much depended on the informal contacts that a small closed system could engender. This is discussed further in Chapter 3. The key point to note here is that Scottish politics were frequently invisible when compared to the politics of Westminster.

This welfare state was in large measure a response to the growth of support for the Labour Party, to which we will come shortly. But, given the legacy of the nineteenth-century paternalism, it is hardly surprising that the principle of state involvement commanded support far beyond the Labour movement. This consensus was not only a consequence of the popularity of the Liberal Party in Scotland, and with it of the socially reforming policies of the Liberal Government of 1906–10: it was also the result of the split which took place in the Liberal Party in 1886 over Irish Home Rule. The faction which left to form the Liberal Unionist Party displaced the Liberals from large parts of west-central Scotland, drawing on the newly enfranchised skilled working class, which in Scotland was over-whelmingly Protestant. Because of this strength, the amalgamation of the Liberal Unionist and Conservative Parties in 1912 was, in Scotland, effectively the takeover of the Conservatives by the Union-ists. The joint party in Scotland was then known as the Unionist Party until 1965 (and its official title is still 'the Conservative and Unionist Party'). Thus the Scottish political right came to be represented by a party that believed in state intervention, if only because it relied on working-class votes. Being a strongly Protestant party, the Unionists also drew on the Presbyterian ethic of civic responsibility that had dominated Scottish liberalism in the nine-teenth century.

Nevertheless, although the politicians who initiated reform were in the Liberal and the Unionist Parties, the pressure which induced them to make these moves came from the fear that their working-class support would drift to more radical parties. Radicalism had firm roots in Scotland: for example in the 1880s MPs affiliated to the Highland Land League were elected for constituencies in the north of Scotland. But the new Labour Party was in fact quite slow to develop in Scotland, essentially because of the strength of the Liberal Party, and it did not start to have a significant electoral impact until after the 1914–18 war. Even then, Labour in Scotland was dominated by the Independent Labour Party (ILP), which was affiliated to, but on the left of, the British Labour Party: in the general election of 1922, for example, 18 of Scotland's 29 Labour MPs were from the ILP. The ILP declined only after 1932 when it broke its links with the Labour Party. From the early 1920s Labour came to local power in the urban areas, but on the whole with the kind of consensual programme that was eventually acceptable to many supporters of the Unionist Party, and which helped almost to wipe out the Liberal Party by the 1940s.

The other source of unease for the established parties at this time was the extension of the vote to women. There was concern in the 1920s that women would not be happy about voting for conservative parties, and might even desert to a Women's Party. Although women had not been allowed to participate in most areas of electoral politics, women's organisations did have a record of successful and sometimes radical political action stretching back to the eighteenth century. The suffrage campaign of the first two decades of the twentieth century picked up on that radicalism, and in Scotland had a particular national flavour (tartan and the Scots language being prominent in suffrage demonstrations, for example). The campaign was quite successful in securing the support of large numbers of Scottish MPs and local authorities. The parties' new concern with social welfare was believed to make them especially attractive to women, as the state came to intervene in the life of the family to an unprecedented extent. But despite these efforts to attract the votes of women, the parties did not promote any more than a tiny number of women into elected office, as we will see in Chapter 8.

The system of government that emerged to deal with the new state role in welfare was, by the 1940s, commanding the support of most Scottish politicians. It was broadly agreed that the state should be the direct provider of health, education and financial support to people living in poverty. The state also took on a responsibility to plan the economy in such a way that unemployment would be reduced, if not ended altogether. And it was even agreed that the state should have some role in actually owning certain key industries and services: for example railways, coal mining and the generation of energy. The consensus also existed in England, but it was more extensive in Scotland.

So, when we put together this agreement on the need for state intervention with the view that the Scottish Office should be the defender of Scotland's national interest, we find by the 1940s that the focus of Scottish politics was on what was a Scottish semi-state of its own. The key political figures in the expansion of the Scottish Office were Walter Elliot, the Unionist Secretary of State in the late 1930s who prepared for the shift of the Office from London to Edinburgh in 1939; Tom Johnston of the Labour Party, who was Secretary of State in Churchill's wartime Coalition Government and who secured from Churchill a guarantee that the Scottish Office would be free to pursue its own solutions to Scotland's problems; and James Stuart, Conservative holder of the Office in the 1950s who consolidated its independence and who ensured that the new welfare state in Scotland would be managed with a distinct Scottish accent. Labour had abandoned its early belief in a Scottish Parliament in favour of managerial control of the implementation of policy and largesse from the UK state. Unionists opposed some of the state activity rhetorically, but in practice – when in government – they pursued it almost as enthusiastically as Labour.

All the parties also inherited that nineteenth-century view that Scotland was a partner in the Union: it could best realise itself as a nation if it remained within the Union, and could best ensure its status as a partner by always reminding England that Scotland was a nation, not a region. So the Unionist Party was nationalist and unionist at the same time, protesting against some of the 1945 Labour Government's proposals to nationalise industry on the grounds that it would remove control from Scotland to London. And the Labour Party asserted the needs of the areas of declining heavy industry in nationalist terms, couched in the language of the rights of the Scottish people to work. The politicians and civil servants in the Scottish Office used this opposition nationalism to put pressure on London for more resources. Nationalism of this moderate sort therefore became the taken-for-granted framework for all Scottish political debate.

The legacy of this system of governing Scotland provides the immediate background to the politics of the period from the 1960s onwards. There are two key components:

- that state intervention is justified to alleviate the harmful effects of the market and to promote social welfare;
- and that the Scottish Office should act as the defender of Scotland's national interests, providing the framework in which the state should intervene in Scotland.

Nationalist challenges

Alongside this official nationalism was campaigning of a more militant sort, advocating a directly elected Scottish Parliament. There was a long tradition of support for such a Parliament, stretching back to the middle of the nineteenth century. It was present in the campaign that secured a Scottish Secretary, although only as a minority view. It also grew in the Liberal Party towards the end of the century, partly in response to Gladstone's offers of Home Rule for Ireland. There was a belief in some Liberal circles that Scotland was a more radical country than England, and that Scottish preferences for welfare legislation were being held back by English conservatism.

There was also a view that the Westminster Parliament was congested, and that by devolving legislation on domestic matters to Parliaments for Scotland, Ireland, Wales and England, Westminster could be left free to concentrate on the Empire. Supporters of appointing a Scottish Secretary believed that such a post would also contribute to alleviating the pressure on Westminster, by helping to channel Scottish concerns more efficiently into draft legislation.

The ILP inherited these kinds of view, and ensured that they would become the standard outlook of the Labour Party at least until the 1920s. It was believed that Scotland was potentially socialist, and that it should therefore have the same freedom as Dominion countries such as Canada or Australia. Several Home Rule bills were presented to Parliament by ILP and Labour MPs in the 1920s, none of them being passed, but all of them commanding a majority of Scottish MPs.

It was the failure of one of these bills which provoked the setting up of the National Party of Scotland (NPS) in 1928, growing out of the cross-party Scottish Home Rule Association. The NPS was at first vague about the status it wanted for a Scottish Parliament – whether independent or subordinate to Westminster – but it drifted towards favouring independence as it gave up trying to attract supporters of more moderate Home Rule from the Labour movement. In 1934 it formed the SNP by amalgamating with the much smaller Scottish Party, which was on the right of politics and wanted Home Rule, not independence. The tension between independence and Home Rule has been felt in the SNP ever since.

The new party had a negligible electoral impact in the 1930s, although prominent Conservative Secretaries of State such as John Gilmour and Walter Elliot used the threat from the SNP to secure more autonomy for the Scottish Office. The SNP did flower briefly during the 1939–45 war, taking advantage of the truce among the Labour, Unionist and Liberal Parties, and it won a by-election in Motherwell in 1945, losing it in the general election that followed a few months later. The party had little impact from then until the 1960s.

As the SNP moved towards fundamentalism and against Home Rule, some campaigners returned to the 1920s route of cross-party movements. The most successful project was the Scottish Covenant of the late 1940s, which attracted about two million signatures to a petition in favour of a Scottish Parliament with control of domestic social policy. But that, like the SNP, had no direct success, although – again as in the 1930s – the strength of the Covenant was used by Labour politicians in the Scottish Office to put pressure on their colleagues in London.

The conditions were not right for a nationalism of this sort in the 1950s and early 1960s. Most people – and especially most politicians – were happy with the compromise that had been reached between the 1920s and the 1940s, which created a distinctively Scottish branch of the administrative state. They were content because this was delivering the goods: material welfare for the mass of the population on an unprecedented scale, dispensed according to Scottish traditions. For example the education system was built up within a separate structure of Scottish examinations, Scottish curriculum and Scottish teaching practices. Likewise the health service maintained separate patterns of training, a greater integration than in England between hospitals and general practice, and a stronger concern with the social origins of disease. These Scottish differences were not a matter of the broad sweep of legislation but of the details of implementation, and so the Scottish politics that contributed to the nation's continued identity were local and particular. This system of government is discussed further in Chapters 3 and 5.

The credibility of the system started to decay, however, as the state became less able to deliver the material welfare, and it was then that support for a Scottish Parliament began its rise. To say that is not to claim that the sole explanation of that support is material; it is merely to point out that the Scottishness that people in Scotland seem to want for their politics is in the framework through which material welfare is administered. It is possible to care about the framework passionately, but to judge any framework on offer first of all on whether it is believed to bring prosperity. Compromise on the Scottishness of a framework can be justified only on these grounds. In particular, for as long as prosperity seemed to be more likely through a British realm of legislative politics, there was no need to press for anything more Scottish than an administrative realm. Of course, beliefs about the economy are themselves influenced by attitudes towards the state: as we shall see in more detail in Chapter 4, one of the main constitutional problems for the UK state in Scotland since the 1960s has been a popular Scottish perception that it is economically incompetent.

The change which happened in the 1960s was that the economic credibility of the UK state began to be questioned as never before. The long expansion of the post-1945 period was coming to an end, thus showing up how anachronistic were large parts of the British economy. The Scottish economy, still resting on the same staples as in the second half of the nineteenth century, was especially threadbare. The Labour Government of 1964–70 attempted to modernise these legacies on the basis of social democracy, but failed, and the Labour Government of 1974–9 barely managed to survive from one political crisis to the next, far less to embark on a new ideological project. In this respect British social democracy was following a European trend, where the welfare-state consensus of the previous 40 years was crumbling and in desperate need of intellectual renewal.

What made Scotland peculiar in this context was not the perception that the post-1945 welfare state was failing to live up to expectations but that it was the UK link itself that was blamed, rather than the political progenitor of the welfare state, social democracy. As we shall see, social democracy remained the dominant political preference in Scotland. The first signs of the tension with England were evident in the late 1950s, when the Unionist Party started its 40-year slide from over half the popular vote in the 1955 general election, to 1997, when it reached its lowest point in a general election of just 18 per cent. There were two main reasons for this decline. The first was that the Protestant working class slowly stopped voting on religious grounds, and shifted to the Labour Party (and later the SNP). The Catholic working class had always been with Labour. The second is that the Scottish middle class never abandoned a belief in the public provision of welfare, and so was unwilling to follow the Conservative Party in its 1970s move to the free-market right. The middle class therefore shifted to all three non-Conservative parties. (These electoral trends are analysed more thoroughly in Chapter 7.)

That first sign of Scottish voting distinctiveness was not immediately evident, however: it became so only when the continuing strength of the Conservative Party in England in the 1980s showed up the national differences sharply. But the second sign of Scottish difference was immediately apparent: the rise in popular support for the SNP in the late 1960s, culminating in their winning the Hamilton by-election (from Labour) in 1967, and in their widespread electoral success in local elections shortly after. Although the party did not sustain this success into the 1970 general election, they started growing again under the Conservative Government of 1970–4. They turned this fairly modest expansion into what seemed to be an unstoppable surge by tying their campaign for independence to the discovery of oil off the Scottish coast under the North Sea, a resource that seemed to remove any doubts that a Scottish state would be economically viable. The growing anti-Conservative mood in Scottish politics helped inspire nationalism: for example, when the Upper Clyde Shipbuilders company was threatened with closure in 1971, the Scottish reaction was both nationalist and socialist. The high point of the SNP was in the general election of October 1974, when they attracted over 30 per cent of the vote and won 11 of the 71 Scottish Parliamentary seats (coming a close second in most of the others).

The most immediate interpretation of this growth of the SNP was that it was a challenge to the UK state; not necessarily an endorsement of the SNP's goal of full independence, but at least a preference for a Parliament. And that was how the SNP and its opponents chose to see events. In response to the Hamilton by-election, the Conservatives set up a committee under the former prime minister, the Scottish landowner and MP Alec Douglas-Home. It recommended a form of weak but directly elected Scottish assembly that could take the second reading, committee and report stages of Scottish bills from Westminster. It would thus be a sort of second chamber for Scottish legislation.

The Labour Government's reaction had the greatest effect, however. It set up a Royal Commission on the UK Constitution, which eventually reported in 1973, recommending that a directly elected Scottish assembly be established with legislative powers covering the main areas of social policy dealt with by the Scottish Office, though leaving significant parts of that Office still answerable through the Secretary of State to the Westminster Parliament: for example powers over economic development, the universities, and law and order. The Labour Government of 1974–9 acted on these proposals, and managed to get the legislation through Westminster against the opposition of the Conservatives (now, under Margaret Thatcher, opposed to a Scottish assembly) and Labour sceptics. But the price for passing the bill was that the proposed powers of the assembly were restricted even further, and that a referendum should be held in Scotland in which at least 40 per cent of the total electorate would have to vote in favour before an assembly would be set up. The referendum took place in 1979, and the proportion in favour was only 33 per cent (although this was a majority – 52 per cent – of votes cast). The subsequent Conservative Government repealed the legislation. In the election which brought that Government to power, the SNP lost all but two of its seats and its vote fell to 17 per cent.

Why did the apparent popular enthusiasm for the SNP in the mid-1970s become this merely lukewarm support for mild Home Rule in 1979? The answer probably lies in what is, in retrospect, a more important feature of the SNP's success than constitutional politics directly. The SNP was, and is, an essentially social democratic party, just like the Labour and Liberal Parties. The votes for the SNP were as much votes for continuing the social democratic project in Scotland as they were a preference for a particular form of Scottish Parliament. When it looked as if the Labour Government could continue to deliver that project, the SNP waned. In this analysis, the reason why support for an assembly was fairly weak was that the Labour Government had put in place several new agencies by which the existing constitutional system could continue to act in the way it had been doing since 1945 (notably the Scottish Development Agency, intervention to help failing industries, and the transfer of powers over regional development grants to the Scottish Office). That was why the conjunction of nationalism and socialism in the Upper Clyde Shipbuilders of 1971 could fall apart; if jobs could be secured by these new agencies, then nationalism seemed to have done its work. An assembly was believed to be unnecessary if the existing structures could be made to work, especially if an assembly also threatened to bring with it new problems (for example, the possibility that rural areas would be dominated by the Labour-voting central belt).

So the rise and then weakening of the SNP can be interpreted as the same phenomenon as the steady decline of the Scottish Conservatives. It shows the Scottish electorate expressing a continuing preference for a welfare state, delivered through distinctive Scottish agencies. Only if that was not available from the Union would these agencies have to include a separate Parliament.

What, then, happened in the 1980s was that the Thatcher Government placed in question whether that welfare state would continue to be available at all. The main sources of the Government's Scottish unpopularity in the 1980s were social and economic: a perception that it was attacking the principles of government which were shared across the political spectrum. This became especially evident in the late 1980s when the Thatcher reforms moved from the economy to social policy. In the early part of the decade the Scottish Office, under George Younger, had managed to maintain a consensual approach to social policy even while the Scottish manufacturing economy was collapsing. But after about 1986 Thatcherism extended to those areas of policy that the Scottish Office administers (for example health and education). At the same time the Government's restriction on the autonomy and budgets of local government prevented the opposition parties (especially Labour) from being able to do much to counteract the effects of these changes.

In social policy the Thatcher Government was never able to command a majority of Scottish support and, even in social groups which were staunchly right wing in England, in Scotland the Conservatives were weak: for example, the skilled working class and the middle class (see Chapter 7). This division over social policy along national lines propelled Scottish opinion towards interpreting the problem in constitutional terms, even though the underlying causes had to do with social welfare rather than national identity as such. In particular the Labour Party shifted from its grudging support for a weak assembly in the 1970s to the belief that such a body could have protected Scotland from Thatcherism in the 1980s. After the 1987 general election it joined the Liberal Party and other groups in the Scottish Constitutional Convention to prepare a consensual scheme for Home Rule (more on which is in Chapters 3 and 5).

Accompanying this tension with England was the growing importance of the EU. Again, as with SNP voting, this sometimes appears to be directly about constitutions. The EU is attractive both to supporters of limited self-government, such as the Labour or Liberal Parties, and to the SNP. For the SNP, the EU provides a new framework of external security and trading opportunities to replace the UK: they argue that accusations of separatism are irrelevant if the policy is independence within the EU. For Labour and the Liberals, the key point is that the EU favours subsidiarity: the principle that decisions should be taken at the lowest level possible. The Governments of John Major and Margaret Thatcher interpreted this as favouring the central state against the European Commission, but the arguments they used were picked up by proponents of a Scottish Parliament in support of decentralisation within the UK. Underlying these Scottish preferences for Europe is a cultural shift that is unprecedented in the period since the Union. No longer is England admired as the source of progressive ideas: that role has been taken over by Europe. Thus to call yourself 'European' in late twentieth-century Scotland has something of the same modernising connotation as calling yourself 'British' did in the period between the middle of the eighteenth century and the middle of the twentieth.

Equally as important as the constitutional relevance of the EU is the perception that it has been close to the welfare-state consensus that Scotland seems to favour. On the position of women, the rights of workers and public spending on social infrastructure, the EU Commission was in conflict with the UK Conservative Government, and therefore has seemed an ally to many left-of-centre politicians in Scotland. Indeed it is a perception of a European agreement over these matters that has given the constitutional issue its European dimension in Scotland. All the non-Conservative parties believe that a self-governing Scotland could readily find allies in the EU, and thus could have influence far greater than its size would indicate. In this context, the apparently sharp differences between independence and a more limited type of Scottish Parliament become, in the long term, fairly unimportant. Eventually, the big legislative decisions will be centralised at the European level anyway: decisions on macro-economic policy, foreign affairs, and probably defence. That leaves Parliaments – whether independent or devolved – with control of social policy, precisely the area in which the Scottish Office has had administrative discretion throughout the twentieth century.

It is this European dimension – in both its constitutional and its social implications – that ensures that the campaign for a Scottish Parliament has a recurrent tendency to keep coming back on to the agenda. For example it ensured that the constitutional issue returned after the 1992 general election, despite the Conservative Party's having done slightly better than in 1987, and therefore having escaped the wipe-out that many opposition politicians had pre-dicted. The Scottish interpretation of subsidiarity produced a demonstration of some 30 000 people in Edinburgh at the time of the meeting there in December 1992 of the heads of government of the EU. The most remarkable feature of this demonstration was that it united the non-Conservative parties, a highly unusual event in the acrimonious world of Scottish politics. Europe still had this capacity to inspire the Scottish debate because the result of the 1992 election had still left the Conservative Party with just over a quarter of the vote, and therefore had not in reality brought into question the fact of Scottish preferences for a continued welfare state and a new constitutional mechanism to ensure that.

That this is the best interpretation of the 1992 election result and its aftermath was finally confirmed in 1997. The continuing Conservative Government after 1992 did little to respond to the underlying reasons for Scottish discontent – the preference for public welfare and so on – and instead interpreted the problem as being about symbols. They produced various minor reforms to the procedures by which Scottish business was dealt with at Westminster, and – especially after Michael Forsyth became Secretary of State in 1995 – they indulged in a great deal of flag-waving to try to place the Scottish Office and its ministers once again at the head of a national crusade. But the time for such an approach had long passed: it belonged to the 1950s, and failed to address the specific policy issues on which the Scots had been alienated. Local government was reorganised against the wishes of almost all expressed opinion in Scotland. The health service was broken up into trusts and semi-autonomous local practices, the relationship among which was supposed to resemble a market. There were further attempts to reduce the role of the local authority in overseeing school education, and – just before the 1997 election – there was a proposal to allow public sector schools to compete with each other by selecting their pupils on academic grounds.

So the Conservatives misread the popular mood. They mistook dissent from policies as a desire for a merely symbolic Scottishness. Right up to the end, they did not understand the Scottish predilection for state action. And they continued to alienate Scottish political elites with their strident hostility towards the European Union (which came across as a form of English nationalism), with their enthusiasm for competition in social life, and with their disdain for consensus wherever that would produce results that contradicted their policies.

The result in 1997 was the loss of every Conservative seat in Scotland, to the surprise of all observers. In this the party was badly served by the electoral system, because it actually obtained 18 per cent of the popular vote (five points more than the Liberal Democrats, who won 10 seats). The catastrophe left the Conservatives unable to lead the campaign against a Scottish parliament when the new Labour Government held a referendum on the matter on 11 September 1997. The referendum had been Labour's way of defusing the issue during the general election itself: by seeking separate endorsements of the principle of a Parliament and of the proposal to give it some limited power to vary tax, the Conservatives could be denied one of the main lines of attack that they had used in 1992. The idea of a referendum had originally caused disquiet in the party when the intention to hold it was announced in the summer of 1996, but that dissent was not widely voiced by the time of the general election (Jones, 1997a).

The new Secretary of State, Donald Dewar, was a lifelong campaigner for home rule. At the end of July 1997 he was able to produce a widely admired set of proposals for a Scottish Parliament (discussed further in Chapters 3 and 5). He achieved something that was remarkable considering the divisions in the previous referendum campaign in 1979: almost all the forces that favoured home rule came together behind one single campaigning strategy, led jointly by Dewar, Alex Salmond of the SNP and Jim Wallace of the Liberal Democrats (Jones, 1997b). The campaign against, by contrast, was amateurish and poorly funded. On 11 September the result was more decisive than anyone expected, even considering the wipe-out of the Conservatives at the general election. On a respectable turnout of 60 per cent, 74 per cent voted in favour of a Parliament, and 63 per cent voted to give it tax-varying powers. This clarity ensured that even the Conservatives did not demur any longer, and when the ensuing Bill to set up the Parliament emerged at the end of 1997, they promised not to obstruct its passage through Westminster. So Dewar's timetable seems likely to be achieved: elections to the Parliament in May 1999, and its assumption of power at the beginning of the year 2000.

The electoral events of 1997 marked the culmination of three decades during which the issue of a Scottish Parliament had come to dominate Scottish politics.   There are four main legacies of this movement:

- the belief that Scotland is more left-of-centre than England;
- a preference in Scotland for maintaining the welfare state;
- a belief, therefore, that the Scottish national interest which the Scottish Office had been leading since the 1930s was now not being served by an unreformed Union with England;
- and a feeling that Scotland's social welfare goals would be better furthered in the European Union than solely in the UK.

The Scottish Parliament will inherit that legacy. But it will also be drawing on the previous three centuries, notably the belief in liberal democracy, the preference for public provision of welfare, and – perhaps most fundamental of all, despite some nationalist claims to the contrary – a belief that Scottish interests have been best served when the country ties its destiny to its more powerful neighbours. The main novelty is that these neighbours are now seen as lying beyond England.

2

Politics, State and Society

Does Scottish politics exist? This might seem an odd question to ask in the light of the narrative outlined in the last chapter. Scotland's political story since the Union of 1707 seems to be lively and distinctive, and in no need of justification. And yet the conventional conceptual tools for making sense of that story seem inappropriate. How are we to make sense of Scotland? In conventional terms, it does not seem to have a 'politics' because Scotland is not a nation-state, and much of political analysis is premised on a high degree of self-containedness of the state. Most of the time Scotland and its politics have been treated as an adjunct to those of Britain, and we do not ask whether British politics exists. At best, the conventional wisdom goes, Scotland is 'British with a difference' (McAllister and Rose, 1984). Similarly, critics ask, how can Scotland have a political system when it does not have an independent legislature (Midwinter, *et al.*, 1991)?

State, society or nation: how to describe Scotland? Before we answer this question, it is important to spell out what we mean by these terms, for it is all too common to assume that they are synonyms; on the contrary. The argument that the state, society and nation are in alignment is a central assumption of modernist social and political theory which we have inherited from the Enlightenment. We argue that there is nothing synonymous about them. In that scheme of things self-governing territories are judged to be culturally homogeneous and socially bounded with the right of self-determination. These 'nation-states' are deemed the proper actors in world affairs. In this book we refer to Scotland as a 'stateless' nation. We mean that while there is a considerable apparatus of government with a high degree of autonomy, Scotland does not have a fully independent legislature. The conventional wisdom is that a 'stateless' nation like Scotland has no independent existence outwith the unitary state, the UK, which rules over it. These old orthodoxies, however, appear to be losing their power. The alignment of state, society and nation seems far less secure, for reasons we will outline later.

Let us first examine what we mean by these terms. The 'state' connotes 'an impersonal and privileged legal or constitutional order with the capability of administering and controlling a given territory' (Held, 1992). It is in essence a political concept.

What is the state?

First, the state has a unity (Poggi, 1978). Each state operates in its own territory as the exclusive fount of all powers and prerogatives of rule. This unity is expressed through the medium of a single currency, a unified fiscal system, a single 'national' language (national culture being acquired through a powerful education system) and a unified legal system.

Second, the state is ineluctably modern. That is, it appears as an 'artificial, engineered institutional complex', a deliberated constructed framework vital for state and nation-building. Poggi comments: 'The modern state is not bestowed upon a people as a gift by God, its own geist, or blind historical forces; it is a "made" reality' (Poggi, 1978, p. 95). The state, in other words, is viewed as a machine, internally structured as a formal, complex organisation. He argues: 'In sum, the state is designed and is intended to operate as a machine whose parts all mesh, a machine propelled by energy and directed by information flowing from a single centre in the service of a plurality of coordinated tasks' (Poggi, 1978, p. 98).

The third characteristic of the state is that it embodies, in Max Weber's phrase, rational-legal legitimacy, expressed above all in law: that is, 'positive law, willed, made and given validity by the state itself in the exercise of its sovereignty, mostly through public, documented, generally recent decisions' (Poggi, 1978, p. 102). In other words rule-making is no longer conceived of as custom, nor as a set of partial immunities for some but not others, and neither is it the expression of the will of God or nature or the monarch. The legitimacy of the modern state rests on rational and open procedures of law.

In practice, the most common idea of the modern state is to characterise it as the 'nation-state', in which the political realm (the state), the social (society) and the cultural (the nation) are as one. In the words of David Held (1992): 'All modern states are nation-states – political apparatuses, distinct from both rulers and ruled, with supreme jurisdiction over a demarcated territorial area, backed by a claim to a monopoly of coercive power, and enjoying a minimum level of support or loyalty from their citizens.'

Defining society

What are we to make of our second concept, 'society', and how does it relate, if at all, to the state? If the 'state' is in essence a political concept, then 'society' is a sociological one. Broadly speaking we can identify two ways of talking about society. Most sociologists use society in a fairly unproblematic and implicit way. It is, simply, the state. In the words of the sociologist Zigmunt Bauman (1992a, p. 57): 'It seems that most sociologists of the era of modern orthodoxy believed that – all being said – the nation-state is close enough to its own postulate of sovereignty to validate the use of the theoretical expression – the "society" concept – as an adequate framework for sociological analysis.'

The second sense of society is as 'Society' (capital S). This is a higher level of abstraction and is used to refer to the broad, common patterns of human organisation, to how people relate to each other, as well as its subsets (industrial society, capitalist society and so on). In the main, however, when sociologists today talk about 'society' they are usually referring to 'nation-states'. Alain Touraine (1981, p. 5) commented over a decade ago:

The abstract idea of society cannot be separated from the concrete reality of a national society, since this idea is defined as a network of institutions, controls and education. This necessarily refers us back to a government, to a territory, to a political collectivity. The idea of society was and still is the ideology of nations in the making.

This somewhat diluted image of 'society' carries its own difficulties. It implies that the conventional state is a bounded and self-contained social system. The two dominating paradigms of Western sociology in the twentieth century both adopted this convention. On the one hand, Parsonian structural functionalism has equated society with 'social system', a limited and enclosed world within which all meaningful social interaction takes place. On the other hand, Marxism has used the concept 'social formation' in much the same way. Economic and social exchange has taken place largely within the confines of a (national) market, and policed by the state. In practical terms society was simply the state. For example 'British society' is a term which has been in common currency as long as sociology has had a professional foothold in these islands, and it has been used extensively since the coming of the welfare state in 1945.

In recent years there have been attempts to refine society as an analytical concept by using the prefix 'civil'. The term 'civil society' refers to 'those areas of social life – the domestic world, the economic sphere, cultural activities and political interaction – which are organised by private or voluntary arrangements between individuals and groups outside the direct control of the state' (Held, 1992, p. 73). In other words, whereas the state can be treated as a unitary entity which functions externally (through warfare) and internally (through law), society is composed of an extensive though bounded network of self-activated individuals and groups. State and society are not wholly independent of each other, but are largely formed and maintained within the context of the other.

Within the Marxist tradition, civil society has come to stand not simply for the economic (market) dimension, but for the set of social and civic institutions, including the whole range of public institutions from courts, welfare agencies and educational bodies, mediating between the individual and the state. In Kumar's words: 'Civil society is the sphere of culture in the broadest sense. It is concerned with the manners and mores of society, with the way people live' (1993, pp. 382–3). The fall of communism in central and Eastern Europe has helped to boost the revival of the concept 'civil society'. Kumar is critical of commentators on eastern Europe who, he argues, imply too much consensus in the sphere of civil society at the expense of the real degree of coercion involved in the maintenance of political power in modern societies. Others counter that civil society provides 'the space or arena between the household and the state, other than the market, which affords possibilities of concerted action and social self-organisation' (Bryant, 1993, p. 399).

Discovering the nation

The final concept in our trilogy is probably the least understood: the 'nation'. There is considerable debate about what 'nation' means. To classical writers like Weber it referred to 'a community of sentiment which would find its adequate expression only in a state of its own and which thus normally strives to create one' (Beetham, 1974, p. 122). The essentially ideological nature of the concept is best captured in Benedict Anderson's (1983) definition of nation as an 'imagined political community' with the following characteristics:

- it is imagined as a 'communion' of people (whom one has never met);
- it has finite territorial boundaries;
- it implies sovereignty and self-determination of its members;
- the community is viewed as deep and horizontal comradeship.

It is the nation which, according to the conventional model, cements state and society together. Bauman (1992b, p. 683) comments:

> In the course of modern history, nationalism played the role of the hinge fastening together state and society (represented as, identified with, the nation). State and nation emerged as natural allies at the horizon of the nationalist vision (at the finishing line of the re-integrating race). The state supplied the resources of nation-building, while the postulated unity of the nation and shared national destiny offered legitimacy to the ambition of the state authority to command obedience.

The conventional way of looking at state, society and nation is to see them as aligned with each other so as to be coterminous: state–society–nation coming together to form self-contained, free-standing, ethnically homogeneous 'communities'. Each state is the embodiment of these distinct communities, self-originating and self-empowering, operating exclusively in pursuit of its own interests. Note that the state is judged to have a 'will' generated by the principle of nationality.

The notion that the world consists of these free-standing communities is also gender-laden. Put simply, society–state is divided into the public and private spheres. In a useful syllogism, man = public; public = political, therefore man is political. Conversely, woman = private, private = apolitical, therefore woman is apolitical. In other words: 'If politics is assumed to be the prerogative of the public sphere, and women are taken to be firmly located within the private domain, then the access of women to politics would appear to be understandably problematic' (Siltanen and Stanworth, 1984, p. 195).

Such models of politics assume that political environments like political parties and Parliaments are gender-neutral, and the absence of women from active participation in them is due to their lack of motivation. The argument here is that 'politics' presents a restricted face to women; it excludes them. As we shall see in Chapter 8, simply relying on encouraging women to participate in an implicitly male-stream set of institutions does not raise the proportion involved in active decision-making. Redefining 'politics' requires re-mapping the public–private spheres, as the debate over a Parliament for Scotland makes plain. It is not a coincidence that politics in 'stateless' nations tends to involve the redefinition of the public and the private.

In sum, then, although we can find analytical differences between state, society and nation, these have become fused in our models of society and treated as coterminous with the 'nation-state'. Our problem is that, on the one hand, the covert influence of nation-state building in the nineteenth and twentieth centuries dominates politics, sociology and history alike. On the other hand, societies bounded in geographical and social space are less and less likely to be unified totalities in the late twentieth century when economic, political and cultural forces have eroded the homogeneity of states. Let us examine the key changes.

Shifting state–society relations

The first set of changes concerns the relationship between state and society. In general terms, the state has encroached on society, and society on the state, making it much more difficult for us to distinguish between the two. Just as citizens demand more of the state, so the political dimension has required legitimacy for its actions in the social and cultural spheres. In Poggi's words: 'some encroachments on the state–society line result not from the state being "pulled over" the line, as it were, but from its "pushing" itself over it' (1978, p. 131).

Why should this have occurred? The two key domains of civil society are the family/domestic sphere, and the economy. In their classical forms, both are judged to be beyond the influence of the state, defined as the public sphere. The public refers to the sphere of 'work' (employment), authority, power, responsibility and management of the world – by men. The private relates to the 'domestic kingdom', where women and feminine virtues are said to prevail. As Stuart Hall (1992, p. 20) comments:

> The private/public distinction is . . . rooted in a particular sexual division of labour, and one of the principal means by which the exclusion of women from public affairs has been constructed and secured. The maintenance by the state of the public/private separation is therefore sometimes taken to exemplify the patriarchal aspects of the state.

Similarly, in its classical form the privately owned economy stands outside the influence of the state. The breaking down of the state–society line results from economic developments (the market is no longer self-equilibrating), the extension of the franchise resulting in increased demands on the state, and the emergence of a sizeable state sector with its own interests to protect and enhance.

In the late twentieth century the domestic and the economic spheres are no longer separated from the state in any meaningful way. The boundaries of the state and civil society were, of course, never fixed but have been constantly redrawn, with obvious implications for relations between men and women. However, in modern times the state can no longer stand outside social, political and cultural relations and institutions which make up society. In other words, as Hall points out, the 'empty' state – without a social content – does not exist. The state constitutes society as well as being constituted by it.

'Civil society' indicates that there is a sphere which is autonomous from the state. Neither is it simply the economy writ large. Similarly, what is meant by the state and society have themselves changed over time, as well as the relationship between them. The distinction between the two was probably much more meaningful to Victorians than it is to us today. That is because, as Poggi has pointed out, the last century or so has seen an increasing fudging of the boundary between state and society. Notably, the extension of the franchise has brought to bear new political and social pressures on the state, and increasingly the state is constituted to exercise rule over society. He comments: 'the state tends to increase its power by widening the scope of its activities, by extending the range of societal interests on which rule is brought to bear' (1978, p. 135). The state is required to address the concerns of its citizens more directly, and this presents the task of societal management for modern governments.

Nations and states

The second set of changes which have an impact on how we understand Scotland and other 'stateless' nations concerns the relationship between the state and the nation in the second half of the twentieth century. If anything, nationalism has waxed rather than waned in importance as this century has progressed. The usual way of identifying this is to point to the rise of nationalisms from regions or territories which wish to break away from existing state formations. Hence when we think of nationalism in the West, we think of its rise in Scotland, Wales, Catalonia and Quebec and other formally 'stateless' nations. In the post-war period, however, there has also been a core form of nationalism which is frequently implicit. As the modern state became the appropriate instrument for guaranteeing the life chances of its citizens and ironing out social inequalities, governments became major actors in economic competition between states in the quest for economic growth 'in the national interest'. This is state nationalism expressed in economic and political competition. Nationalism, in this form, became more, not less, common in this process of post-war international competition. This nationalism of the 'core' developed alongside counternationalisms on the periphery which sought to redraw the limits and responsibilities of central state power, and in many cases secede from it.

Yet just as nationalism was growing in importance, so the 'nation-state' appeared to be losing its powers. The growing interest in nationalism coincides with the apparent decline in the powers of the state. How is it possible to explain this apparent contradiction? One possibility is that the sovereignty of the nation-state was always a trick of the eye. In the words of one writer, 'The era of the homogeneous and viable nation-states is over (or rather the era of the illusion that homogeneous and viable nation-states are possible is over, since such states never existed) and the national vision must be redefined' (Tamir, 1993, p. 3).

What are these forces which seem to require a redefinition of the national vision? In short, the loss of sovereignty – economic, political and cultural – which has occurred in the late twentieth century under the impact of global forces. More and more power appears to have flowed upwards from the nation-state. It is far less able to control its 'national' economy; it no longer has a monopoly over the means of its military protection and destruction in a nuclear age; and the correspondence of cultural and political dimensions are such that the state no longer speaks for a single mono-cultural 'nation'. The shorthand for this complex of social changes is 'globalisation'. It recognises that, in Daniel Bell's words, the nation-state has become too small for the big problems of life, and too big for the small problems of life. There is also an unprecedented flow of goods and ideas. Information, comments Zigmunt Bauman, 'cannot be arrested by any border guards, however zealous and heavily armed' (1992b, p. 691).

Globalisation can of course imply a shift to universal standardisation, to a sociology of one world. But there appears to be a complex dialectic between the global and the local. It involves 'the intersection of presence and absence, the interlacing of social events and social relations "at a distance" with local contextualities' (Giddens, 1991, p. 21). Globalisation involves not simply 'broadening' but also 'deepening'. It can enhance 'threats from below', and stimulate searches for new identities or the refurbishment of old ones. In other words, a global–local nexus emerges, a process of relocalisation and a reordering of time and space.

What are the cultural and political implications of this? Stuart Hall (1992, p. 309) argues:

> Globalisation does have the effect of contrasting and dislocating the centred and 'closed' identities of a national culture. It does have a pluralising impact on identities, producing a variety of possibilities and new positions of identification, and making identities more positional, more political, more plural and diverse; less fixed, unified or trans-historical.

In this context, social identities are reformed in such a way that they become amenable to choice, and hence less predictable. Issues of gender, class, race and ethnicity are remixed in powerful and unpredictable ways. We discuss this point further in Chapter 9.

Nation-states appear to lose their authority to forces above as well as below. Global and multinational forces shift centres of power upwards, while 'civil societies' – which have been submerged by broader state forces – reassert their right to autonomy. State-based societies become heavily porous. Globalisation carries with it an implication for locality; the global and the local become part of the same dialectic. We enter a world not of standardisation and homogenisation, but of difference and unpredictability.

Not all commentators accept that the demise of the nation-state is inevitable. They argue that while some of its functions decline in importance, others grow. In Michael Mann's words, 'Where countries lack an effective nation-state, they would dearly like to have one. The nation-state is not hegemonic, nor is it obsolete, either as a reality or as an ideal' (Mann, 1993, p. 139). States remain important sites for political democracy and, despite the extended role of multinational capital, are key centres of social citizenship.

It is not our aim to take sides in this debate about the future of the 'nation-state', but to point out that the changing terms of reference about the relationship between political, social and economic power have important implications for Scotland and other 'stateless' nations. We have seen that the long-held assumption about the correspondence of state, society and nation, which removed Scotland as a conventional arena for analysis and action, has been eroding. If we recover the idea that states are essentially political entities with no necessary correspondence with civil societies, then Scotland's institutional autonomy within the British state takes on added relevance. Similarly, Scotland as a nation, as an 'imagined community', is not determined by its formal political independence. As we shall see in the next chapter, Scotland has in fact had more constitutional autonomy than many formally more independent states in Western Europe.

Where does this conceptual review of state, society and nation leave us with regard to understanding the politics of Scotland? It is manifestly not a state, if by that term we mean a sovereign, independent polity with a seat at the United Nations. We might, however, quibble that Scotland is a semi-state with, as we saw in the previous chapter, a high degree of civil and political autonomy over its institutions despite nearly 300 years of belonging to a unitary UK. We would be on firmer ground if we referred to Scotland as a civil society, because it corresponds to Giddens' practical definition of society as 'a group of people who live in a particular territory, are subject to a common system of political authority, and are aware of having a distinct identity from other groups around them'.

In the previous chapter we saw that over the last hundred years increasing demands for internal reform in Scotland have resulted in increased responsibilities accruing to the Scottish Office to the extent that a fairly high degree of *de facto* self-government or limited sovereignty has existed. The demands for concomitant democratic accountability over the Scottish semi-state in the late twentieth century represent recognition of the limits which mere administrative devolution has reached. There is irony in the fact that the Scottish Office has given political meaning to Scotland. If it had not existed then it would have been much harder to address Scotland as a meaningful political unit.

Fundamentally the Scottish Office is the expression of a complex network of social organisations – which is what we mean by Scottish civil society – which have made political demands for more self-determination so much easier to make. In these terms Scotland is indubitably a society, or rather (in Adam Ferguson's phrase) a civil society with 'a political life which more than anything else calls forth and strengthens intellectual and moral powers'. The Union of 1707 saw Scotland keep virtually intact much of its active political life, its institutional autonomy in particular.

Is Scotland, then, a 'nation'? To say that nation belongs firmly to the ideological realm is not at all to imply that it is in some way false or inaccurate, contrary to material reality. In Benedict Anderson's useful phrase, which we introduced earlier in this chapter, nation is an imagined community. Nations are imagined communities because they require a sense of belonging which is both horizontal and vertical, in place and in time. The idea of the nation is to be conceived of, says Anderson, as a solid community moving steadily down (or up) history. The notion of historical community is a vitally important part of the nation as imagined community.

Let us underscore this point. 'Nations' as such do not have some external or objective reality. We cannot identify those characteristics which inevitably lead to nationhood, and those which do not. The search for objective definitions legitimises nationalistic claims that it is the sharing of certain attributes that 'makes a nation' (Bauman, 1992b, p. 677). To argue that nations are not 'real' goes against the conventional wisdom that nationalism is simply the expression of fundamental, pre-ordained cultural and social differences. As the anthropologist Fredrick Barth (1969) pointed out, the continuous existence of an 'ethnic' category depends on the maintenance of a phenomenological boundary with others. Nationalism is not the expression of objective differences, but the mobilisation of those differences which actors believe to be salient. The 'nation', then, is not a primordial form of social organisation, but an idea, an aspiration. It should be considered not so much as 'place' but as 'process'.

There can be little doubt of the ideological power of Scotland as a nation in these terms. It implies that Scotland is not simply a piece of geography but a transcendent idea which runs through history, reinterpreting that history to fit the concerns of each present. To say that Scotland, or England or Wales for that matter, are 'figments of the imagination' is not at all to imply that they are false, but that they have to be interpreted as ideas, made and remade. Above all they are places of the mind. The phrase 'Scottish people' invokes a historical idea stretching back over centuries, implying that four-teenth-century peasants and twentieth century workers share some common identity.

Scotland and the British state

We are now in a position to turn our attention to Scotland and its place in the UK. What does the debate about state–society relations tell us about Britain? First of all, and revealingly in the issue of naming, it is unclear what the state and its citizens are to be called. Its official one is the United Kingdom of Great Britain and Northern Ireland (or UK for short); a title, as Benedict Anderson pointed out, which denies nationality in its naming. However it also refers to Great Britain, or simply Britain, which of course *strictu sensu* only covers the British 'mainland'. To confuse the state with 'England', as is frequently done, is to make the point. If political and social scientists equate Britain and England, that is more than a slip of the pen: it implies by definition the equivalence of state and society and nation.

The creation of Great Britain in the early eighteenth century before the wave of modernising states transformed our world is the key to understanding the relationship. The British state managed to contain within it quite distinct self-governing 'civil societies', which co-existed within its formal boundaries quite contentedly as long as a fairly high degree of limited autonomy was afforded them. We can now see with hindsight that by the middle of the twentieth century the relationship between the state and these civil societies had been radically altered in such a way that peaceful co-existence was no longer logically possible. Above all, the generic shift between the boundaries of the state and civil society in the modern world created particular difficulties for relations between the British state and its constituent civil societies.

The focus here is on the relationship between Britain and Scotland because that was the basis of the creation of the new state of Great Britain in 1707, and is and always has been the most problematic and intriguing one. This is not to deny that other civil societies existed within the state, notably those in Wales and (after 1801 when the state became the UK) Ireland, as well as local and regional ones within England itself. However their relationships to the political centre were different. On the one hand, the national societies of Wales and Ireland had been the subject of successful conquest by England from the thirteenth century, and had elements of colonial status attached to their civil and political institutions. On the other hand, regional autonomy within England did not have to contend with competing national identities and institutional residues of historical statehood as north of the border.

The Scottish view, then, of state–society relations in these islands tends to be quite different from those encountered the closer one gets to the English core. The conventional orthodoxy is that Britain is a highly centralised and homogeneous state/society, with very little meaningful difference across its territory. Anthony Giddens, for example, cites Britain (and France) as 'the two instances usually given of a smooth coincidence of "nation" and "state"' (1985, p. 270). We must assume here that Giddens is referring to 'society' rather than 'nation' as such, because national identity has been consistently and significantly different in Scotland so as to make that reference inappropriate. However, even if we substitute 'society', there are problems. We may use terms like 'British society' as a political shorthand, but it is a sociological inaccuracy.

What the emergence of nationalism did not alert sociologists and political scientists to was that 'British society' was a misnomer. The assumption that class cleavages were all that mattered seemed to square with strong Labour support in the political peripheries. Growing divergence between Scotland and England, as well as within England between 'North' and 'South', indicated that the old homogeneous models were out of date. In Scotland as in Wales a new sociology began to emerge which did not take the old certainties for granted. By the 1970s, imported models of 'colonialism' were being tried out to make sense of economic, social and political change on the 'periphery'. If these models were found wanting as analytical devices rather than simply as metaphors, they did open the way for a fresh look at the old assumptions about the homogeneity of the UK.

Above all, social and political science began to take seriously the relationship between state and society. How, for example, had Scottish (or Welsh) civil society developed in the context of the unitary British state since 1707? Given that all formal political power resided in Westminster, how much (or little) autonomy could these nations continue to have? There was a consensus of political opposites on this issue. For nationalists, Scotland had ceased to exist in 1707 when it was incorporated into greater England. Its project was and is that Scotland should rise and be a nation again (nation, of course, implying statehood). For unionists, a new, integrated society was born called Britain (or the UK), and they argue that it would be disastrous if the whole was unscrambled into its weaker constituent parts. The problem with these two stark representations is that they play fast and loose with history as well as sociology.

Scotland in the Union, and the Union in Scotland

What is nearer the truth is that Scotland did not cease to be a nation or a civil society in 1707, and neither was it incorporated into greater England. Instead, the political settlement which was the Treaty of Union (note the word Treaty) was, in Tom Nairn's phrase, a settlement between two patrician classes for economic and political gains.

This settlement took place in 1707, long before what we now know as 'modern' processes began, and well in advance of the French and American Revolutions in the last quarters of the century which were to give political change a democratic impetus. The Treaty of Union in 1707 did create something new. Greater England it was not. Instead, Scots took full advantage of opportunities which England and the Empire provided, and were in no way confined to the subaltern tasks.

A genuine sense of Britishness was created with reference to two related aspects: war with France, and Protestantism. The invention of Britishness was forged in the long period of virtual or actual warfare with France from 1707 until 1837. As Colley points out, these wars were religious wars, and were perceived as such by both sides. The overthrow of the Catholic Stuarts in 1689 and their replacement with the Protestant William of Orange reinforced the political-religious nature of the settlement. Indeed she says (1992, p. 5) that Britain

> was an invention forged above all by war. Time and time again, war with France brought Britons, whether they hailed from Wales or Scotland or England, into confrontation with an obvious hostile Other and encouraged them to define themselves collectively against it. They defined themselves as Protestants struggling for survival against the world's foremost Catholic power. They defined themselves against the French as they imagined them to be, superstitious, militarist, decadent and unfree.

This struggle against the French may seem like an integrating mechanism, a forging of a new national identity, but Colley argues that 'Britishness was superimposed over an array of internal differences in response to contact with the Other, and above all in response to conflict with the Other' (1992, p. 6). In other words it worked with rather than against the grain of older national identities which were to persist, and outlast the later British one.

This is a crucial point in the argument. It was precisely the fact that Britishness sat lightly on top of the constituent nations as a kind of state identity which is the key to understanding state–society relations in the UK. The British state was quite unlike later state formations which sought to integrate political, cultural and economic structures in the classical 'nation-state'. These formations demanded the lining-up of state, nation and society, and even economy and culture, in such a way that 'national identity' ran through all of these institutions. Being a citizen in these nineteenth-century modern states demanded allegiance, and in return the state was made accountable and its sovereignty was limited, often by means of the doctrine of popular rather than Crown/Parliamentary sovereignty as in Britain.

Here we encounter familiar themes. The British state was a 'nightwatchman state', content to concern itself with matters of defence, foreign policy and maintaining a stable currency. It was a state externally oriented to managing its dependent territories and arranging their defence. Above all, it left civil society to its own devices, and only intervened where it perceived a threat to social and political order. This it did most notoriously after the Jacobite Rising of 1745, but only at the behest of and largely by the hands of lowland Protestant Scots.

All in all, the Anglo-Saxon state, especially in its British form, was viewed, as Poggi points out, as a 'convenience'. In contrast the continental European state was seen as an 'entity', as 'The State'. The point here is that the British state sat lightly upon civil society, whereas continental European states were thoroughly interwoven with theirs.

The unreformed, *ancien régime*-like quality of the British state has been commented upon by many writers. David Marquand, for example, has called the UK an 'unprincipled' society because its state structures are fundamentally deficient. He comments:

> Thanks to the upheavals of the 17th century – thanks in particular to the victory of the English landed classes over the Stuart kings – one cannot speak of a 'British state' in the way that one speaks of a 'French state' or in modern times of a 'German state'. The UK is not a state in the continental sense. It is a bundle of islands (including such exotica as the Channel Islands and the Isle of Man which are not even represented at Westminster), acquired at different times by the English crown, and governed in different ways. Its inhabitants are not citizens of a state, with defined rights of citizenship. They are subjects of a monarch, enjoying 'liberties' which their ancestors won from previous monarchs. (1988, p. 152)

Marquand's point is not that the British state represents an *ancien régime* in a pre-French Revolution sense, but one which suffers from a form of arrested political development. It was a minimal state with a small bureaucracy which was clearly suited to market-driven adjustment in the eighteenth century, but which failed to make the transition to become a 'developmental state' in the late nineteenth century. At its root lies an ethos of market liberalism which has survived long after the doctrine which created it has been abandoned.

A similar point is made by Linda Colley, who points out that for a time the British state (at the turn of the nineteenth century) was one of the most modernised and democratic in Europe. Its Protestant 'ethic' gave it a commitment to civil and economic liberalism which helped to make it the premier power until the late nineteenth century. The problem was, she comments, that whereas the reforms of 1832 established a high degree of civil and democratic rights, by 1865 it had been overtaken by most continental powers. Its political development had been arrested, possibly because its route to modernisation was much more conservative than is usually made out: a kind of conservative liberalism in which by means of that 'antiquated compromise' a thoroughgoing reform of political and constitutional structures did not take place. By the end of the nineteenth century this was even being celebrated as the strength of the British constitution by apologists such as A. V. Dicey:

> No one of the limitations alleged to be imposed by law on the absolute authority of Parliament has any real existence, or receives any countenance, either from the statute book or from the practices of the courts. This doctrine of the legislative supremacy of Parliament is the very keystone of the constitution. (1950, p. 70)

How was it that the *laissez-faire* British state had the doctrine of Crown sovereignty at its core, whereas continental states, which were more interventionist, did not? The answer is that the price for greater state–society integration on the continental model was precisely that it was more accountable to its citizens. Indeed its population could consider themselves citizens, rather than subjects of the Crown, albeit the Crown in Parliament. In the British case, sovereignty had been transferred from the monarch to Parliament (which became the Crown), but the power of the state remained fairly crude and primitive, and so, it could be argued, accountability mattered less.

It is this relationship between state and civil society which is touched upon by commentators such as Tom Nairn and Neal Ascherson when they speak of the British state as an *'ancien régime'*. In Ascherson's words: 'It is closer in spirit to the monarchy overthrown in 1789 than to the republican constitutions which followed in France and elsewhere in Europe' (1988, p. 148). The doctrine of the Crown-in-Parliament, the Royal Prerogative, under-pinned the British state at that crucial period in its formation in the late seventeenth and early eighteenth centuries, between the self-styled Glorious Revolution of 1689 and the Treaty of Union in 1707. On paper, from the vantage point of the late twentieth century, it looked authoritarian. In eighteenth-century practice, probably little changed in the lives of the subjects.

This, then, is the context in which the Union took place between Scotland on the one hand, and England (and, to all intents and purposes, Wales and Ireland) on the other well before the period now characterised as 'modern'. With hindsight, we might argue that the only kind of state which allowed the Scots and others to retain a high degree of civil autonomy was a 'pre-modern' one in which the links between high and low politics were tenuous indeed. It is doubtful if the Scots would have agreed to submerge their institutional autonomy into the British state if it had been a thoroughly modern formation.

In contrast to other states of a more modern ilk, the British state found itself with a particular difficulty as time passed. It too had to respond to these new demands on it, but its essentially pre-modern character meant that there were few checks and balances on its power. The irony of the Thatcher epoch is that a Government elected ostensibly on the mandate of correcting Government overload and rolling back the state managed to extend state power in an unprecedented way. Scottish civil society, which had achieved a high degree of self-governance, found itself subject to greater central state powers.

The governance of Scotland was increasingly in the hands of the Scottish Office, which became the means of imposing London rule on the Scots. The Scottish Office, which had evolved partly as the expression of a complex network of self-governing social institutions in Scotland, became more obviously the instrument of the Westminster Government. For much of its history, this did not create problems because, more often than not, the Scots voted for the majority party south of the border. However the growing divergence in political behaviour, coupled with a succession of Conservative Governments in London, called into question the delicate balance of Scotland's place in the Union.

In both Scotland and Wales, the political vehicle for incorporating the enfranchised working class into the political system had been the Labour Party. As long as the party had a chance of winning power at Westminster, and it held its working-class support, the Union was likely to hold. For much of the last century Scotland behaved much like England did in terms of its electoral behaviour. It was not until the late 1950s that patterns of electoral divergence began to show between the two countries, with long-term constitutional consequences. The emergence of an explicit nationalist party, the SNP, with substantial support in the late 1960s and 1970s, began to erode the position of both of the main unionist parties, and even when that party fell away electorally (as it did in the 1980s) the political divergence between Scotland and England did not diminish.

The SNP had managed to get itself into the right place at the right time, providing a political alternative when the British settlement began to fail. Secular trends which were present south of the border found a different political expression north of it. In the 1960s and 1970s, rising affluence, full employment and upward social mobility were to be found in Scotland also. To be sure, Scotland differed little from the rest of the UK with regard to these changes, but 'Scotland' was an ideological category in terms of which socio-political change could readily be interpreted. In this regard the relative autonomy of the Scottish press and media was vital, because it helped to frame these social changes in a Scottish way. Crucially, the SNP was a political party which could more easily capture the Scottish label, because it was a taken-for-granted reference very like the 'national' identity implicitly assumed by the Conservative Party in England. The collapse of the SNP in the late 1970s did not mean that nationalism was off the Scottish agenda, because other parties (notably Labour) played the Scottish card with vigour.

By the 1990s, the delicate balance between Scottish civil society and the British state had been transformed. It had begun on the implicit understanding that Scotland would retain a high degree of self-governance of its social institutions. Parliamentary politics were a fairly unimportant sideshow for much of the history of the Union. However, the pre-modern and largely unreconstructed British state had retained the doctrinal incubus of Parliamentary sovereignty which became a central element in politics in the second half of the twentieth century. The ushering in of the welfare state after 1945 was an attempt to modernise British state structures in the light of demands for reform from civil society. This project, which represented the high-point of Labour power in Britain, required state-led social change but without major reforms of the British state itself. The state was required to do more, but it did not have a modern and integrated institutional base.

Conclusions

In this context, the shifting balance between the state and civil society which all modern countries have been confronted with in the twentieth century has been compounded by the delicate constitutional balance between Scotland and the British state. As this largely unreconstructed state has confronted these problems, it has taken refuge in the powers it has in its constitutional locker. In a Scottish context, the balance between civil society and the state has been transformed in such a way as to throw considerable doubt on the future of Scotland in the Union. Middle-class management of civil institutions has been eroded by central state power, and its allegiance to its historic political party, the Unionists (as the Conservatives were called until 1965), has been severely and probably irrevocably damaged.

  If we characterise modernity as requiring the alignment of state, civil society and nation, then Britain never became a thoroughly modern state formation, possibly because it could not hope to do so without destroying the autonomy of Scottish civil society. In the late twentieth century, at the end of 'modernity' as it were, the lack of alignment between state, society and nation in the British context might be judged as a positive if peculiar advantage. In the next chapter we will examine the politics of the constitution in Scotland.

3

Politics and the Scottish Constitution

Introduction

We saw in the last chapter that state, society and nation are more complex ideas than is commonly supposed in the rhetoric of politics. The problem is exacerbated in a state such as the UK where there is no written constitution. It is impossible to go to an authoritative document to settle disputes about where power and sovereignty lie.

Nevertheless, appeals to the constitution are frequently heard in UK political debate. Ever since Dicey wrote in the nineteenth century, the great virtue of this constitution has been held to be its flexibility. Indeed the very fact that it is unwritten is believed to enhance that quality: an authoritative document can become, it is alleged, authoritarian, especially if its interpretation is mainly in the hands of unelected judges.

Whatever the advantages may be of an unwritten constitution, however, it does pose difficulties for trying to understand the ground rules of Scottish politics. We have to infer constitutional principles from observing political practice, rather than by reading a single document. That is what we do in this chapter, in three main parts: the *laissez-faire* state of the nineteenth century, the welfare state of the mid-twentieth century, and the debates since the 1970s about whether and how the Scottish and UK constitutions should be modified.

As well as studying Scotland, we also look at other similar nations and regions: Bohemia, Ireland and Finland in the nineteenth century, and the federal states of Germany, the USA and Canada in the twentieth. The point of this comparison is to achieve some perspective on what could be reasonably expected as far as national autonomy is concerned by societies of similar size or international position to Scotland. Some of these places do or did have written constitutions, but – even for them – observing the practice of politics is more revealing about the meaning of these constitutions than the written document.

A useful distinction is drawn here by W. S. Livingston, writing about federalism. He argued that outward constitutional forms are neither necessary nor sufficient for the operation of federalism: '[A] society may possess institutions that are federal in appearance but it may operate them as though they were something else' (Livingston, 1952, p. 84). Moreover – and here he cites the UK in the mid-twentieth century – '[A society] may possess a unitary set of institutions and employ them as though they were federal in nature' (p. 84). The deciding factor, he argues, is not the written rules, but whether or not the society itself is truly federal. The same could even be said about formal statehood. A state might appear to be independent, but actually be highly constrained because all sorts of unwritten rules are imposed on it by its powerful neighbours. On the other hand, a part of a state might be allowed so much freedom that, in important respects, it behaves like an independent state.

So the main argument of this chapter is that the constitutional categories which dominate political debate can be misleading. The distinctions among 'independence', 'federalism', 'devolution' and a 'unitary state' are just as slippery as the distinctions among 'state', 'society' and 'nation'.

Four ideas provide the keys to understanding the Scottish constitution; these summarise the more extensive discussion of the nature of the state in Chapter 2. The first is Poggi's concept of the legal state: the argument that the great innovation of nineteenth-century government was that it started operating through the legal system. This has sometimes subsequently been called the rule of law. Equally important is that access to the state for the citizen was through that same legal system: bureaucrats were to an increasing extent recruited from the legal profession, and – partly as a consequence – so too were the members of the legislature.

The importance of this idea for understanding Scottish politics is that the Scottish legal system was and still largely is self-governing. So, in its relations with people in Scotland, the UK state has been Scottish.

The second idea is the important role which civil society plays in separating the state from the people. In the nineteenth century, Scottish civil society operated independently of 'high politics' at

Westminster. The lawyers mattered in this respect too, because their national Scottish networks and training gave coherence to that civil society, and so allow us to draw out principles that can be reasonably described as a Scottish 'constitution' for domestic politics. The relation between the state and civil society became more complicated in the twentieth century, as professional experts became incorporated as partners in government; this 'technocracy' is discussed in more detail later in the chapter.

The third point is about sovereignty. This is a hotly debated concept in political theory, but its essence is that a body claiming sovereignty is asserting its right to rule. That right could exist even if, in actual fact, its power was limited. The right to rule has frequently been claimed through ceremonies and symbols: in the words of the anthropologist, Clifford Geertz (1983), 'at the centre of any complexly organised society . . . there is both a governing elite and a set of symbolic forms expressing the fact that it is in truth governing'. For our purposes here, what matters is that Scotland never ceased to regard itself as a partner in Union. It had voluntarily given up power in the interests of gaining access to British trade and so on, but it always had the right to claim that power back. That right was embodied symbolically again in the highest reaches of the legal system – the High Courts – but also in the solemnity of the Scottish churches and the traditions of the Convention of Royal Burghs, the national body that could date its origins back to well before the Union, and which has been succeeded in the second half of the twentieth century by the Convention of Scottish Local Authorities. In these senses, Scotland could be said to have retained sovereignty.

The final idea is legitimacy. Beetham argues that a state is legitimate if it follows the rule of law, if it commands frequent 'acts of consent' from its citizens, and if it is justifiable in terms of the beliefs of the society. In all these respects, the UK state has retained legitimacy in Scotland only so long as it respects distinctively Scottish beliefs and practices: a distinctively Scottish constitution. It has had to follow the rule of Scots law. It has commanded consent, but only in Scottish terms: for example, throughout the nineteenth century the support for the British Empire that was widespread in Scotland always incorporated Scottish symbols (such as the Lion Rampant) into these celebrations. Throughout most of the twentieth century Scotland has participated enthusiastically in British wars and in support of the British governing institutions. And the state remained attractive to people in Scotland only because, at least until the 1960s, they broadly shared the same beliefs as people in England (in the nineteenth century, beliefs in free trade and the superiority of the Protestant religion, in the twentieth the ideals of the welfare state).

The nineteenth century: the era of the legal state

What, then, did the Scottish constitution in the nineteenth century look like? The key point is that it was, above all, local. Henry Cockburn described the 1832 Reform Act as giving a constitution to Scotland for the first time. By this he meant that government would henceforth be based on agreed rules rather than on patronage. These rules, so far as the governing of Scotland was concerned, operated at the level of the city, the burgh and the county, ruled over by the newly enfranchised middle class. These local councils and the accompanying local and national boards were far more powerful than their counterparts today. They ran the poor law, what there was of public health, and the asylums for lunatics. They managed the prisons and the police, and regulated housing. They were in charge of registering births, marriages and deaths. And by the end of the century they had taken responsibility for elementary schools, agriculture and the development of the Highlands. The councils of the large towns also, crucially, regulated trade. The people who staffed these councils and boards were the professional middle class, led by lawyers and, in particular, sheriffs (the local judges whose powers extended far beyond administering justice). The local boards were increasingly co-ordinated as the century progressed by national boards based in Edinburgh.

So the government of nineteenth-century Scotland consisted essentially of this network of councils and boards. This autonomous system of local powers built on the already existing Scottish civil society, and so ensured that Scotland would remain distinctive. The Scottish constitution in the nineteenth century, then, consisted of the conventions and traditions governing that network.

All this could happen because British politicians had little interest in interfering. The Parliament in London paid attention to domestic Scottish affairs only at the behest of factions within Scottish civil society; when they could sort things out among themselves – and that usually meant getting agreement among particular factions of Edinburgh lawyers – they could get their way by means of legislation. The UK state can best be thought of (at least for Scotland, England and Wales) as a foreign-policy instrument loosely placed on top of essentially self-governing localities. It was one of the most decentralised states in Europe.

An example of the relatively smooth operation of this system is in the campaign which led to the inclusion of Scotland in the Sale of Goods Act of 1893. The initial inclination of English ministers was not to include Scotland, but Scottish business leaders firmly believed in harmonising commercial legislation between the two countries, in pursuit of their ideal of free trade. They sponsored a campaign which also included lawyers in Edinburgh, Glasgow and Aberdeen, and prominent Liberal politicians. Faced with this pressure, the Government in London acceded readily. The key point is that the Act was not imposed on Scotland: the desire for uniformity with England came from Scotland.

An example of delay caused by an absence of Scottish agreement is in the campaign for a national system of elementary schools. This campaign started after the Disruption in the Church of Scotland in 1843: the split debilitated the capacity of both it and the new Free Church to continue to provide a school in every parish, and ended any possibility that they could respond adequately to the educational needs of the new industrial areas. But a national system was not established for another 30 years (in 1872). The delay was due, however, not to deliberate English obstruction, but to the religious divisions in Scotland; not only between these two churches, but also between them and the United Presbyterian Church and the secularists. The change by 1872 was that the religious passions had waned somewhat.

The governing system retained legitimacy in Scotland for a mixture of pragmatic and principled reasons. The pragmatism ensured that the people in the losing faction in any particular dispute were always able to look forward to being in the winning faction in some other battle. So, although Scottish majorities were sometimes defeated by English majorities when these were in alliance with the Scottish minority, the system itself was not brought into disrepute because the Scottish majority changed from issue to issue. The main dividing line in Scottish politics was, on the whole, not between Scotland and England, but around the principles which were used to justify the alliance with England in the first place: free trade, liberty, limited government.

In particular, Scotland did not need to develop a separatist nationalism in the nineteenth century because no faction in the country's politics ever felt sufficiently disenfranchised from the political system to want to change it. The nationalism which did develop was cultural, and Unionist, as we saw in Chapter 1. These nationalists celebrated Scotland's great achievement in having voluntarily entered and sustained a Union that brought great benefit to the nation. If Scotland had surrendered sovereignty, it had chosen to do so, and could always assert its identity as a nation to remind England not to take its friendship for granted.

Nineteenth-century Scotland in a European context

How does this relative autonomy for Scotland in the nineteenth century compare with other places in Europe? Answers to this question in political debate since the 1960s have often compared Scotland to big countries such as France, Prussia, Russia or, indeed, England; but the appropriateness of that is dubious. Big countries are bound to be able to exercise more autonomy than small ones, and a place like Scotland could hardly have reasonably expected to have had as much influence as a Prussia. Indeed many Scots of the nineteenth century would have argued that only the Union with a friendly neighbour could allow Scotland any influence in international affairs at all.

The more appropriate comparison is with countries that resemble Scotland in size or geopolitical situation. At one end of the scale are places which had considerably less autonomy than Scotland, and where in fact local liberals and nationalists looked to Britain for a model of a free constitution. Examples include Bohemia and Ireland.

Bohemia was part of Austria–Hungary, but had a history of semi-independent statehood dating back to the Middle Ages. The relative autonomy which it enjoyed in the eighteenth century was eroded from the mid-century onwards, provoking nationalist reaction in favour of limited self-government based on a liberal constitution. The nationalists wanted to retain the link with Austria because of the importance of the Austrian economy for the expanding industries of Bohemia: like Scotland in Britain, Bohemia was one of the centres of the industrial revolution.

However attempts at pragmatic reform were crushed in recurrent bouts of repression. In contrast to Scotland, elected local government lost powers as the nineteenth century progressed. It also came to be supervised tightly by officials appointed from Vienna, who had powers which even the Scottish sheriffs did not (and the sheriffs were, it should be emphasised, appointed from Edinburgh, not London). The Austrian Government also restricted free trade, and so business leaders in Bohemia had moved behind the liberal-nationalist programme by the end of the century.

Thus Bohemia differed from Scotland in failing to secure the rights which Scotland could take for granted. If there was no need for the dominant Scottish liberals to became separatist nationalists – because they had secured their liberal goals in the British realm – there was an equal need for Bohemian liberals to treat nationalism as a serious option.

Even more revealing than Bohemia for the Scottish case is Ireland – because it belonged to the same state and sent MPs to the same Parliament. But Ireland was never a partner in the Union; it was in certain important respects a colony. Outside the strongly Protestant areas around Belfast, there was no self-sufficient entrepreneurial middle class that could see its destiny as the wider British Empire. The mass of the population – the Catholic peasantry – was alienated from the British rulers on ethnic, religious and economic grounds, again in contrast to Scotland where culture, religion and a widespread belief in free trade made the partnership with England popular. The British Government attempted to build a programme of 'constructive unionism' in Ireland towards the end of the century, encouraging civil society by setting up truly autonomous local government, and encouraging investment in rural industry. But this was too late, and in any case failed to address the growing sectarian bitterness between the Catholic majority and the north-eastern Protestants.

From the point of view of the respective constitutions, Scotland was more fortunate than Ireland because it had inherited the self-governing institutions that Ireland lacked. It was more fortunate than Bohemia because Bohemia's institutions were eroded or abolished by a regime that eventually became authoritarian.

Scotland was not the only place that was constitutionally lucky, however. Finland found itself in a very similar position. It had been ruled by Sweden from the late Middle Ages, retaining autonomy in domestic matters. It kept that freedom when Russia annexed Finland in 1809. The Tsar's concern was to ensure that Finland could not be used as a base from which Sweden or some other power could invade Russia. Provided that Finland did not interfere with this military aim, it was therefore left free to get on with its own domestic policy. This it did largely through the agencies of civil society: its legal system, its schools, its local government, its cultural organisations. The country did retain something which Scotland did not have, namely a parliament (called the diet). But that mattered far less to Finnish autonomy than did civil society. The diet did not in fact meet for 60 years after the annexation, and thereafter it mostly had a purely advisory role. In that respect it resembled the many national bodies in Scotland that were used by government ministers as sources of ideas on Scottish development: for example the Faculty of Advocates, the Convention of Royal Burghs, the meetings of county landowners, the chambers of commerce.

This relatively stable situation in Finland changed only as the Tsarist Government grew much more oppressive after about 1890. Finland eventually became an independent state in the chaos of the Russian Revolution of 1917, but the new state retained the administrative structure that had grown up under Russian rule: that governing system was felt to be indigenously Finnish.

Thus Finland, while retaining a nominal Parliament, had a form of autonomy that resembled Scotland's quite closely. The conclusion we can draw from this and the other comparisons is that Scotland was relatively fortunate among small nations in nineteenth-century Europe. The actual autonomy of any small country depended on its being able to use its inherited institutions in the endless negotiation that went on with neighbouring big powers. Far from the century seeing the flowering of the nation-state – as is sometimes supposed – Europe can be thought of as having been governed by five empires with an assortment of nations and regions underneath and alongside them. The ultimate power lay with the big five: the UK, Prussia (and later Germany), France, Russia and Austria–Hungary. Small nations could hope, at best, to be left free to govern their domestic social policy, and to retain some wider international influence through a partnership with one of these five. In constitutional terms,

Scotland's partnership with England, and its domestic autonomy, were therefore worth having.

The twentieth century: the era of the technocratic state

The central idea for understanding the Scottish constitution in the twentieth century is again from Poggi. He argues that the century saw the growth in a belief that political problems could be solved by technical means. The most efficient way of ensuring that welfare could be delivered to the whole of society was believed to lie in rational planning. The new welfare state could become an instrument of redistribution only by removing decisions about how to allocate resources from the hands of politicians. Non-political experts would be fairer and more efficient.

In this kind of state, there was a central role for bureaucrats. They would not only control the implementation of policies – deciding how to interpret the inevitably vague legislation coming from Parliament – but would also be involved in helping to draft the legislation, and even in lobbying for change in the first place. The experts in the civil service shared a culture with similar experts in pressure groups, trade unions or employers' organisations. This common professional outlook was more important in shaping the character of legislation – and, through that, of social development – than the rather amateurish activities of MPs or even of ministers.

Thus the politics that really mattered was administrative politics. This dominance was helped by the political consensus over the aims of the welfare state. When most of Britain – even most of Europe – agreed that the state should provide basic levels of education or of health for all its citizens, the scope for national distinctiveness lay in how these broad principles were implemented, rather than in whether they should be adopted as national goals.

In this context, by the middle of the twentieth century Scotland had as much autonomy as could reasonably be hoped for, because it had its own indigenous bureaucracy in the Scottish Office and the other Scottish branches of the bureaucratic state. The Scottish Office grew out of the breakdown of the nineteenth-century constitution that we have surveyed. When the new mass electorates were demanding the mass provision of welfare, the local state was no longer powerful enough to be satisfactory. Centralisation therefore happened in Scotland just as much as in England or anywhere else. But in Scotland, centralised control mostly meant control by the Scottish Office, rather than by the ministries in London.

The Scottish Office acquired this type of autonomy gradually, the main impetus coming between the 1930s and the early 1950s. It was most evident in those areas which were regarded as essentially Scottish, such as education or law. In education, for example, reforms came from non-partisan committees, not from the political parties. The members of the committees were appointed by the senior civil servants in the Scottish Office, and were chosen according to expertise rather than partisan affiliation. They produced new examinations, new curricula, new teaching methods and – most notably of all – new ways of allocating children to secondary schools from 1965 onwards, abolishing selection by academic ability to establish the new system of comprehensive secondary education. But these committees, and their sponsoring civil servants, did not impose their ideas on Scottish education or Scottish society. They negotiated compromises that would be acceptable to the key interest groups: the teachers, local authorities, parents, employers and so on. Out of the consensus that was thus constructed, the civil servants would implement the policy, either by administrative fiat where that was possible, or by special Scottish legislation that – until the 1970s – mostly passed through Parliament with no serious challenge.

Similar points can be made about a whole range of social policy, in other words those topics which, in the nineteenth century, were governed by the boards and councils we have discussed. Housing, child law, health, roads, agriculture, the environment and the structure and financing of local government: all were shaped more by this process of consensual decision-making than by fierce partisan controversies. In housing, for example, the Scottish Office favoured rental from public agencies (mainly local authorities) over private ownership from the 1920s until the late 1970s. This was believed to be the only sensible way of dealing with the legacy of nineteenth-century slums. In child law, a welfare model of justice was developed from the 1960s onwards, replacing the courts with a new system of Children's Panels. This structure is quite distinctive not only from England, but from most other countries in the world.

The Scottish Office has in fact acquired growing powers of this sort, beyond the traditionally Scottish areas. Being able to influence the Scottish economy mattered a great deal to the legitimacy of the Office because the economic advantages of the Union were probably what saved it from disintegration in the first part of the twentieth century (see Chapter 4). The Secretary of State for Scotland was being pressed to speak for the Scottish economy as early as the 1930s, even before the Office had significant economic powers, and during the 1950s the convention developed that the Secretary of State was 'Scotland's minister'. It can be argued that one of the reasons why political nationalism grew in strength in the 1960s was that the Scottish economy was continuing to decline (following the British economy as a whole). The response to this new nationalism was to transfer new economic powers to the Scottish Office. For example, in the 1970s the Labour Government gave the Scottish Secretary responsibilities for significant aspects of economic development from London ministries. Oversight of regional policy has become especially important as grants from the EU have grown in size in the 1980s and 1990s.

The domestic policy areas where the Scottish Office did not have a large role were those in which it was felt that sharing resources or culture with the rest of the UK mattered more than national autonomy. By the 1990s the only notable remaining example was the large topic of social security (representing about one quarter of all public expenditure), but in the early years this argument was used to justify keeping control of economic development, transport and the universities in Whitehall. However, even in areas that were not under the direct control of the Scottish Office, it had a significant say: for example, its responsibility for housing and social work ensures that it can influence aspects of social security policy.

So the Scottish constitution that emerged between the 1920s and the 1960s can be seen in the workings of the Scottish Office and its interactions with the committees, pressure groups, professional organisations and so on, which it partly sponsored, but which also were partly independent of it. Thus, as in the nineteenth century, the Scottish constitution had the character of a network of informal rules emerging through the relationship between civil society and the state. The workings of the system are discussed in more detail in Chapter 5. The general conclusion here is that, if control over administrative politics was what made a country's politics distinctive, then Scotland – with its own special branch of the welfare state – had as much scope for exercising its own choices in domestic policies as any small nation. It did not have full independence, of course, but it retained its autonomy by reminding England repeatedly that the Union was a partnership (for example, in the campaigns for a Scottish parliament in the 1940s, or in voting for the SNP in the 1970s). This was a sort of reserve sovereignty, as it were. The whole system retained legitimacy up to the 1970s (and even thereafter, as we will see) largely because these reminders to the rest of the UK did extract more autonomy for the Scottish Office, so that the state continued to be seen as flexible enough to accommodate Scottish differences.

Twentieth-century Scotland in an international context

As in the nineteenth century, whether this autonomy was worth having can only be decided by comparing Scotland's situation with similar places elsewhere. Scotland chose not to try to become independent, and so the country was not as influential in international affairs as, say, Norway or Belgium. Until the 1960s, it still seemed reasonable to many Scots to try to influence world affairs through a continuing British connection. This view has waned only since then, as the British Empire has disappeared.

The main comparative question, however, is whether Scotland would have been more autonomous if it had had a Parliament while remaining within the UK state. The most relevant comparative model for that type of arrangement is federalism, in which legislative powers are shared between a central Parliament for some areas of policy and regional Parliaments for others. Indeed recent debate about the UK constitution has suggested that only a restructuring on federal lines could give Scotland what it wants. Whether this claim is true for the 1990s is discussed in the final section of this chapter. For the present, the argument is that the UK in the mid-twentieth century was in fact a pseudo federation (the point argued by Livingston in the source quoted at the beginning of the chapter). We look at this claim by examining the federations of the Federal Republic of Germany (FRG), the USA, and Canada.

The FRG was founded by the victorious Allies after the 1939–45 war to try to prevent the emergence of a state as centralised as the one that had been defeated. The Basic Law, which provided the constitution of the FRG, separated legislative competence between the *Länder* (the regions) and the *Bund* (the federal level). Broadly, the *Länder* were supposed to be responsible for domestic social policy and the *Bund* for foreign affairs and macro-economic policy.

In practice, however, the system has worked quite differently. Legislative powers have moved steadily from the *Länder* to the *Bund*, and administrative responsibilities have shifted in the other direction. As a result, the *Bund* has become the main level at which all laws are made – whether foreign or domestic – and the *Länder* have become the agencies through which the domestic laws are implemented.

This centralisation of law-making and decentralisation of administration has come about for three main reasons. The first is political consensus. There was such agreement across the FRG as a whole that no individual *Land* would want to deviate on fundamentals from the others. This agreement was partly because most of the *Länder* (with the main exception of Bavaria) were somewhat artificial creations in the first place, there being no real recent tradition of German regional distinctiveness, and partly because the main political parties – the Christian Democrats (and their allies in Bavaria), the Social Democrats and the liberal Free Democrats – all agreed about the need for a welfare state in a mixed economy.

The second pressure for legislative centralisation was the sheer cost of public services. Resources had to be transferred from richer areas to poorer to achieve something like equal access to state welfare. This was done by means of *Bund* grants to the *Länder*, but with conditions attached ensuring that uniform principles would be applied throughout the state. Because of the political consensus, these conditions attracted no effective opposition.

The third pressure was, however, for administrative decentralisation. There was a feeling that the spending of these transferred resources did require detailed knowledge of local circumstances (sometimes even at levels more local than the *Land* as a whole). That was why the *Länder* governments were increasingly charged with putting the legislation into practice. Through the second chamber of the central Parliament – the *Bundesrat* – they also could influence the content of legislation, but again only if they could achieve a political consensus among themselves.

Thus the actual operation of the German constitution has resembled the relationship between the Scottish Office and London for most of the post-1945 period. In fact there have been fewer differences in policy among the *Länder* than between Scotland and England. For example none of the *Länder* have anything like the degree of distinctiveness which Scotland has in education, child welfare or public housing, and none has a separate legal system.

A similar analysis can be made of the constitution of the USA since the 1930s, which has been described as 'cooperative federalism'. Federal powers expanded from the 1930s onwards to fulfil the welfare-state ideals embodied in President Roosevelt's New Deal. As in Germany, the federal level could prevail because it had access to far greater resources than did individual states. Other pressures for uniformity came from the growing bodies of professionals such as planners, economists, teachers, social workers and others. Organised across the USA as whole, they pushed for similar policies and practices in all the states, and – even more than the federal government – were in a position to ensure that the uniformity would be respected in practice, through their individual members' work at their own jobs.

However there was also administrative decentralisation. As with the *Länder* and the Scottish Office, the states became responsible for spending the money. The federal government made resources available through grants in aid, attaching conditions that ensured uniformity, but the ways in which the money was spent could be adapted to local conditions. The professional associations contributed to this too, because part of the culture of professionalism – as in other countries – came to be that the individual professional should have some rights to decide how policy would be implemented in each particular case.

For a country that had its origins in the voluntary coming together of the states, this system appears to be strong centralisation. On the other hand, it can be argued that without this pooling of resources the federal system would have completely collapsed. Better to keep control of the administration, it was argued, if the only real alternative is no local control of anything.

The third example is of Canada. This is the most decentralised federation of the three we are looking at. For example, by the 1980s the federal level in Canada was responsible for only 44 per cent of public spending, in contrast to 59 per cent in the USA and Germany (Moreno, 1993). The reason for the difference is that Canada lacks the national unity which Germany and the USA have, there being tensions most notably between Quebec and the rest, but also between the rich western provinces and the poorer Atlantic ones.

It is true that Canada has experienced many of the pressures for centralisation that we have observed in the UK, Germany and the USA. From the 1920s onwards, there grew up the same belief as in these other states that welfare spending had to be shared if it was to be efficient. Joint decisions between the provinces and the federal government gave the provinces a say, and allowed them to have control over the ways in which federal money was spent.

The fundamental difference from the USA and Germany, however, is the unresolved conflict among Canada's provinces. A federation will work if there is a quite fine balance between respect for diversity and an acceptance of uniformity in the interests of efficiency and fairness. Where one part of the state periodically seems to be questioning the state's very existence, that balance is upset. There have been no such disruptive influences in the USA, Germany or – until quite recently – the UK. Indeed, even after the absorption of the five *Länder* that used to make up East Germany (and despite the economic problems which this has caused) German federalism still operates on broadly the same principles of sharing resources; there is no serious move for some parts of the federation to separate from the rest. In Canada, however, the cultural and political conflicts involving Quebec have always stood as an obstacle to a fully cooperative federalism.

All three of these federal states have lessons for Scotland and the UK. Most obviously, the actual working of German and US federalism has looked quite like the constitutional position of Scotland, in that legislation has come from the centre and has been administered by the Scottish Office. By comparing the UK with Canada we can see why that has been politically acceptable. At least until the 1960s, political and cultural tensions in the UK were never as severe as those which have recurrently separated the provinces of Canada. Scotland and England shared the same political majority for all but three of the years between 1945 and 1970, and the still-dominant Britishness ensured that most people felt that Scottish culture was best served within a wider Britain. Scottish differences were accommodated even in the formally non-federal UK, which has allowed more distinctiveness in policy to Scotland than the German state has to its *Länder*. We shall discuss in the final section of the chapter whether Scotland has now diverged sufficiently from the rest of the UK to prevent the post-1945 constitution from working as it used to do. The point for the middle of the twentieth century, however, is that a Scottish Parliament in the UK would probably have produced much the same social outcomes for Scotland as did the Scottish Office working with the central Parliament in London.

A new constitution for Scotland?

Debate about the Scottish constitution has grown since the 1960s, and has become intense since the late 1980s. There are three main reasons for this.

The first is shared with many other countries where some form of popular democracy is the guiding principle. The essence of the question that is raised is whether loss of popular participation is a price worth paying for technocratic efficiency. The version of this that can be found in federations bears an obvious resemblance to the debates in Scotland. For example the *Länder* in Germany have asserted their rights against the federal control of legislation, especially if that control is in danger of slipping away to an even more remote level in the EU.

Suspicion about technocracy can be found further in what Daniel Bell (1976) has called the 'participation revolution'. On the political left, this took the form of student rebellions in the 1960s, and the emergence of such movements as feminism, sexual politics, environmentalism, and the politics of race and ethnicity: all of these have in common an assertion of the rights of human beings to shape their own lives. This leftist critique of the welfare state complained that the professionals in the bureaucracy had gained too much control of the lives of individual people.

On the political right – the so-called 'New Right' – the most famous and influential exponents of individualism and popular participation were Margaret Thatcher and Ronald Reagan, who believed that the only way to reduce the stultifying power of bureaucracy was to convert all social relations into relations of the free market. These politicians and their allies shared some of the leftist critique of bureaucracy, although their hostility to it also rested on a belief that the welfare-state professionals had subscribed too thoroughly to the political beliefs of social democracy.

Scotland has produced its version of all of these critiques of technocracy. As in the federations, one of the origins of the idea of a Scottish Parliament is as a democratic check on the Scottish Office. In particular the Scottish Office has been accused of governing Scotland through 'the quango state': the network of committees staffed by professionals that we discussed earlier as forming the core of the twentieth-century Scottish constitution. Only a Parliament, it is claimed, could bring the system under popular scrutiny.

In the leftist critique of the technocratic state, arguments for a Scottish Parliament have increasingly found support among people whose political philosophy has decentralisation at its core: environmentalists or feminists, for example. These ideas found a forum in the magazine *Radical Scotland*, as influential on the Scottish left in the 1980s as *Marxism Today* was on the left in England. For these people, a Scottish Parliament is a first step towards even more thorough devolution of power to communities and individuals.

The decline of the Conservative Party in Scotland has reduced the impact of the rightist critique of technocracy, but it has not been absent. Many of the ideas that became associated with the New Right had their origins in St Andrews University in the 1960s: and when Michael Forsyth was Scottish Minister of Education and Health between 1987 and 1992, he tried to further the same free-market revolution as his colleagues in England. In particular, he followed Thatcher's general suspicion of the autonomy of civil society, regarding it as a source of corporatist conspiracy against the individual consumer. He therefore sought to reduce the independence of the various agencies that were the bulwark of Scotland's autonomy in the welfare state: for example local government itself, or the boards that ran the health service, or the professional committees that advised on educational questions. Powers were removed from elected local government altogether; for the committees that were appointed by the Scottish Office, the Conservative strategy was to fill them with their ideological supporters. This rightist version of constitutional reform has almost always gone along with opposition to a Scottish Parliament, because that is seen as simply another source of bureaucratic inertia. When Forsyth became Secretary of State for Scotland in 1995, he claimed to have recanted from some of his earlier confrontational style, and he proposed to return power to local government, but in this he largely failed.

The second impetus to debate about the Scottish constitution has been political divergence between Scotland and England. Control of how policy is implemented might have been enough when Scottish and English policy preferences were much the same, but since the 1970s Scotland has retained an essentially social-democratic majority, while large parts of southern England have moved to the right. This difference has been controversial because the English majority has provided the government that controls the Scottish Office. As the Scottish Conservative vote declined to under one fifth, the ministers in the Scottish Office became increasingly embattled. Their attempt to create a rightist revolution from above – restricting local government and so on – merely exacerbated the Conservative Party's unpopularity.

Political divergence within the UK has helped the SNP in its battle with the Labour Party. A problem for the proponents of a domestic Scottish Parliament is that the disagreements between the Scottish and English majorities might be so profound as to push Scotland towards outright independence. As we have seen, federal arrangements work only if there is broad agreement between the component units.

The third source of ideas on the Scottish constitution is the slow reorientation of Scotland towards the EU and away from Britain. The Empire has ended, the monarchy has declined, and the British economy has long since passed its Victorian peak. Some of the original arguments for a Union with England have therefore now become arguments against it. If wide markets are to the benefit of business, then the EU offers more opportunities than the UK. If a small country needs to share in cultural developments beyond its borders, then there might be more security in the EU – which has had to respect the enormous diversity of its members – than within a UK dominated by England. The European dimension has now permeated the constitutional proposals of all the political parties. The SNP advocates independence in the EU; Labour and the Liberal Democrats want a domestic Scottish Parliament to have membership of the UK delegation to the Council of Ministers; and the Conservative Government had already set up a lobbying body in Brussels which acts as an umbrella for any Scottish organisation that wants to influence EU policy. Scottish Office ministers also occasionally take part in the UK delegation.

The eventual outcome of this frustration with the existing Scottish constitution is not certain, however, even though we now know there will be Scottish Parliment. The weakness of the support in the 1979 referendum for a Scottish assembly seemed to reflect a desire to continue with the compromise on autonomy which the welfare state had offered. If that compromise had continued to be available – say, under a continuing Labour Government – then it is possible that the movement for a Scottish Parliament could have stagnated. That it did not was as much due to Thatcher's hostility to the welfare state – and therefore to the Scottish majority – as to any passionate wish in Scotland for a Parliament. Although the opportunity to restore the legitimacy of an administrative autonomy has passed (because of there having been so long a period of fundamental political disagreement between the Scottish and English majorities) the issue of a Scottish Parliament has not provoked a complete breakdown of the system of Scottish government. Many Scots – although now no more than a minority – still hope that the system which worked quite well in the middle of the twentieth century can be revived. That is one explanation of the result of the 1992 general election, where the Conservatives did slightly less badly than had been forecast, and claimed this as a victory for the Union. That it was not was confirmed by the electoral events of 1997, when the Conservatives lost all their Scottish seats, and when, in the referendum, the electorate clearly endorsed the Labour Government's proposals for a Scottish Parliament.

These proposals owed a great deal to the work of the Constitutional Convention, which had been set up after the 1987 general election, in which the Scottish Conservative vote declined to 24 per cent and they retained only 10 seats, despite winning in the UK as a whole. The Campaign for a Scottish Assembly established a group of Scottish notables, who produced a 'Claim of Right' which asserted the right of the people of Scotland to decide on their own constitution, and indicated that the UK state had become too centralised. The Convention which resulted from this declaration first met in March 1989. It included representatives of four political parties: Labour, the Liberal Democrats, the Greens and the Communists. The Conservatives refused to join, and the SNP withdrew shortly after the discussions that preceded its inaugural meeting on the ground that it would not take independence seriously enough. Alongside the parties were representatives of many civil-society bodies (for example, the trade unions, cultural organisations, the churches and local government).

The Convention was a curious combination of rhetoric about a renewal of democracy with a continuation of the semi-secretive world of the committees and boards that had run the Scottish welfare state: the closed system that radical critics such as Michael Forsyth were determined to abolish. There was some reality to the claims that the Convention represented a broad spectrum of Scottish society. It did, after all, contain 59 of the 72 MPs, and it did embrace a much wider range of civil-society groups than the government could claim to speak for. But it was also socially narrow and very traditional in its composition and style. The committee which had formulated the Claim of Right was as firmly part of the Scottish establishment as could be imagined, containing as it did a mixture of professors, ministers of religion, retired diplomats and retired senior civil servants. The title of the declaration unintentionally located the Convention in a firmly Protestant tradition, although the intention was to evoke the radicalism of the religious reformers who issued the two previous claims: the Free Church of Scotland in its break with the Established Church in 1843, and the Presbyterians who asserted their rights in 1688. The Claim of Right committee was also mainly male, although less predominantly so than the Convention itself, which simply reflected the male-dominated nature of Scottish civil society in general.

This dual character of the Convention – radical as well as conservative – is hardly surprising because it was drawing on the various strands that had led to the questioning of Scotland's current constitutional position; both the leftist critique of the bureaucracy, and the frustration by Scotland's political elite that the Conservative Government had excluded it from power for so long.

The core idea of the Convention's scheme is that a Scottish Parliament should have legislative powers in all the areas administered by the Scottish Office. Thus as far as Scotland is concerned, the main legislation that would remain at Westminster would be foreign affairs, defence, macro-economic policy and policy on social security. The relationship between a Parliament of this sort and Westminster would therefore resemble the structures in a federal state. The difference would be the absence of parallel Parliaments in other areas of the UK (except, probably, Wales and Northern

Ireland). The current Labour Government's scheme for a Scottish Parliament is closely based on the Convention's proposals.

The implications of this scheme for policy-making are discussed in Chapter 5. We consider here their constitutional significance. Four key constitutional features distinguish the scheme from the proposals that were not implemented after 1978:

- The legislation setting up the Parliament specifies what is reserved to Westminster rather than what is transferred to the new Parliament. This approach is generally regarded as a stronger form of home rule, because in effect it confers on the Scottish Parliament the power to act in very general ways in the interests of the people of Scotland. In debates about local government in the rest of Europe, this is often referred to as 'power of general competence' (Bogdanor, 1994). It will probably encourage the Parliament to be adventurous and deter Westminster from interfering, at least so long as the latter is governed by a party that is reasonably sympathetic to the idea of a Scottish Parliament.
- The elections to the Parliament will be by a form of proportional representation (PR), broadly ensuring that the number of seats allocated to each party is proportional to the number of votes won. The form of PR adopted by the Convention and in the Government's scheme is a version of the Additional Member System used in Germany. There will be 73 members, chosen from individual constituencies in the same way as for the Westminster Parliament: that is, the candidate who gains the most votes in a constituency will be elected for that constituency (Orkney and Shetland having been separated into two constituencies). The remaining 56 seats in the Parliament will be used to compensate for the extent to which the party distribution of seats in the constituency section differs from their distribution of votes (as happens frequently in the case of Westminster). These seats will be filled by candidates chosen by the parties, and the calculations will be done separately for the eight regions of Scotland (corresponding to the eight constituencies represented in the European Parliament), with seven seats in each region. PR is almost unprecedented in elections on the British mainland (although the education authorities in Scotland were elected by PR between 1918 and 1929).

- The scope for Westminster to interfere in the running of the Scottish Parliament will be limited, and will be entirely confined to constitutional matters. Under the 1978 proposals it would have been able to interfere in policy as well, which would have created endless opportunities for partisan conflict. It is likely that the resolution of disputes will become a mainly judicial matter, as it is in fully federal states.
- Although the legislation does not allow for a direct link between the Parliament and the European Union, it is likely that secondary legislation will provide for that, so that Scottish ministers will be able to take part in the UK delegation to the EU Council of Ministers. This will be analogous to what happens in Germany and Spain.

Each of these constitutional innovations shows that the setting up of the Scottish Parliament will have profound implications for how the UK as a whole is governed. The long-term consequences are difficult to foresee, partly because – if the experience of federal states is a guide – the effects will arise as much through slowly evolving conventions as through formal rules enacted in the founding legislation. In this sense the Scottish constitution will continue to draw on the informal versions of autonomy that have been in place throughout the period of the Union. The new system will require goodwill and compromise from both the Edinburgh Parliament and Westminster, establishing during its first few years a set of working practices that will shape constitutional relations for many decades. The form of these conventions will depend not only on the Parliaments themselves but also on civil society. For example, although most health matters will be transferred to the Scottish Parliament, most health professionals will continue to be members of UK-wide associations such as the British Medical Association or the Royal College of Nursing. Such associations will help to mediate the overtly political relations between Scotland and London, just as they have done in the federal systems we have looked at briefly in this chapter.

In some respects the new settlement could be seen as a first step towards a more formally federal UK. This is certainly how the Liberal Democrats would see it. The main political problem with federal ideas, however, is that there seems to be an uneven desire for regional assemblies in England. Moreover, as we have seen from our discussion of Germany and the USA, a federal system might not be able to give Scotland the degree of autonomy which the political divergence between Scotland and England would seem to require.

The SNP, of course, could answer all of the constitutional complications of the Convention's scheme, or federalism, by pointing out that an independent Scottish state would operate in exactly the same kind of way as, say, independent Denmark. It would be up to the Scottish Parliament to decide on matters of taxation, the method of election, how to get more women elected and how decentralised government should be within Scotland. If the Scottish majority were to be different from the English one, that would no more produce a constitutional problem than would a similar disagreement between Denmark and Sweden. So in theory the option of independence seems to answer the constitutional dilemmas, at least as far as they can be answered by any state. The problem for the SNP is a political one: how to persuade a majority of Scottish voters that an independent state would be economically viable and would not culturally sever Scotland from its British neighbours.

In fact, the Scottish electorate are fairly cautious (as we have seen) and prefer to postpone the question of independence until after a more limited form of autonomy has been achieved. The meaning of independence is in any case changing, as the states of Europe are converging towards a greater sharing of responsibilities. Independence no longer means the same as it did in the nineteteenth century. It could be that, once independence in Europe is seriously on the agenda, it will be barely distinguishable from the limited autonomy that the new Parliament will offer after 2000, because all the matters that the Scottish Parliament will not control – such as foreign affairs, defence and macro-economic policy – will have been transferred to the European level anyway.

Whatever the outcome of the debates about the constitution, one conclusion can be drawn with certainty: no settlement will be final. The constitution will continue to evolve, partly in response to pressures from outside the country, and partly because Scottish civil society will continue to be important despite the addition of a Parliament, and will continue to change independently of it.

4

The Scottish Economy

Introduction

Is there such a thing as the Scottish economy? Some would answer 'no'. This is because of Scotland's relationship to the UK economy, where key macro-economic decisions over monetary and fiscal policy are made at a highly centralised level, although they may have a specific impact on economic conditions in Scotland. It is also a relevant question to ask with regard to the position of Scotland within the EU and the wider world economy. In the context of growing globalisation of markets and increasing power and mobility of international finance, the level of control which any state has over its own economy is diminishing. This has raised particular issues in Scotland, which has existed within the UK and without its own parliament.

This difficulty of understanding the economic position of Scotland within the capitalist world economy is not new. Scotland's structural position has been doubly unique. While Britain was the first state to undergo the industrial revolution, in Scotland this revolution took place in a country which did not have all of the political and institutional structures of statehood. Added to this, and unlike the industrialisation process experienced by most countries in Europe, change occurred before the ideological input of nationalism (Nairn, 1977).

Despite the fact that Scotland does not yet have its own legislature, and, it can be argued, has never been independent of influence from the rest of Britain or of trade with the rest of the world, it is nevertheless possible to distinguish a Scottish economy in respect of the key economic actors involved and features and conditions relevant to Scotland. Although Scotland was part of the post-war economic consensus associated with the Keynesian welfare state, it was also successful in constructing its own national economic interest (L. Paterson, 1994). The existence of distinct policy networks and institutions in Scotland (see Chapter 5) and the role of the Scottish Office in promoting Scottish interests helped to ensure the articulation of this separate Scottish national economic interest.

We wish to place an understanding of the Scottish economy within broader political and social discourses. It is not our intention in this chapter to provide a comprehensive account of the development of the Scottish economy, and neither is it our aim to enter into what could be regarded as a technical economic debate. Rather we are concerned to explore the way in which the perceived health of the Scottish economy influenced the policy of political parties and other groups in Scotland and helped fuel many of the political arguments for constitutional change.

In this chapter we outline the key features of the Scottish economy which have affected both its past and present before identifying some of the strengths and potential weaknesses which could influence its future development. In common with other developed economies, the Scottish economy has been subject to major structural changes in the twentieth century. The impact of some of these changes has given rise to different interpretations and debates, which we shall discuss. For example it is argued that the decline of traditional industries and the dependence on a limited number of export markets, together with the rising trend in mergers and takeovers by foreign-controlled companies, has left the Scottish economy increasingly vulnerable to economic changes outwith its control. The decline in control over economic decision-making in Scotland is said to have been exacerbated by the electoral divergence between Scotland and England and the centralisation of political decision-making after the election of the first Thatcher Government. The Conservative administrations of 1979–97 stressed their rejection of Keynesian demand-management techniques aimed at full employment, in favour of giving priority to the reduction of inflation and public expenditure. This macro-economic approach, coupled with other free or liberal market policies, was at odds with the policies advocated by all the main opposition political parties in Scotland. The pressure to establish a Scottish Parliament with greater control over aspects of the Scottish economy, or an independent Scottish Parliament within the EU, gained momentum in the 1980s as the negative economic consequences of so-called Thatcherism and monetarism affected the Scottish economy. The view that there was and still is an alternative to the economic policy approach of the Conservative Government has been sustained by the opposition parties and other institutions in Scottish civil society.

The Scottish economy: past and present characteristics

There are several factors which have specific relevance to an understanding of the Scottish economy. It has rarely if ever been self-contained or independent; rather, it has always been an open economy, reliant on external capital and technology, and subject to the vagaries of the broader economic and political environment. The size of Scotland's population and the dependency of economic development on traditional industries are also important features.

In relative terms, Scotland is sparsely populated with a heavy concentration of the population in the central belt. Gavin McCrone (1993, p. 5) explains that this 'means that Scotland alone cannot provide an adequate market for the majority of modern industries and the economy must therefore be heavily dependent upon exporting.' One consequence is that Scotland exports a higher proportion of its output per head than the UK as a whole.

As one of the first countries to experience the industrial revolution, Scotland developed its economy around heavy industries, including ship-building, steel, engineering and coal. For example, in the nineteenth century 80 per cent of the world's ships were built in Scotland. The textile and woollen industries also formed part of the basis of the Scottish economy. As J. Scott (1983) states: 'Scotland evolved an economy focused around textiles and heavy industry.' As a result of the concentration of the heavy industries in west central Scotland, people migrated to the area from the Highlands of Scotland and from Ireland in search of work. The social and other costs of this mobility of labour were high, and Aitken (1992, p. 233) makes the point that the nation's wealth was 'built on the poverty of the people'. For example, in late nineteenth-century Scotland the average life expectancy was 30.

The initial buoyancy of demand in Scotland's industries and favourable trading conditions meant that insufficient attention was given to the structure of industry, future investment or new technology. When market conditions changed, the vulnerability of the Scottish economy became exposed. After the 1914–18 war the market for Scotland's goods was open to increasing competition, and the inter-war depression years had serious consequences for Scottish industry. As in other parts of Britain, unemployment soared, with the male unemployment rate increasing to 35 per cent in 1933 (Aitken, 1992). The number of company mergers and acquisitions also rose during the recession. Similar to the experience in other countries, the economy was lifted out of depression in the late 1930s, mainly because of production required for the war effort of 1939–45. The outbreak of war necessitated government intervention and investment, which provided a boost to private industry.

The post-war period witnessed a continuation of Keynesianism and the expansion of the welfare state. It also involved the extension of a nationalisation programme under Attlee's Labour Government, with the railways, coal, gas and electricity all coming under public control. This latter development affected the ownership and control of industry in Scotland and shifted decision-making south of the border. A major problem facing the Scottish economy in the post-war period was the continued decline of traditional industries. One consequence was that unemployment in Scotland was about twice the UK average (Dey and Fraser, 1982). For example, at the end of the Second World War 187 coal-mining pits were operating in Scotland; by the 1970s the number had decreased to 18; and by the early 1990s, following the closure programme pursued by British Coal in the 1980s, just one pit survived – at Longannet (Aitken, 1992). Another pit – Monktonhall Colliery – was saved following a unique venture which involved a small group of miners forming their own company in order to lease the pit from British Coal. The 110 miners each invested £10 000 to finance the venture. However the colliery continued to face financial problems, which led to the intervention of a private company in 1995. Monktonhall's difficulties did not end there: and in 1997 Caledonian Mining withdrew interest, thus threatening the future of the colliery.

Post-war British governments, both Labour and Conservative, used regional policy to tackle rising unemployment in Scotland. This involved two approaches: providing resources to encourage workers to move to higher employment areas, and providing incentives to potential employers to locate in areas of high unemployment. In other words, regional policy meant 'taking workers to the work, or work to the workers'. One of the senior civil servants in the Scottish

Office responsible for implementing regional policy in Scotland, Gavin McCrone (1985), records the beneficial impact of this on Scotland's economic growth, employment and average earnings. However there are differences of opinion between commentators on the extent to which these benefits can be attributed to regional policy (A. Brown, 1989; L. Paterson, 1994). Regional policy was supported by the establishment of the Highlands and Islands Development Board (HIDB) in 1965, aimed at providing economic assistance and encouragement to the area. Ten years later, in 1975, the Scottish Development Agency (SDA) was set up with responsibility for economic development in other areas of Scotland.

Additional factors which contributed to changes in the Scottish economy in the post-war period were the increase in investment by multinational enterprises; the investment in insurance companies and pension funds; the development of new industries, including electrical engineering, electronics, chemicals and clothing; and the growth of the tourist trade. The result was a diversification of Scotland's industrial base and increased convergence with the economy of the rest of the UK, but also a significant shift in ownership and control.

The world recession which followed the 1970s oil crisis exposed the underlying weaknesses of the Scottish economy. Even the discovery of oil and gas in the North Sea in the 1970s, which contributed to Scotland's natural resources and the possibility of economic growth, was insufficient to cushion Scotland from the recession. The traditional heavy industries were particularly badly hit by the collapse of demand, and manufacturing jobs were most at risk. Aitken (1992) estimates that in just three years (1979–81), Scottish manufacturing lost 11 per cent of its output and 20 per cent of its jobs, and the decline coincided with the time when the consensus on government intervention to boost demand had been shattered by the election of the first Thatcher Government. Clearly Scotland was not the only country in Europe to suffer the costs of structural change in the economy and the decline of traditional areas, but all of the heavy industries most adversely affected by restructuring were to be found in a concentrated geographical area.

To some extent, but not entirely, the growth in the service industries helped offset some of the most adverse effects of restructuring. Table 4.1 shows the shift in employment between major industries and the service sector in the period 1979–94.

Table 4.1   *Employees in employment in Scotland by major industry or service sector*

Sector	Number in employment (thousands)			Change in employment (percentage)		
	1979	*1989*	*1994*	*1979–89*	*1989–94*	*1979–94*
Agriculture, forestry, fishing	48	29	26	−40	−10	−46
Energy and water supply	72	57	49	−21	−14	−32
Manufacturing	604	402	354	−33	−12	−41
Construction	155	130	101	−16	−22	−35
Distribution, hotels and catering, repairs	392	400	416	+2	+4	+6
Transport and communication	135	113	107	−16	−5	−21
Banking, finance, insurance and business services	123	176	204	+43	+16	+66
Education, health and other services	573	651	704	+14	+8	+23
All industries and services	2 102	1 957	1 963	−7	+0.3	−6.6

Source: Hughes (1994).

The figures in Table 4.1 highlight the decrease in the contribution made to employment in the Scottish economy by the manufacturing industries: some 41 per cent between 1979 and 1994. It also demonstrates the decline in other areas, including agriculture, forestry and fishing (−46%), construction (−35%), energy and water supply (−32%) and transport and communication (−21%). The most rapid growth area was banking, finance, insurance and business services, which had a 66 per cent increase in employment over the 15-year period. Two other areas experienced growth in employment, namely education, health and other services at 23 per cent, and distribution, hotels and catering, and repairs at 6 per cent. There was an overall drop in the number of employees over the period, from 2 102 000 in 1979 to 1 963 000 in 1994, in spite of a minor recovery after 1989, representing a fall of 6.6 per cent.

There are competing analyses of the strengths and weaknesses of the Scottish economy which can be divided into two main perspectives: the pessimistic view and the optimistic view. The pessimistic view is that the growth of the service sector will be insufficient to fill the gap left by job losses in the industrial sector, that the export trade is overdependent on two main products (electronics and whisky), and that Scotland is disadvantaged in being located on the periphery of European and international markets and has been denied the investment in transport which is essential in order to compete. Concern is expressed for the future prospects of the economy because of the continued closure of key firms and industries, the erosion of Scotland's industrial base, takeover bids by non-Scottish companies, and the replacement of management functions, research and development programmes and high value-added, skilled employment by assembly-line, low-skilled work, which is more vulnerable to market changes. An extension of this view is that Scotland has suffered disproportionately in comparison with other parts of Britain, and has been adversely affected by macro-economic policies targeted at economic problems specific to the south-east of England.

The optimistic view of the Scottish economy acknowledges that Scotland has undergone major structural change with the decline of heavy industries and the closure of manufacturing plants, but contends that the economy is now more competitive, more technologically advanced and, with the growth of service industries, more broadly based than it has ever been. Scotland is also rich in natural resources and enjoys economic benefits from the North Sea oil and gas industries. Unlike other parts of Britain, it is argued, Scotland has survived the 1980s and 1990s recessions remarkably well. The optimists are confident about the longer-term trends in the economy, including future productivity, investment and growth rates, the opportunities provided by the European market, and Scotland's performance relative to the rest of the UK.

One problem with assessing these differing interpretations is that the arguments are often based more on political differences and competing approaches to economic policy management than on economic evidence. Also, they inevitably involve sweeping generalisations about the economies of Scotland and England. While there are identifiable differences between the Scottish and English economies, these differences are complicated by the variations which exist between different regions in the two countries, and may be offset by similarities between them. For example the industrial differentiation within Scotland has been higher than industrial differentiation between Scotland and the rest of Britain. Similarly the occupational structure of Scotland is close to the

British mean, the significant difference in white-collar employment being between the south-east of England and the rest of Britain (McCrone, 1992).

However it is with the political nature of some of these economic disputes that we are most concerned. Some of the key debates are discussed in the section which follows.

Key debates

The performance of the Scottish economy has been subject to academic debate and much political controversy. The most dominant debates surround issues of underdevelopment/dependency, branch-plant economy status, de-industrialisation, the north–south divide, the changing role of women in the economy, the impact of European integration, and the consequences of constitutional change.

Underdevelopment/dependency theory

Both the 'underdevelopment' and 'dependency' theories influenced the research agendas and commentaries on Scotland in the late 1960s and early 1970s (McCrone, 1992). Such theories were used to explain the perceived disadvantaged position of the Scottish economy. The debate between Immanuel Wallerstein and Christopher Smout is one example of this discourse. Working within the framework of analysing capitalism as a world-system and dividing countries between 'core' and 'periphery', Wallerstein (1980) examined Scotland's dependence upon external factors for its development, and argued that Scotland could be categorised as a country on the periphery and as one to which the terms underdevelopment and dependency could be applied. Within this analysis, countries on the periphery are disadvantaged in their trading relationships with core countries, which in turn reinforces the inequality in the balance of power between core and periphery. For his part, Smout (1980) questioned the application of the term 'dependency' to some countries, and challenged the view that dependency was necessarily a barrier to economic development. In Scotland's case, according to Smout, trade was not an engine of exploitation, but on the contrary was a cause of growth. He contended that Scotland had been able to move from periphery to semi-periphery and then to core status precisely because of its early dependency. The debate between the two academics continued with Wallerstein challenging Smout's data and claiming that Scotland experienced 'development by invitation', by which he meant that Scottish capitalists were able to develop markets only by invitation from their English counterparts. Some took the view that Scotland was a colony of England, and that Scottish capitalism developed a 'complementary' rather than a 'competitive' relationship with English capitalism.

We can question the extent to which underdevelopment or dependency theories are applicable to the Scottish case, but in the late 1960s and early 1970s the intellectual climate in Scotland was receptive to such perspectives. Without doubt the concept of colonial status has played an important part in the development of a specifically Scottish political consciousness, especially at times of economic decline when the SNP has gained electoral support.

Branch-plant economy status

Linked to the theme of underdevelopment/dependency is the view that, with changing ownership patterns away from indigenous capital, Scotland is increasingly becoming a branch-plant economy with control of Scottish industry lying outwith Scotland (Firn, 1975; Young, 1984). It is difficult to obtain accurate data in this area. From the available evidence, it is estimated that in just two years (between 1985 and 1987) Scotland lost control of more than 20 per cent of its listed industrial companies, and that around 70 per cent of Scotland's industrial sector is now owned and controlled from outside Scotland (Rosie, 1991). At the beginning of the 1990s the magazine *Scottish Business Insider* estimated that of the top 200 companies operating in Scotland more than 36 per cent were owned by outside interests. In addition it was estimated that only one in five of the top 50 manufacturing companies in Scotland had headquarters in the country, prompting Aitken (1992, p. 262) to comment that 'Scotland in the 1990s is conspicuously, many believe alarmingly, short of headquarters'. The rapid increase in takeovers – especially of firms with a long history of operating in Scotland, household names such as House of Fraser, Bell's, Coats Patons, Distillers, Britoil, Govan Shipbuilders – and bids for other companies, including Scottish & Newcastle Brewers and the Royal Bank of Scotland, caused concern. A significant feature of the growth of takeovers and mergers in the 1980s was that it was not confined to failing industries. Some of Scotland's 'best' performers were also vulnerable. In addition the Conservative Government's policy of privatising of the nationalised industries in the 1980s resulted in very little ownership returning to Scotland. This trend is commented on by Aitken (1992, p. 265): 'Perhaps there is some irony in the fact that Margaret Thatcher's Government, while steadfast in defence of political sovereignty, appeared so tolerant of the loss of economic sovereignty. In Scotland the linkage between the two has been more consistently understood.'

The issue was given extensive media attention in Scotland and formed the basis of a television documentary by George Rosie. Rosie argued that the extent of takeovers, mergers and acquisitions was only just being realised and the consequences assessed, and he concluded that 'we are, quite literally, losing the heid' (Rosie, 1991). In answer to the question 'does it matter?', he asserted that a growing number of Scottish business people, industrialists, union leaders and commentators thought that it mattered a great deal.

Those who consider that the shift in ownership has negative implications for the Scottish economy base their case on several points. It is contended that the extent and speed of the removal of ownership from Scottish entrepreneurs mean that key economic decisions are taken outside Scotland, which leaves the Scottish economy vulnerable to changes in corporate plans; that 'predators have picked the plums and left the crab apples alone' (Aitken, 1992, p. 263); and further that the extent of reciprocal investment or takeovers by Scottish entrepreneurs is small by comparison. Concern is expressed that the removal of company headquarters from Scotland and their replacement with a branch office has negative spin-off effects for the range of professionals needed to sustain and support the operation of a head office. From his studies of the effect of takeovers on the Scottish economy, Love concludes that although takeovers may not necessarily be bad for the companies involved, they are almost invariably bad for their suppliers: 'Not so much with the suppliers of materials, but with the suppliers of professional services. And that's an area in which Scotland has traditionally prided itself' (quoted in Rosie, 1991). The case against takeovers is summed up by the Standing Commission on the Scottish Economy: '[It] erodes our skill base, saps our entrepreneurial potential, and leaves us vulnerable to arbitrary decisions by multinational companies over which we have little control, and whose investment and disinvestment decisions invariably seem to catch policymakers by surprise.'

The counter-argument put by others, most notably the Scottish Office, is that takeovers do not matter as markets themselves are international; that Scotland can benefit greatly from inward investment whatever the source; that jobs will be protected and new jobs created in Scotland; that most of the companies taken over continue to operate in Scotland; and that Scotland has been successful in attracting many of the world's well-known manufacturers. In stating the benefits of what it describes as 'overseas participation in Scottish manufacturing', the Scottish Office estimated that in 1988 the gross value-added per employee in Scotland was over 90 per cent higher in overseas-owned plants than in the equivalent UK-owned units, and that the electronics industry provides a good illustration of the success of the inward investment programme: 'after more than 40 years of development and expansion, the industry in Scotland is sophisticated, innovative and flourishing' (Scottish Office, 1991, p. 41).

Clearly different perspectives and strongly held views on the issue of branch-plant economy status exist. Claims that takeovers and mergers are 'all bad' are just as difficult to support as the counterclaims that they are 'all good'. The perception of the negative effects of increased foreign ownership of Scottish companies has nevertheless helped fuel the belief that Scotland is losing the ability to control its own economy, and that the blame for this can be attributed to Conservative macro-economic policies which were hostile to conditions in Scotland. Such a view increased the support for political and constitutional change and greater control of the activities of foreign-owned companies.

De-industrialisation

As we have already discussed, there has been a marked shift in the balance between the manufacturing and service sectors of the Scottish economy, and in particular Scotland has experienced a rapid decline of its traditional industries, including coal, steel, shipbuilding and engineering. This structural shift in the economy has led to considerable debate about the appropriate balance between the manufacturing and service sectors. Some contend that the shift from manufacturing to services does not matter, while others argue instead that a strong manufacturing base is essential to underpin the service sector. Attention is drawn to the problem of de-industrialisation, characterised by a sustained growth in import penetration, a decline in British industry and manufacturing output, and mounting unemployment.

Much of the blame for the de-industrialisation process was laid at the door of the 1980s Conservative administrations. The collapse of manufacturing industry and investment was argued to be the result of the monetarist stance followed by successive governments post-1979. The overriding desire to keep inflation low meant cuts in public and local government expenditure, and implied relatively high interest rates at times of inflationary pressure. Capital investment, both public and private, suffered as a consequence. Consumer demand was also adversely affected by these changes, and when the government boosted demand in its giveaway tax budget before the 1987 general election, much of the spending went on imported goods and on speculation in the housing market.

For a highly industrialised country such as Scotland, the collapse of industries and plant closures meant a drastic loss of jobs. It was difficult for people in Scotland to understand or accept the wholesale loss of many of its manufacturing industries and the rising trade deficit, particularly for a country which prided itself on its international trade and which saw the revenue from North Sea oil and gas apparently being wasted. The discovery of oil and gas resources in the North Sea had added considerably to the revenue of the Exchequer and to the balance of payments figures. The argument was then made, especially by supporters of the SNP, that Scotland was experiencing all the costs of oil and gas production without gaining many of the benefits. The allegation is that the resources were being used to subsidise the Conservative government's economic policies including tax cuts to the higher paid; that oil revenue was being used to protect the UK's balance of payments from the worst effects of the government's deflationary and de-industrialisation policies; and that the revenue from oil should instead be used for longer term investment in industry and in the infrastructure of Scotland. Other concerns surround the potential destabilising effect on the rest of the Scottish economy caused by the oil and gas industries, the operation and employment practices of the oil companies, and the longer term implications of high extraction rates. The arguments being advanced in Scotland echo the thesis put forward by William Keegan (1984), that the government was pursuing the worst form of short-termism and squandering the investment potential and longer term benefits which oil revenues offered.

It is not difficult to see how these concerns about de-industrialisation, balance of trade deficits and the revenues from oil and gas have influenced demands for policies which are relevant to Scotland's needs.

North–south divide

The trends discussed above contributed to concern in Scotland that the UK economy was becoming increasingly divided between the north and south (Ashcroft, 1988). Following the 1979–81 recession, Scotland, in line with the rest of the UK, enjoyed a period of economic recovery and growth. In 1986, however, the relative performance of the Scottish economy deteriorated, and Ashcroft argued that the principal reason for the reversal in Scotland's economic fortunes was to be found in the fall in the price of oil during late 1985 and early 1986. Concern over the relative performance of the Scottish economy was also fuelled by the publication of the 1984 Census of Employment in January 1987. The Census highlighted 'regional' disparities in unemployment rates, showing for example that while the employed labour force in Britain had fallen by 3 per cent between June 1979 and June 1986, the Scottish fall was 8 per cent for the same period. This led the Scottish Council, the STUC and the Fraser of Allander Institute to draw attention to the imbalance between the north and south (especially between Scotland on the one hand, and East Anglia, the south-east and the south-west of England on the other). The claim that the UK was being divided in regional terms was strongly rejected by the Government and the then Secretary of State for Scotland, Malcolm Rifkind.

The debate re-emerged in the 1990s recession, but in somewhat different terms. This time it was the south of England which was said to be suffering most in terms of plant closures, lack of investment, rising unemployment, growing debt levels, negative equity (where the value of a house is less than the mortgage held on it), and house repossessions. The argument was put by economic commentators that Scotland had weathered the 1990s recession somewhat better, with its unemployment rates lower than in other parts of Britain. Several explanations are advanced to support this view. First, the Scottish economy did not suffer the same kind of structural shock which it experienced in the early 1980s, and other service industries expanded over the period. Second, the increase in saving levels at the time when the economy was going into recession was a particular feature of the south of England. And third, Scotland has a different housing structure from England (for example, 68 per cent owner-occupation in England compared with 52 per cent in Scotland), and house prices in Scotland in the owner-occupier sector did not follow the same trends as south of the border. Thus Scotland suffered less from the problems arising from the slump in property values. In the early 1990s the Secretary of State, Ian Lang, argued that, in comparative terms, Scotland had survived the recession well and was in a good position to take advantage of the Government's expected upturn in the economy.

The north–south divide debate provides a classic example of the dangers inherent in overgeneralising about differences between Scotland and England, without reference to the conditions in different regions in the two countries. While Scotland as a whole had a marginally lower unemployment rate in 1993 and 1994 than the rest of Britain (Table 4.2), there are substantial variations in the rates between different parts of the UK and within Scotland itself (Tables 4.3 and 4.4). Substantial differences also exist within the large cities in Scotland. For example in 1995 Glasgow had an overall unemployment rate of 10 per cent, which was only slightly above the Scottish average. Yet in parts of Glasgow around one quarter of people of working age were unemployed. The problem was especially acute for male unemployment, with one in three men without a job in some areas, and in long-term unemployment, with almost half the city's jobless being out of work for a year or more. Comparing employment change in Glasgow with the rest of Scotland also reveal significant differentials. Employment in manufacturing dropped by 21.9 per cent for Scotland as a whole but by 43.8 per cent for Glasgow, and although employment in the services increased by 17.2 per cent in Scotland, Glasgow experienced a drop of 5 per cent (*The Scotsman*, 27 February 1995).

Table 4.2   *Scottish and British unemployment 1990–5* (seasonally adjusted)*

Year	Scotland		Great Britain	
	Rate (%)	Total	Rate (%)	Total
1990	8.4	208 100	5.4	1 513 100
1991	8.2	206 300	6.8	1 880 800
1992	9.2	231 700	9.2	2 532 900
1993	9.9	247 500	10.4	2 853 300
1994	9.5	236 800	9.7	2 653 500
1995	8.3	207 900	8.3	2 274 100

* As at February each year.
Source: Fraser of Allander Institute (1995); *Quarterly Economic
Commentary*, 20 (March).

Table 4.3   *Unemployment in the regions of England, and in Scotland and
Wales (seasonally adjusted)*

Regions and nations	Unemployment rate in February 1995
England:	
East Anglia	6.4
London	9.9
Rest of south-east	6.7
South-west	7.4
West Midlands	8.4
East Midlands	7.9
Yorkshire and Humberside	8.9
North-west	8.7
North	10.6
Wales	8.5
Scotland	8.3

Source: Fraser of Allander Institute (1995); *Quarterly Economic
Commentary*, 20 (March).

The concept of a north–south divide does not refer to the division
between Scotland and England, but it was popularly translated as
such. The case has been made that many parts of England
experience similar economic conditions to Scotland, and that the
north-east or the north-west of England have more in common with
Scotland than they have with the south-east of England. However
the image of the border between Scotland and England as forming

Table 4.4 *Total unemployment in the Scottish regions (unadjusted series)*

Region	Unemployment rate in February 1995
Borders	5.6
Central	9.2
Dumfries and Galloway	9.3
Fife	10.8
Grampian	5.1
Highland	9.7
Lothian	7.2
Strathclyde	10.0
Tayside	8.7
Orkney Islands	5.7
Shetland Islands	3.2
Western Isles	11.3

Source: Fraser of Allander Institute (1995); *Quarterly Economic Commentary*, 20 (March).

the natural division between the north and the south continues to have a powerful influence on Scottish political consciousness.

Women in the Scottish economy

Structural changes in the economy and other social changes have resulted in the increased participation of women in the labour market. So much is this the case that women now form the majority of the paid workforce in Scotland (Table 4.5), albeit not in terms of full-time work. As men have lost full-time, unionised jobs in the traditional industries, there has been an expansion of part-time, non-unionised work in the service sector. This work has mainly been taken up by women, but it should be noted that many women also lost full-time, unionised jobs in the traditional industries, and in the public sector because of cutbacks. Male employment fell by 234 000 between 1979 and 1994. Over the same period there was a modest increase in female employment, but the number of full-time female employees was lower in 1994 than in 1979. The increase was therefore made up of a rise in part-time employment for women (332 000 in 1979 compared with 451 000 in 1994: Hughes, 1994).

Table 4.5   *Employment in Scotland*

Year	Employees in employment (thousands)			Self-employed (thousands)		
	All	Male	Female	All	Male	Female
1979	2102	1205	897	146	118	28
1989	1957	1020	937	221	174	47
1994	1963	971	992	234*	172*	62*

* The figures for self-employed relate to December 1993.
Source: Hughes (1994).

This 'feminisation' of the Scottish economy has met with different responses. One line of argument is that 'real' jobs (those associated with male employment in heavy industry and manufacturing) are being replaced by 'women's jobs' (those associated with caring and the service industries). The strategy advocated is to return to the 'halcyon' days of 'real' work and full employment for men. This argument has common features with the de-industrialisation debate, but can be distinguished in that it is based on conventional views of gender segregation in the labour market. It runs the risk, therefore, of reinforcing the barriers faced by many women in entering traditionally male areas of employment, and of confining them to the low-paid, low-wage sectors of the economy. Other concerns have been raised in the media and by commentators about the impact on the self-confidence and esteem of men caused by women entering the labour market in increased numbers and taking over the role of main earner in many households. The more extreme advocates of this point of view blame the so-called crisis in masculinity on the feminist movement, and it is contended that men are now in more need of equal opportunities than women.

A more reasoned debate surrounds the disadvantaged position of women in the economy. There is no doubt that some women have gained real benefits in the labour market in recent years through improved access to jobs, opportunities for training and promotion, and legislation on pay and sexual discrimination; yet many problems still remain. Women are still concentrated in areas of work which are non-unionised and unprotected by legislation; they still earn on average just over 70 per cent of the pay earned by men in full-time employment; and they form 70 per cent of low-paid workers in Scotland. The unpaid work undertaken by women in the home and community (for example, as carers of the young and old) remains unrecognised by official economic statistics. In addition the government's official unemployment statistics, produced by the Department of Employment, understate the level of female unemployment. The switch in 1982 to a calculation that counted only people who were claiming unemployment benefit excluded many married women from the register. Mothers of young children were also excluded by the availability-for-work test, which includes questions on childcare provision. Unemployment, poor wages and insecure employment all contribute to the poverty faced by many women and their families in Scotland.

The general experiences of women in the labour market in Scotland are shared by women in other parts of the UK. The *Gender Audits* (Engender, 1993, 1994, 1995, 1996, 1997) and information published by the Equal Opportunities Commission (EOC) do, however, discuss some of the differences. The relevance of the debate on women's position in the Scottish economy is the link with constitutional change. As we shall discuss in Chapter 8, women in Scotland have entered the campaign in a particular way and have been motivated by their vision of a Parliament which will offer equal representation and the prospect of different policy priorities and outcomes for women. It is their belief that issues which are of key concern to them, such as low pay and poor conditions and rights at work, are more likely to be addressed in the context of a Parliament in Scotland.

The European dimension

The 'European question' is another area of debate in Scotland where arguments have surrounded 'costs' and 'benefits', here associated with membership of the EU. However, for opposition parties and other organisations in Scotland, European membership and European policies provide a potential alternative to the free-market ideology so enthusiastically promoted by Conservative administrations post-1979. Areas of Scotland have benefited from European funding, and European policies including childcare, equality issues and workers' rights are cited in political discourse as examples of a different approach to social and labour market problems, an approach which is argued to be more compatible with Scottish public opinion. As William Paterson (1994, p. 4) puts it, 'Scottish dissatisfaction with its internal status focuses on the EU as an alternative site for Scottish aspirations.'

There have been attempts to assess the potential economic costs as well as the benefits for Scotland of European Union. Andrew Scott (1991) takes issue with a study quoted by the European Commission which suggested that completing the internal market would improve employment and growth, reduce the average level of prices, and enhance Europe's external trading position. Scott argues that much less attention has been paid to assessing how the gains from the internal market will be distributed between the different regions of the EU, and states that there is a clear concern that the already weak regions will be further disadvantaged as producers locate or relocate their activities closer to the centre of the newly completed internal market. Should the trend towards core/periphery development increase (note the new importance to the European dimension in this debate), there will be obvious disadvantages and risks for a country such as Scotland. Scott refers to a study conducted by the Louvain group, which considered three issues to be crucial in determining the regional impact of the internal market: technology, training and infrastructure. But it is precisely these areas which are argued to have been starved of central government resources in Scotland: 'From the periphery of Europe it seems that many of the other member states are involved in a giant game of chess, with each moving those pieces from which they expect to gain most strategic advantage come 1992. We, on the other hand, are still playing Happy Families' (Scott, 1991, p. 42).

A more optimistic assessment is provided by Gavin McCrone (1993), who argues that Scotland could benefit from the special 'Cohesion Fund' set up under the Maastricht Treaty because it has had a major problem of industrial restructuring, and it suffers from the handicap of peripheral location. Thus Scotland should be able to continue to take advantage of European structural funds. However he cautions that, in order for Scotland to gain from European integration, a higher level of investment in the economy is needed, namely investment in transport infrastructure, investment in human capital in the form of education and training, investment incentives to companies and the carrying out of studies on different sectors of the economy: 'Nothing can guarantee Scotland a prosperous future in a more integrated Europe, but the opportunities are there and the aim of the policy should be to ensure that Scotland is well placed to take advantage of them' (McCrone, 1993, p. 21). Given his view of the potential benefits of European membership, McCrone expressed concern about the Conservative Government's negative attitude towards Europe and the potential impact on the Scottish economy. He argued that if Britain were to withdraw from Europe, then Scottish exports to the EU and the amount of inward investment in Scotland would fall. At present Scotland is seen as an attractive location to serve the European market. For McCrone, the future of the Scottish economy, is therefore, dependent on what happens on the European question.

In the run-up to the 1997 general election, the political opposition parties in Scotland re-affirmed their support for membership of the EU. The Scottish Labour Party and the Scottish Liberal Democrats argued that, in order to give Scotland a greater say in Europe, the Committee of the Regions would be the most appropriate forum for articulating Scottish interests (along with the attendance at the council of ministers of appropriate ministers from a Scottish Parliament). The SNP has supported a policy of independence within Europe from the late 1980s on the ground that Scotland would need to be an independent state before it could participate effectively in Europe. The significance of the European question for the broader constitutional debate is summarised by William Paterson (1994, p. 10): 'Participation in the European Community has thrown some of the central features of the unmodern British state into sharp relief. It has increased, rather than weakened, a pre-existing Scottish sense of distinctiveness within the United Kingdom.'

The constitutional question

The campaign for constitutional change in Scotland was influenced by the experience of so-called 'Thatcherism' in the 1980s, and the perceived negative economic effects on the Scottish economy. With regard to economic policy, it was argued by the participants in the Scottish Constitutional Convention, including the Labour Party and

Liberal Democrats, that a Scottish Parliament with revenue-raising powers would be best placed to determine the priorities and needs of the Scottish people. A Scottish Parliament could pursue its own industrial, labour market and energy strategies that would be markedly different from the policies being imposed by Westminster. The type of powers proposed by the participants in the Convention included strategic planning, the strengthening of the development agencies, competition policy and regional incentives, responsibility for training, and policies to attract overseas investment (Scottish Constitutional Convention, 1990, p. 10). They also advocated power to initiate some form of public ownership or control of industries in the public interest. There is, of course, considerable debate as to whether it will be possible to have a meaningful influence over the economy when central government still controls the key levers of macro-economic policy. The point is made most forcibly by the SNP, which advocates an independent Scottish Parliament which would benefit directly from North Sea oil revenues and control over macro-economic policy.

The issues were publicly debated by the Conservative Secretary of State for Scotland and the leaders of the three main opposition parties in Scotland at the 'Great Debate', held at the Usher Hall in Edinburgh just before the 1992 general election. The main argument put by the Secretary of State and by Government spokespeople was that a Scottish Parliament would mean levying extra taxes on Scotland and would act as a disincentive to those seeking to invest in Scotland. Far from providing a boost to the Scottish economy and improving employment levels, a devolved or independent Scottish Parliament would be detrimental to the economic interests of the country.

After the 1992 election the debate grew in sophistication but there was still no agreement on the economic impact of constitutional change. The debate can be divided into two main categories. The first related to the impact on taxation levels which would result from the establishment of a Scottish Parliament, while the second focused on the potential advantages and disadvantages of the different options of devolution or independence.

The scheme proposed by the Scottish Constitutional Convention, and which formed the basis of agreement between the Convention partners at that time, can be summarised under four main recommendations: first, that all Scottish income tax and all Scottish value added tax (VAT) should be assigned to a Scottish Parliament; second, that the Scottish Parliament should have the power to vary the income tax rate up or down, but within a narrow margin; third, that equalisation across the UK should continue to be based on assessment of needs, using the present formula as a basis of calculation; and fourth, that it would be necessary to review the arrangements regularly. The broad consensus on the financing of the Scottish Parliament was maintained after the 1992 election, although there was a move from 'assigned' taxes to a block grant, and the Scottish Labour Party placed a limit on the variation of taxation: 'the Parliament will have revenue varying powers to increase or cut the basic rate of income tax for Scottish taxpayers by a maximum of three pence in the pound' (Scottish Labour Party, 1995).

The Labour Party's devolution plans came under sustained attack from Government ministers, including the Prime Minister, John Major. Heald and Geaughan (1995) state that these attacks took two forms: the 'tax horror' version and the 'irrelevance' version. The 'tax horror' version claimed that Labour's plans would cost the average Scottish family £6 per week and would mean an additional 20p on the basic rate of Scottish income tax. The first of these claims 'makes the assumption that the Scottish Parliament would in fact choose to exercise in full the right to increase income tax by 3p', while the second 'makes the assumption that the establishment of a devolved Scottish Parliament would be accompanied by the cancelling of all Scotland's claims on the basis of relative need to have access to the pool of UK resources' (Heald and Geaughan, 1995, p. 4). Somewhat contradicting the 'tax horror' approach, the 'irrelevance' version of the argument was that, even if the full rise of 3p tax was implemented, the amount available for spending by the Scottish Parliament (approximately £450 million) would be insufficient to make any significant difference. In taking issue with the criticisms advanced by the Conservative Government, Heald concludes that the 'devolution finance proposals of the Constitutional Convention are soundly based and should not be modified because the political temperature is rising' (Heald and Geaughan, 1995, p. 12).

The taxation debate was to have an impact on the events that followed. It was the Secretary of State, Michael Forsyth, who made most political capital from Labour's taxation plans for the Scottish Parliament, with his reference to the 'Tartan Tax'. The perceived success of the Conservative campaign on taxation at the time is argued to have played a key role in the decision by the Labour Party in 1996 to include a question on taxation in the planned referendum.

In assessing the second debate, namely the potential advantages and disadvantages of the different options of devolution and independence, several factors have to be considered. For example Neil Hood (1995) explores the claim which was made, mainly by Conservative spokespeople, that there would be a negative effect on inward investment if a Scottish Parliament was set up. Focusing largely on manufacturing investment, Hood analyses the various issues involved such as the level of uncertainty, the characteristics of foreign investment in Scotland, the behavioural patterns of international companies, and potential changes in the EU economic environment. His main conclusion is that 'there is no prima facie case for claiming that devolution as currently proposed will have a negative effect on Scotland's position for either inward investment attraction or development', and that the uncertainty associated with devolution is relatively minor and can be minimised by developing a working relationship between the prospective policy-makers and the business community (Hood, 1995, p. 18).

In the run-up to the 1997 general election there was evidence that the Scottish Labour Party was taking steps to enter into a dialogue with the business and financial community in order to explain Labour's plans for home rule and minimise opposition.

The economists David Bell and Sheila Dow (1995) have developed the debate to include the option of an independent Scottish Parliament. The authors examined the constraints placed on the fiscal and monetary options of a Scottish Parliament because of membership of the EU and wider global economic pressures. While acknowledging that such constraints exist, they nevertheless conclude that there is the possibility of developing a distinctive Scottish economic policy. They support their argument on the grounds that the logic of constitutional change rests on the view that there is something distinctive about Scottish society which should allow a distinctive role for the state: 'the combination of distinctive institutional arrangements and economic behaviour within a co-operative ethos can allow for a partnership role for government which could have dynamic effects on the Scottish economy' (Bell and Dow, 1995, p. 66).

Finally, there is a long-standing debate concerning the difference between Scottish fiscal revenue and the level of public expenditure. Put rather crudely, the devolutionist wing of the constitutional change argument acknowledges that there can be benefits for Scotland in remaining within the UK. One such benefit is that Scotland has received a higher share of public expenditure than the size of its population would strictly allow. This view is challenged by those arguing for an independent Parliament on the grounds that Scotland is a rich country and people living in Scotland would be better off financially if North Sea oil revenue and other tax receipts were spent directly on investment in Scotland. The difference of view is complicated by the inadequacy of official statistics, the method of calculation, and what is included or excluded from the figures. For example it was argued during the property boom in the late 1980s that Scottish taxpayers were subsidising mortgage tax relief for owner-occupiers in the south-east of England.

Jim Stevens (1995) returned to this debate and provided figures for 1992–3 which show that while Scotland accounted for 8.8 per cent of the UK population, Scottish expenditure (that is, the amount of expenditure which is readily identifiable as being allocated to Scotland from the available data) was 10.3 per cent of the UK total. While tax receipts from Scotland amounted to 8.2 per cent of UK receipts without, and 8.6 per cent with, North Sea taxes and royalties, he estimated that the share of total public expenditure and services provided to Scotland was 9.8 per cent of the UK total. Further, the Scottish budget deficit was higher than for the UK as a whole. According to Stevens, such statistics do not undermine the case for devolution or provide an argument for a reduction in the allocation to Scotland. He does argue, however, that they do not provide comforting reading for those who support independence.

This perspective was challenged by the SNP, which provided alternative figures to support its case for independence. The SNP took the argument further in January 1997 by provoking a written Parliamentary answer from the then Treasury Chief Secretary, William Waldegrave, to the SNP's question on whether Scotland was in surplus or in deficit to the rest of the UK. The response, that almost £27 billion more had been raised in revenues in Scotland than had been spent since the Conservatives came to power in 1979, provided the ammunition the SNP had been hoping for. This allowed the SNP to undermine the advertising campaign launched by the Scottish Office (under Michael Forsyth) under the heading

'It's the Scots Wha Pay' with its own response: 'It *is* Scots Who Pay
. . . and the Tories admit it!' (*The Herald*, 28 January 1997).

The 1997 general election and the referendum

In the previous section we briefly summarised some of the key
debates and issues in the academic literature and the extent to which
they have been part of the political discourse on the Scottish
economy during the last forty years. The key focus for such dialogue
and media attention immediately before and after the 1997 general
election was the perceived impact of constitutional change.

The White Paper on devolution and the Scotland Bill published in
1997 re-stated the Labour Government's position on financing the
Scottish Parliament. The Scottish Parliament will continue to receive
a block grant calculated on the basis of the Barnett formula and the
Parliament will have the power to vary the basic rate of income tax by
up to 3p in the pound. A Scottish taxpayer will be defined as someone
who is resident in the UK for tax purposes and for whom Scotland is
the part of the UK with which she or he has the closest connection.
This is likely to be determined by the period of time a person spends
in Scotland or has his or her main UK home in Scotland.

Given the general opposition of the business and financial
community to the plans for devolution in the 1970s and the way
in which some key employers in Scotland made known their
opposition to home rule during the 1992 general election, there
was some concern by supporters of constitutional change that
history might repeat itself in 1997. Their fear was unfounded,
however, as the business and financial communities were largely
silent during the election campaign. In spite of various attempts, the
Conservative campaign in Scotland was unable to harness widespread opposition to the plans for constitutional change. On the
contrary, the Labour Party was successful in gaining support,
evidenced by the announcement made by two of Scotland's largest
insurance companies, Scottish Widows and Standard Life, that they
were not unhappy with the party's plans for home rule (*The
Scotsman*, 23 April 1997). Neither did the business community
provide significant resources to help fund the campaign for No votes
during the referendum.

There were some notable exceptions to this general picture. For example in his capacity as Governor of the Bank of Scotland Sir Bruce Pattullo made a controversial attack on the plans for constitutional change and European monetary union. He was reported to have warned that both policies carried grave risks and that the tax plans proposed for the Scottish Parliament would handicap business and discourage investment (*The Scotsman*, 22 May 1997). When Pattullo reiterated his warning about what he believed were the dangers of the tax powers of the Scottish Parliament, he received an adverse response from all the parties campaigning for Yes votes in the referendum and also from some customers of the bank, who decided to move their accounts elsewhere (*The Herald*, 23 August 1997). To counter some of the potentially damaging effects of the Pattullo intervention in the referendum campaign, the pro-home-rulers published their own list of major companies who were investing in Scotland and had not been deterred by the planned taxation powers of the new Parliament (*The Herald*, 29 August 1997). In the run-up to the referendum in September 1997, the claims and counter-claims continued, and the CBI in Scotland entered the fray, but with differing points of view being expressed by its members. In the event, opposition from a small sector of the business community was by far outweighed by those who supported the case for constitutional change. Indeed the business community in Scotland is considering ways in which it can play a positive role in developing the plans for the new Parliament and in finding avenues for engaging with the new institution once it has been established. The Scottish Council Foundation (1997) has published a business guide to devolution in which it discusses the potential opportunities for business and recommends that business people should 'stand for a parliament which is close to home', 'take advantage of the pre-legislative process', and 'contribute more forcefully to the newly invigorated debate about Scottish policy options' (Scottish Council Foundation, 1997, p. 47). Whether or not a Business Party will ever be formed to take forward some of these aspirations is a matter for speculation; it was rejected as an option by the Conservative Party in Scotland.

So economics has continued to play a key part in political discourses in Scotland and influenced different perspectives on constitutional change.

Conclusions

As has been discussed in this chapter, there are fundamentally different perspectives on some important debates surrounding the Scottish economy, not least on the effects of constitutional change. They do, however, help us answer our original question – 'is there such a thing as the Scottish economy?' – because they illustrate the characteristics of Scotland's polity and society and the key economic actors involved, Scotland's place in international markets and the world economy, and the factors that are perceived to be of most relevance to Scotland and the economic and social needs of the Scottish people. They also serve to explain why there was a strong consensus in Scotland that there was an alternative to the economic policies pursued by the Conservative Governments in the 1980s and 1990s. Expectations in Scotland are high that the new Parliament will deliver many benefits, including more jobs and better education, health and housing (Surridge *et al.*, 1998). However the constraints will also be significant, and much will depend on economic developments in Europe as a whole and more generally. Nevertheless this alternative vision of the Scottish economy will pose a real challenge to the Scottish Parliament and all those involved in the policy-making process.

5

Policy-Making in Scotland

Introduction

Scottish policy-making will be deeply affected by the setting up of a Scottish Parliament in the year 2000. So any account of policy-making is bound to be provisional. Nevertheless there are three reasons to be interested in how policy is currently made, and how it has been made for the last half century.

The first reason is about the content of policy. The existing systems of policy-making have shaped the policies that the new Parliament will inherit. An understanding of where public policies have come from in recent years is, therefore, necessary if we are to understand how the Parliament will deal with its legacy. For example, in cases where a policy is felt to have come from a Conservative Government in London that was insensitive to Scottish preferences, then we might expect the Parliament to be keen to replace it. On the other hand, when a policy has been made or modified in Scotland, then influential groups in the Parliament will feel that they own it, and so are likely to want to preserve that inheritance.

The second reason is about the style of policy-making. Looking at the current systems of policy-making can help provide an understanding of where the pressure for a Parliament has come from. The Parliament's reform of the policy-making process will be shaped by the history of that process. What features of the current system will the Parliament want to reform? What features will be felt to have served Scotland well?

The third reason is about inertia in the policies themselves and in the styles of policy-making. The parliament will not be able to change everything overnight, even if it would like to. It will simply take over policies that have been set in motion over the last few years

– including those Conservative Government policies that did so much to provoke support for a Scottish Parliament. More profoundly, it will inherit styles of policy-making that are so common in Western democracies that they are unlikely to be changed even by the most radically inclined Scottish Parliament. Part of the reason for the common international experience is that administering a large and complex public sector requires rules, a bureaucracy to oversee them and autonomous professionals to implement them locally, and little of this is amenable to national political interference. The Parliament might be able to move the system towards greater openness and accountability, as we shall see, but it will probably not be able to inaugurate a revolution.

This chapter therefore asks where Scottish policy comes from. Does it make sense to talk of Scottish policy before the Parliament is set up: is not the system of policy-making part of the unitary UK constitution, whereby all the important decisions are taken in London? How have the current styles of policy-making emerged? What realistic scope is there for the Scottish Parliament to have any impact?

Who is involved in Scottish policy-making?

Before we get into various theories of how policy is made and why it has evolved in the way it has, we start with a summary of who makes policy, and where. There are four main arenas for Scottish public policy, and these intersect each other.

The first arena is the most obvious to anyone who is familiar with the UK constitution: the Westminster Parliament. Scotland elects 72 members of the House of Commons, while 578 are elected in other parts of the UK. This makes Scottish representation per head of population rather higher than in England, and that has been defended on the grounds that Scotland requires separate legislation to cope with its distinctiveness. For example when a UK government wants to legislate changes to education, it has been standard practice for it to have separate pieces of legislation for Scotland and for England and Wales, simply because the Scottish education system is distinctive and therefore can not be easily accommodated by making qualifications to the legislation for the rest of Britain. This separate stream of legislation requires the existence of enough Scottish MPs to staff the committees that scrutinise it. Analogous over-representation has been in place since the Treaty of Union in 1707, although before the coming of mass democracy this over-representation was in relation to the value of the property that then formed the basis of the franchise, rather than in relation to the size of the adult population.

Nevertheless, despite this over-representation of Scotland the 72 Scottish MPs can be easily outvoted by the other 578, as repeatedly happened in the period between 1979 and 1997, when the Conservative Party held a majority of English constituencies but only a small minority of Scottish ones (and as has happened less frequently for over a century).

The special circumstances of Scotland and of Scottish legislation are reflected in three features of the management of Scottish business in the House of Commons. First, there is the Scottish Grand Committee, which is entitled to debate Scottish matters but not to vote on substantive motions. Since its reform by the Conservative Government in 1981, the Grand Committee has consisted only of the 72 Scottish MPs. Before that it could include up to 15 MPs from elsewhere, so that the UK governing party could gain the majority of places, but even that would not have given the Conservatives a majority at any time after 1979. After 1992 the Conservative Government of John Major reformed the Grand Committee in some further, minor ways – for example it was now able to question ministers (including those with UK-wide responsibilities such as the Prime Minister and the Chancellor of the Exchequer) – but these changes were seen by opposition politicians and the media as symbolic rather than substantial.

Second, for scrutinising Scottish legislation there are two smaller Scottish Standing Committees, each with having a guaranteed government majority; and since 1979 there has been provision for a Scottish Affairs Select Committee (also with a Government majority) to scrutinise the operation of Government departments and public bodies in Scotland. the latter was introduced as part of the wider system of departmental Select Committees set up by the new Conservative Government.

Third, from the Westminster Parliament is drawn that other part of the governing system – the Executive, consisting of the ministers responsible for government policy in Scotland. The top post is Secretary of State for Scotland, a Cabinet rank since 1926. There is also a team of about five other ministers, one of whom is usually from the House of Lords (where Scottish peers are again out-numbered by their counterparts from elsewhere in the UK). These ministers are drawn from the party that commands the majority of votes in the House of Commons, and therefore need not be from the Scottish majority party. Indeed between 1987 and 1992 the Conservatives had so few MPs from Scotland that, once they had staffed the Scottish ministerial posts and a few Scottish MPs had taken on other ministerial responsibilities outside Scotland, there were hardly any non-ministerial Conservative members from Scotland left. As a result the Select Committee on Scottish Affairs did not convene in these years, because the Government could not be guaranteed a majority without importing non-Scottish Conservative members, a move that was deemed too provocative to be politically acceptable at that time (McConnell and Pyper, 1994). Throughout the period 1979–97 the Conservative Government had to rely on non-Scottish members to ensure that the Scottish Standing Com-mittees had a Conservative majority; this caused resentment in Scotland when the legislation before the committees was politically controversial, for example the poll tax, which was introduced in 1989, and the legislation to allow schools to leave the control of local authorities in the same year.

Despite this potential for partisan conflict between the Scottish ministers and Scottish political preferences, the Secretary of State has always played an ambiguous role. He (to date all Secretaries of State have been male) has certainly represented the UK Government in Scotland – a role that has been described as that of a Governor General. But he also represents Scotland within the Government. Because of the secrecy of Cabinet government, his contributions in this respect do not usually become evident until official Government papers are released at least 30 years after the event: thus we could see only in the 1980s how forcefully Scotland's case had been put in Cabinet by a succession of Conservative Secretaries of State in the 1950s, securing for Scotland significant inward investment and Government action to clear slums and develop public services (Levitt, 1994). More recently, Scottish Secretaries have let it be known that they have been fighting in secret for Scotland: thus George Younger, when he was Scottish Secretary between 1979 and 1986, frequently argued successfully against the closure of the Ravenscraig steelworks, and got his way by threatening to resign; his

Table 5.1 *The structure of the Scottish Office, 1998*

Department	Main responsibilities
Agriculture, Enviroment and Fisheries	Agriculture, fisheries, environmental affairs
Development	Local government, housing, planning, transport, roads, European funds
Education and Indusry	Eduction, arts and culture, energy, enterprise and tourism, economic and industrial affairs, training, urban policy
Home Department	Social work, criminal justice, civil law and legal aid, police, fire services, legal services, prisons, Scottish Courts Administration
Health	National Health Service in Scotland
Secretary of State's Office	Scottish Office Personnel, public information, finance, audit and accountancy, liaison with other government departments, management group

Source: The Scottish Office, *Factsheet 1: the Scottish Office* (Edinburgh: HMSO, 1996).

successor, Malcolm Rifkind, fought the same cause, but was less successful and the works closed in 1992.

The second arena of Scottish policy-making is the Scottish Office, together with the other Government departments in Scotland. The Scottish Office has become the Government's executive arm in Scotland. Its civil servants devise legislation and oversee, monitor and evaluate its implementation. Its structure has changed frequently since it was founded in 1885, but since the 1960s, with the founding of the Scottish Development Department and the Scottish Industry Department, it has grown incrementally rather than by fundamental reform. In 1998, just before the advent of the Scottish Parliament, its departments and their main functions were as summarised in table 5.1.

As with all Civil Service departments, the Scottish Office is above all the agent of ministers. But it also has a more subtle role in policy: mediating between Scottish civil society and the UK state. This is especially the case when a department has a professional arm, such as the inspectorates for education, social work and prisons, and the medical professionals in health. For example, although schools inspectors do of course inspect – taking responsibility for ensuring that Government policy on education is adhered to in schools – they also act as the 'ears and eyes of the department' (McPherson and Raab, 1988). They suggest to ministers areas where new policy is needed, they themselves give leads in policy where no legislation is required, and – as by training they are members of the profession they inspect – in principle their primary concern is with the education system rather than with the policies of the government of the day.

An example of this creative policy role in education can be found in the reform of vocational education in the early 1980s. When the Thatcher Government sought to introduce a greater attention to vocational education, the inspectorate in the Scottish Education Department used its network of allies in the education system to insist that Scottish reforms would be distinctive, and would not proceed directly from the headquarters of the Manpower Services Commission south of the border. The result was a set of Scottish vocational courses, independent of those that were eventually developed for England and Wales. This is a good example of the professional civil service operating through compromise: the principle of greater vocational emphasis was conceded to Thatcher in return for Scottish control of how it would be implemented.

The capacity to be creative is greater in some areas of Scottish policy than in others. For example, during the last three decades there has generally been more Scottish innovation in education, child law, housing and social work, than in training, industry, and health. There has been only minimal innovation in those parts of central government in Scotland that do not come under the Scottish Office. For example the Scottish arm of the Department of Social Security merely implements in Scotland the rules governing social security benefits that apply throughout the UK. Because of the growth of the Scottish Office, and because it has greater autonomy in policy than other parts of central government in Scotland, in practice the Scottish Office has come to coordinate most of these departments, and therefore to have some influence on their operation. For example, because housing is ultimately a responsibility of the Scottish Office (although in many respects only indirectly through local government), the DSS has to liaise with the Scottish Office over the payment of housing benefit, just as it has to liaise with the Department of the Environment in London in relation to the same function in England.

The third arena of policy is the network of public bodies that are commonly known as quangos (quasi autonomous non-governmental organisations), although the precise definition of these varies among authors (see for example the debate in *Parliamentary Affairs*, vol. 48, no. 2, 1995). The formation of these bodies is not peculiarly Scottish: they are a feature of modern government. In Scotland as elsewhere, they have grown up for two main reasons. The appointment of experts to a committee to oversee a public service has been a way of distancing the government of that service from direct political interference. Thus the board of Scottish Natural Heritage is composed of people who are meant to be independent of Government, and are therefore able (it is hoped) to devise the details of environmental policy free of political pressure. The second reason for the growth of quangos is that large parts of policy are highly technical and require the systematic oversight of professionally qualified people to make them work. So, for example, the work of the Building Standards Advisory Committee is largely technical and requires specialist knowledge.

The theory of independence and technical competence was challenged during the years of the Conservative Government up to 1997 on the ground that the Government was increasingly appointing its own ideological supporters rather than people qualified on merit; the Government itself would have claimed that it was doing this to help roll back the powers of the state. The changes were especially controversial in the health service, where the Health Boards – which oversee the system regionally within Scotland – were alleged to have been packed with Conservative supporters and business people. These accusations revealed an important function of the quangos – their role in mediating between civil society and the state, in ways similar to those played by the professional branches of some of the Scottish Office departments. Thus the Health Boards, although always unelected, were expected to represent to the Scottish Office the views of their localities and of the professionals in the health service there. When that mediating role broke down or was strained, the Scottish Office started to seem remote, a representative of an alien Government rather than a coordinator of opinion in Scotland.

The fourth arena of policy-making is local government whose powers and autonomy have greatly decreased since the nineteenth century when it formed the bedrock of Scottish politics (see Chapter 3). Since the reform of 1995–6 (on which more later) it has consisted of 32 elected councils, responsible for all the local authority functions in their areas (Fairley, 1995). The main ones are education, social work, housing, leisure and recreation, cleansing, local planning, and some aspects of transport and economic development. Because they are elected, they have special status in the system of policy-making: they are politically independent of central government, and in recent years have often been able to command much more public support than central government. For example the local authorities persuaded public opinion that it was the central government, not they, that was responsible for the cuts in the education budget in 1995. Local authorities are also able to sponsor local civil society networks, analogous to the role of the Scottish Office nationally: for example local government is an important source of financial support to voluntary organisations (SCVO, 1997). Local government is also responsible for some local quangos.

Nevertheless the independence of local government is severely constrained by statute and by the power of the central government to restrict its expenditure. Local government is currently responsible for raising only about one fifth of its revenue (mostly through the council tax and charges for services); the rest comes from a mixture of rating of non-domestic property in the local area (the business rate), the level of which is set by the central government, and direct grants from the central government. Moreover, the central government is able to set limits on the overall expenditure of councils, which in effect limits their ability to vary the rate of the council tax.

The powers of councils were also affected by the reorganisation that was imposed on Scottish local government in 1995–6. The nine large regions and 53 smaller districts that had existed since 1975 were abolished. The biggest regions had been able to take advantage of economies of scale, and of some limited powers to redistribute resources from richer areas to poorer. These were not available to their successors. For example the abolished Strathclyde Region covered both the wealthy suburbs of Glasgow and its impoverished inner city; it could justify redistribution because the residents of the suburbs used city-centre services when they worked or shopped there. In the new system, Glasgow Council has been deprived of its relatively affluent hinterland, and so has a limited local tax base.

Alongside this structural reform were profound changes in the nature of local government. The Conservative Government believed that councils should move away from the direct provision of services, and should instead become 'enablers'; that is, they should solicit tenders for services and monitor the quality of the chosen contractors. In large areas of council work, the opening up of services to competitive contract was compulsory, although, unlike in England, most Scottish councils retained the provision of services simply by being able to compete successfully with tenders from the private sector. The Labour Government elected in 1997 was less enthusiastic about competitive tendering, and replaced it with a scheme called 'best value'. According to this, councils have to demonstrate to their auditors that any services they are providing offer as good value for money as the best of the equivalent services in other parts of the public sector or in the private sector.

Both compulsory competitive tendering and 'best value' reduce the autonomy of local government, insofar as they limit the capacity of councils to decide for themselves what services to provide and how to judge their quality. The comparison with other providers inherent in 'best value' also tends to reduce the scope for political distinctiveness in any particular local authority.

In any case, significant parts of local policy-making are not in the hands of elected local government at all. The most notable are in relation to health and to economic development and training. The Scottish Health Service has been overseen by unelected Health Boards since it was set up in 1947 (their members being appointed by the Secretary of State for Scotland). Under the Conservative Government in the early 1990s, even they lost powers to trusts, which run hospitals and some other services, and to local doctors holding their own budgets and contracting with trusts. Although the Labour Government plans to modify this quasi-market in health care – for example by creating groupings of doctors who will hold a common budget – they do not propose to introduce any formal link between the health service and local government.

Most economic development and training is overseen by a network of 22 Local Enterprise Companies, contracted for these purposes to Scottish Enterprise or Highlands and Islands Enterprise. Because these are private companies, their board members are not subject to democratic scrutiny: the only political oversight is of Scottish Enterprise and Highlands and Islands Enterprise. When the Conservative Government introduced this system in 1990, its aim was to bring together local business people in the service of the local economy; the evidence is that this aim was partly achieved, but that the promotion of local economic development remains fragmented (Fairley and Lloyd, 1995). However the new unitary councils that took power in 1996 had a statutory role in economic development for the first time, and their role is likely to increase. Their relationship with the Local Enterprise Companies is therefore likely to change, and some analysts have suggested that councils are ideally placed to lead the local coordination of development and training (Fairley, 1996).

Theories of policy-making

How are we to understand these networks of policy-making? Political scientists have offered various theories that have helped to explain policy-making, and these have been frequently modified to cope with the great diversity of political systems. In this section we consider some of the main theories, and assess how adequate they are in understanding the situation in Scotland. The point of doing this is not to find a single theory that is able to explain policy-making in Scotland: theories in social science are not like that. Each of the theories is true to some extent, and casts light on some aspect of Scottish government. Moreover, as we will discuss in the next section, these theories might be useful in explaining the transition to a new system of policy-making after the Scottish Parliament is elected in 1999.

Liberal democracy

Liberal-democratic theory was developed by philosophers such as Hobbes, Locke, Bentham and Mill, and became the official ideology of the democratic states of Western Europe and North America.

According to the theory, the people (made up of individuals) are sovereign and behave like the neoclassical consumer in economic theory in that they elect parties on the basis of the policies outlined in their manifestoes. The winning party then forms the Government, the Government implements its policies through state institutions and agencies, and the policies have an impact on the economy and society. In this model, the state is a 'neutral' institution which carries out the wishes of the people via the democratically elected Government.

The main reason for taking this theory seriously is precisely that it is the official account of what goes on in places such as the UK. So whether or not it is true is somewhat beside the point: it is the aspiration towards it that counts. For many democratic countries, it has therefore become as much part of the national myth as more distinctive elements of national history (of the type that we discuss for Scotland in Chapter 9). In Scotland, therefore, the theory that the legitimacy of the Government flows from popular authority has been a source of slowly growing scepticism about the Scottish Office and its network of quangos. When the political power in the land patently does not relate directly to the popular majority – as between 1979 and 1997 – the aspiration for liberal democracy would seem to demand a change of structures.

It has to be said, though, that this is not how it has always been seen. The pioneers of the gradual extension of the franchise in the nineteenth century truly believed that an elected parliament – even though common for the whole of the UK – would inaugurate liberal democracy in one part of the UK. The sheer rationalism of people such as Henry Cockburn and Frances Jeffrey led them to have faith in the transparency and goodwill of an elected legislature. The persisting popular belief in that institution lasted right up until the 1950s, partly because the Scottish popular majority usually coincided with the English one after the universal franchise was achieved in the 1920s, and so there was no fundamental gulf between popular preferences and the stuctures of power. In any case – as we saw in Chapter 3 – liberal democracy in Britain (not in Ireland) operated fairly benignly until the 1950s, tolerating a great deal of local choice.

Even in the 1980s and 1990s, some uncontroversial policy could still be made in this way, and indeed the Conservatives sought to build on that in their reforms after 1992. For example the Children

(Scotland) Act (1995) reflected the majority opinion in Scotland because it was not partisan in a party-political sense.

Pluralism

Nevertheless the theory of liberal democracy has been widely challenged on the grounds that it underestimates the varied and complex ways in which policy is made in specific policy areas, and the exercise of power at different levels of the process. The pluralist view is an approach that recognises the dispersal of power in society and acknowledges that people operate not only as individuals but also within groups with specific interests. Groups will pursue their interests by collective action and pressure. It is recognised that some groups will be more powerful than others in terms of organisational and lobbying strength (as a cursory comparison between the power of the Scottish Confederation of British Industry and the Scottish Council for Single Homeless illustrates), but it is assumed that no group will be dominant over a range of issues or areas of influence. Thus, in addition to their role as voters within a political system of representative democracy, individuals who are members of interest or pressure groups can exert further influence on government policies and decisions in their capacity as members of such groups.

This view of policy-making is itself based on a liberal-democratic view of the state where control over the Government rests with the people, but where the process of political representation and power has more than one dimension. Again the state is perceived as a 'neutral' institution. The Government can act as an arbiter, impartially mediating between contending economic and political interests in society – the arbiter theory. Or it can be involved in the process as an equal participant – the arena theory. The distinction between the two approaches implies different roles for the state. The 'arbiter' theory allows for an interventionist role and some control over the recognition of legitimate groups in society and the balance of power between them. The 'arena' theory implies a participatory role for the state as only one of the actors in the policy-making community.

If we apply pluralist theory to Scotland, we can find examples of policy communities or networks in some areas of autonomous policy such as education, housing, health, planning and others. These autonomous policy communities are reinforced where there are distinctive Scottish institutions, for example in the legal system, education and the church establishment.

The very existence of Scottish policy communities operating within the pluralist UK state is the main reason why there has always been scope for alternative social and political values in Scotland, even though the state has become more powerful and centralised in the twentieth century. Although there have been changes in the composition and influence of Scottish elites, for example a decreased role for local capitalists because of the growing number of takeovers and mergers, it can be argued that Scottish policy remains as firmly in the hands of Scottish elites as it ever has been. Even the Scottish Office under Conservative control had to involve experts in the relevant fields in policy formulation and implementation and to consult with other key groups with a legitimate interest in the discussion. As the journalist Chris Baur wrote in 1978 on the topic of Scottish elites, 'they all know each other – a tight circle of politicians, businessmen, civil servants, lawyers, trade unionists, churchmen, academics, and a nostalgic sprinkling of titled gentry. They fix the nation's agenda' (quoted by McCrone, 1992, p.137). They are also overwhelmingly male and middle class.

Feeding into the networks of power, Scotland has its own pressure groups and organisations (for example the Scottish Low Pay Unit, the Scottish Council for Single Parents, the Scottish Parent Teacher Council, Shelter Scottish Campaign for the Homeless, and the Scottish Council for Voluntary Organisation). These are concerned to represent the interests of their specific groups, taking into account factors relevant to experiences and conditions in Scotland. In addition to participating in policy networks in Scotland and lobbying the Scottish Office, they also seek to influence the policy-making process at the UK level.

Despite the relative autonomy of Scottish pluralism, it too has been a source of pressure for a Scottish Parliament, on two grounds. First, even though the Scottish Office may consult pressure groups and so on, it is not obliged to pay attention to them. Under the Conservatives, and on issues of deep controversy, the sense grew that the consultation was a charade. For example the overwhelming view of groups that submitted views to the Scottish Office in the early 1990s on the reform of local government was that there should be no change until after a Scottish Parliament was set up, and yet the

Conservative Government went ahead anyway (McCrone *et al.*, 1993). Second, there have been difficulties for some groups operating in Scotland where the locus of power rests in Whitehall. For example Stephen Maxwell (1987) has outlined the problems faced by the poverty lobby in Scotland in influencing campaigns and policy decisions that are centred on what he describes as 'unionist mainstream analysis'. It was argued that one way of having a greater say over such issues would be through the creation of a separate Scottish legislature.

Corporatism

A major challenge to pluralist theorists has come from the growth of an extensive and diverse literature on corporatism. Corporatist theory developed as one approach to analysing the relationship between the state and organised interests in most Western countries in the post-war period. The organised interests most often involved in corporatist relationships are representatives of employers and workers. The state has a role in bringing the different organised groups together in order to participate with them in discussions, negotiations and agreements. Having reached a consensus, the representatives then play a part in communicating the outcome to their members with the aim of gaining their endorsement of the decision and their co-operation in implementing the policy. In the process of corporatist relations, the organised interests are drawn closer to the state and at the same time risk losing some of their autonomy

Exact definitions and uses of the term corporatism vary widely, and there is also considerable debate about whether or not corporatism can in fact be distinguished from pluralism. Distinctions are also made between corporatist arrangements at different levels: the 'macro' level, meaning policy decisions that cover the whole of the UK; the 'meso' level, which could include policies that impact on a specific nation, region, industry or policy community in the UK; and the 'micro' level, which may involve policies that influence the operation of a particular firm, branch plant or group of people.

In his analysis of the response of the state to economic, social and political crises, the historian Keith Middlemas (1979) traces the development of a 'corporate bias' in Britain back to 1911. However this interpretation is not accepted by all commentators and there is disagreement about whether corporatism has ever existed or has been successful in Britain. Comparison is drawn with countries such as Sweden and Germany, which are argued to have been much more successful at incorporating the interests of organised labour in the process of capitalist production. It is acknowledged, however, that there have been different attempts by both Labour and Conservative Governments, especially in the post-1945 period, to develop corporatist relations, for example in the area of incomes policy. Reference is made to the efforts of the 1974–9 Labour administration to reach a settlement with the labour movement through the Social Contract, which ultimately broke down in the 'winter of discontent' of 1978–9.

The election of the first Thatcher Government in 1979, which explicitly rejected so-called corporatist solutions and the consensual style of government associated with the post-war period, gave support to those who argued that corporatism was a discredited and 'old fashioned' policy approach. Significant changes have taken place in the relationship between the central state and organised interests in the 1980s and 1990s. 'Rolling back the frontiers of the state' was an oft-quoted intention of Margaret Thatcher, an objective that was pursued through policies of privatisation, contracting-out, deregulation of markets, and transferring civil service functions to autonomous agencies. Her strategy was continued under the premiership of John Major; yet, as was illustrated in Chapters 2 and 3, the rolling back of the state in some spheres has paradoxically necessitated greater intervention and the centralisation of state power.

One approach to analysing the new form of relationship between the state and organised interests is the 'dualist tendency' identified by Goldthorpe (1984). Goldthorpe contends that a dualist tendency re-emerged in the 1980s as the Governments of some states attempted to offset the power of organised interests, especially those of labour, by increasing areas of the economy within which market forces and associated relations of authority and control could operate more freely. Their aim was to decrease the role of organised labour, increase the power of unorganised groups, strengthen employers' interests and encourage the free operation of market forces. While corporatism required the incorporation or inclusion of organised labour, an incorporation that was deemed expensive in terms of wage settlements, dualism has no such requirement and can operate on the basis of excluding organised labour. Goldthorpe cites Britain as an example of a state attempting dualist solutions to economic crisis. The exclusion of representatives of the trade union movement from consultation and discussion with government ministers and from representation on public bodies, the enactment of a wide range of industrial relations laws in the 1980s and 1990s, and the policies of deregulation of the labour market and privatisation, can all be interpreted as part of this trend towards dualism.

Depending on the precise definition of corporatism used, it is possible to cite examples of corporatist relations in Scotland. Certainly we can identify the existence of tripartite organisations – government, employers and trade unions – involved in the policy process in Scotland. Especially in areas relating to the Scottish economy, industry and training, it has been usual for the interests of employers and the trade unions to be represented in tripartite bodies, which have survived longer than their counterparts in England. Further, although the Conservative Government reduced the participation of trade unions in many spheres of policy consultation, the STUC was always recognised as a legitimate interest by other members of the policy community in Scotland. Even during the last few years of the Conservative Government, the STUC still endeavoured to engage in dialogue with the Secretary of State for Scotland when appropriate. It has continued to play a significant role in many aspects of Scottish civil society, for example by being directly involved in the campaign for constitutional change and playing a key role in such organisations as the Scottish Constitutional Convention.

Corporatist relations in Scotland have been noted even in areas of policy that are not directly economic. For example McPherson and Raab found that between the 1940s and the 1970s the education policy community operated with a mixture of pluralism and corporatism. It was pluralistic in the sense that it involved multiple centres of power. Some of these were autonomous of the government – for example the representatives of teachers, headteachers or directors of education (the chief education official in the local authority). Some were creatures of the Government but had acquired a life of their own – for example the colleges of education or the advisory committees on curricular matters. And some were part of the Government but not subject to the will of ministers – most notably the schools inspectors, who were based in the Scottish Education Department (SED) but defended their autonomy from the administrative civil service.

The system was corporatist in the sense that the SED sought to incorporate many of the civil society bodies into committees that would oversee aspects of the system. The board that supervised school examinations included representatives from the teachers' trade unions, the local authorities, employers, the universities and the SED itself. These representatives had relative autonomy from the SED, but in return accepted responsibility for governing a highly influential part of the education system. As Marker comments in his analysis of the colleges of education, 'if the system were, in one sense, pluralist, it was a managed and limited form of pluralism which shades into corporatism' (Marker, 1994, p.171).

However, there is no doubt that there has been a shift towards dualism since the late 1980s, which has meant a decreased role for trade union representatives in some policy areas and an increased role for employers. Such policies as deregulation, privatisation and the introduction of compulsory competitive tendering in local government have all had an impact on the role and power of organised labour. Also the trade union movement in Scotland has found it increasingly difficult to defend the interests and jobs of its members from the effects of central government economic and industrial policy.

Many of the old corporatist networks in social policy have been broken up and even, to some extent, democratised or at least made more pluralistic. For example education policy is no longer tightly controlled by the Scottish Office in negotiation with elites in powerful interest groups. There has been some genuine devolution of managerial responsibility to schools, further education colleges, and universities. The Association of Directors of Education (ADES) is no longer the main partner with which the Scottish Office negotiates: for example a new body representing college principals (the Association of Scottish Colleges) was formed after the colleges were removed from local authority control in 1993. ADES itself is more diverse, partly because of local government reform, partly because it has admitted people immediately below director level to membership (for example deputy and assistant directors), and partly because – in contrast to the era described by McPherson and Raab –

these groups are beginning to include more women, more people with backgrounds outside the high-status parts of the secondary-school sector, and more people from the west of Scotland.

Implementation

Whatever the process by which national decisions are made – pluralism, corporatism or something else – there remains the large area of implementation, the means by which national policies have an impact on people's lives. As Hogwood and Gunn (1984) argue, 'perfect implementation is unattainable', because all policy proposals have to be modified in practice when placed in the hands of professionals such as teachers, doctors and social workers, and when faced with the complexity of society and of individuals. Although the state does influence the activities of professionals, they have retained enough autonomy to affect the character of social policy.

There are three senses in which this could be true. The first is the least under the control of central government, and in a sense is not even an instance of 'implementing' something at all. It is where professionals have to make up policies themselves, either collectively through their professional bodies or individually in their daily practice. The whole point of professionalism is this kind of autonomy. For example it has been found that Scottish doctors have operated devolved budgets in ways that attempt to minimise market-like competition between doctors, and which aim to promote community health (Lapsley *et al.*, 1997). There was no central prescription requiring this, nor was it an interpretation of policy that was at odds with the Conservative Government's intentions. It probably came about because of a somewhat collectivist ethos in the Scottish Health Service, something rather nebulous but which has shaped the professional outlook of Scottish doctors and nurses.

The second sense in which implementation is important is where a policy becomes real, as opposed to simply words in a law or in a policy document issued by the centre. This is as true in Scotland as elsewhere. For example, although the framework of local economic development was created by the 1990 Act that set up Scottish Enterprise, Highlands and Islands Enterprise and the Local

Enterprise Companies (LECs), the precise ways in which these bodies have evolved have depended on the working relationships that have been established between them and a whole variety of professionals working in the field. So the meaning of 'local' varies, and cannot simply be read off the Act. Fairley and Lloyd (1995) report that some LECs have developed strategic partnerships with other local bodies, while others have established partnerships only for putting into place policies devised by the LEC. It is the autonomy of the LECs that allows this variation: and this is an instance of how the general autonomy of civil society shapes the ways in which national policies are turned into workable rules.

One of the ways in which professionals can influence implementation is by participating in the process of monitoring and evaluation. Many aspects of social policy are monitored by official agencies that are to some extent independent of the Government – for example the inspectorates for schools, social work or prisons, the Accounts Commission for local government and other public bodies, or the independent professional associations of high-status professionals such as doctors and lawyers. Insofar as these monitoring bodies build up their own culture and traditions, they act as a conservative force on an innovative Government. In Scotland they also serve to defend Scottish practices against Government attempts to reform them. An example is the reform of vocational training in the mid-1980s: as we saw earlier, this took place only on terms that were acceptable to the Scottish schools inspectorate.

This second sense of implementation – modifying the impact of a policy – shades into the first, but it is worth keeping the two distinct. The second tells how a policy is implemented, often when there was no coordinated practice before; the first is about the persisting culture of a group of professionals, at most modified by a new policy. So in the second the policy does create something new – in the case of the Local Enterprise Companies, a network of relationships around local economic development. In the first, the key feature of interest – such as the community orientation of health professionals – simply persists through something that politicians regard as a major change in policy.

The third sense in which implementation matters is the most politically visible. This is when a policy comes unstuck, being ignored, resisted completely or severely modified. An example is the way in which recent changes in education policy have been, in some respects, nullified by teachers. Brown and McIntyre (1993, p. 117) argue that teachers have control over whether a policy is implemented at all: 'while politicians and managers of education systems have the power to offer rewards and to impose sanctions to encourage teachers to innovate, it is teachers themselves who ultimately decide whether or not an innovation will be implemented in the classroom'. Swann and Brown (1997) found, for instance, that the radical revision of teaching methods and curriculum in Scotland for the age range 5–14 had had little impact on teachers' body of craft skills: they knew what the policy was supposed to be when asked about it explicitly, but made few unsolicited references to its ideas and concepts. Earlier, in 1981, schools inspectors found that primary teachers in Scotland had adopted only selectively the ideas of child-centred education that had been officially inaugurated in 1965.

The first and second senses in which implementation matters underpin the third. There is an inclination and a capacity to subvert Government policy because of strong professional or national cultures and because the Government has to entrust the implementation of policy to civil society. Implementation is the sociological brake on policy. It is the most profound reason why, in a democracy, Governments cannot get their own way. And it is a major explanation of persisting cultural distinctiveness in many countries, even when policy trends are common across the developed world. But not all actions by civil society are disruptive of the Government's intentions, even when the Government is as deeply unpopular as the Conservative Government was in Scotland by the late 1980s. Even while the poll tax was straining the legitimacy of the system to its limits, respectable Scottish professionals were getting on with most of the business of government in a thoroughly uncontroversial manner.

Nationalism

All of these pressures on policy are brought together in Scotland in a diffuse sense of the Scottish national interest. Nationalist sentiment of some sort thoroughly permeates the networks of Scottish government (in a way that has little directly to do with the SNP itself). Moreover, it permeates implicitly – as a background or an ethos of which the actors are mostly not conscious except at moments of overt conflict with England. This Scottishness is therefore an excellent example of what Billig (1995) calls 'banal nationalism' – not usually flag-waving, but flags hanging silently to remind people that they are Scottish.

In holding this taken-for-granted national allegiance – and in being able to draw on the broad popular sense of national identity – Scottish governing groups have shared in a common feature of the modern state. The welfare state was everywhere a *national* project, and in the era of mass democracy to which it was responding it achieved legitimacy partly through constructing a popular sense of the national interest (McCrone, 1992). In Scotland, however, the national interest that has been mobilised is not just British; indeed it has become less and less British since the 1970s.

Each of the four families of policy-making theory we have looked at provides scope for this nationalism to flourish. We have already commented on that for liberal democracy: the ideology that government should be by the people has contributed to the idea that any Government ruling Scotland should be directly responsible to the people of Scotland.

The policy networks of pluralism have bred a sense of a common Scottish interest among the influential elites. Permeating these networks has been an assumption of a fairly homogeneous Scottishness, notably that Scotland is democratic, respectful of education and the intellect, morally rigorous, and has a developed sense of community. The most thorough analysis of these 'myths' has been carried out by McPherson and Raab (1988) for the education system, but they can be observed everywhere. The prevalence of such myths helps explain the resistance of Scottish elites to Thatcherism, which was perceived as promoting individualism, moral irresponsibility and English nationalism. It allowed these elites ultimately to agree broadly on the sentiments of *The Claim of Right for Scotland* after it was published in 1988, which endorsed these supposed national characteristics sonorously (or pompously, depending on your point of view).

This nationalism of the policy-making elites is reinforced to the extent that the system is corporatist, because it has encouraged a willingness to look to the centre for a lead. The Scottish Office has managed to construct a consensually agreed definition of the Scottish interest, in order to be able to put united pressure on

London. This approach has been successful again and again, almost regardless of changes of Government in London. For example it gained the steelworks at Ravenscraig in the 1950s and postponed its closure in the 1980s. It gained a distinctive system of juvenile justice in the 1960s, and an increasingly distinct system of primary, secondary, community and vocational education in the 1980s and 1990s. Above all it protected Scotland's share of UK public expenditure (see Chapter 4), maintaining it at a level that would probably not be justified by a strict analysis of social need.

Although this nationalism operates most obviously at the level of elites, it is grounded in popular preferences through the role of implementation. However partial their view might be, the Scottish elites are closer to Scottish popular feeling than the central UK state tends to be, simply because many of them are in touch with Scottish professional organisations. In the end, after 18 years of Conservative rule that culminated in the loss of every Conservative seat and the overwhelming endorsement of a Scottish Parliament in the 1997 referendum, it turned out that the left-of-centre, pro-home-rule inclinations of Scottish teachers, social workers, doctors and ministers of religion more accurately reflected the popular mood than the policies of a Conservative Government that claimed to be speaking over their heads to the Scottish people.

Prospects for policy-making

The proposals that now exist for a Scottish Parliament have drawn on several of the critiques of the existing Scottish constitution that we looked at in Chapter 3. When the new Parliament takes power in the year 2000, it will therefore be able to respond to the dissatisfaction with the existing styles of policy-making. However, it will also have to deal with broadly the same range of demands on it as are faced by every other Parliament in the developed world, and therefore will probably still adopt styles that are recognisable in terms of the theoretical categories discussed in this chapter.

The current proposals, as we have seen, draw on the work of the Constitutional Convention, and so reflect both the radical and the socially conservative sources of frustration with the Scottish Office. From the radical side come ideas about developing a more open form of government. For example it is intended that the executive in the Parliament will be scrutinised by powerful committees of non-ministerial members, supported by well-funded research services and entitled to take evidence from pressure groups or community organisations as well as civil servants and ministers. Such committees could lead to more open government, and could, in particular, subject quangos to proper democratic oversight for the first time.

These radical ideas were generally uncontroversial in the Convention, and so are likely to be adopted by the Parliament. To this end the Labour Government established a cross-party Committee on Procedures in late 1997 to investigate the standing orders and other technical matters that will allow a more open system of working to be established. That committee started taking evidence in 1998, and one of the most influential sources of ideas for it is a pamphlet by Bernard Crick and David Millar, published by the left-of-centre John Wheatley Centre in 1991 and up-dated in 1995, setting out in detail the ways in which the procedures of the Parliament could be used to make the policy process more open. The committee will report to the Parliament with a set of recommended standing orders and other working practices.

More controversial within the Convention, but still from the same radical sources, were suggestions to entrench the powers of local government, so that in certain respects the Parliament simply could not overrule the decisions of elected councillors. This would be an unprecedented constitutional innovation in the UK, and helps to explain why there has been much less opposition from local government to this scheme than there was to the proposed Scottish Assembly in the 1970s. (The other main reasons for local government support were their frustration with the restrictions on their autonomy that the Conservative Government had imposed since 1979, and a weakening of the fear that a Scottish Parliament would try to take over some local authority functions.) Responding to this concern, in 1998 the Labour Government established a commission to investigate the links between local Government and the Parliament, which will report to the Parliament once it is operating. It is likely that local government will acquire greater powers over time, and hence policy-making will become more decentralised.

A similar desire for radical decentralisation led to calls for a Scottish Civic Assembly – an agency through which civil society could have a direct influence on the Government. The idea emerged from the new Coalition for Scottish Democracy, sponsored by the

STUC after the 1992 general election to maintain the campaign for a Scottish Parliament. Such an assembly met as a lobbying body for the first time in March 1995, involving representatives of trades unions, churches, pressure groups and other non-governmental organisations. Some of its advocates imagine that it might act as a kind of civil-society conscience for the new Parliament, and they propose constitutional mechanisms by which ideas from the assembly could be fed into parliamentary debates. None of these proposals appear in the legislation setting up the Parliament, and so the Parliament itself will have to decide whether formally to acknowledge the Civic Assembly.

The area of radical thinking that provoked most controversy in the Convention was over the electoral system. There were two aspects to this: whether there should be proportional representation of the parties, and whether there should be some system of quotas to ensure that at least a sizeable minority of the members would be female.

The significance of PR is that it will remove Labour's domination, probably forcing it into a coalition with the Liberal Democrats. It is expected that PR will result in a policy process operating more by consensus than Westminster does, because coalition-building will become a matter of routine.

The matter of gender balance has not appeared in the legislation. The significance of the issue lies in the very low level of women's representation among Scottish MPs (or indeed Scottish local councillors). Some advocates of quotas argue that attracting more women into politics would change the whole style in which policy is made, reducing confrontation, encouraging compromise, changing priorities and therefore affecting outcomes. Others, doubting that there are systematic differences between women and men in their approach to politics, nevertheless support quotas as a matter of the civil rights of women. The strongest pressure for quotas has come from the women's committee of the Scottish Trade Union Congress, which proposed a statutory requirement that each constituency elect one man and one woman (subsequently known as the '50:50 option'). This proposal became the policy of the STUC and the Labour Party. The Liberal Democrats have been generally suspicious, as have, privately, many people in the Labour Party (on the ground that the state should not interfere with the electoral process or party constitutions). The compromise that has been reached between these two parties is an 'electoral agreement', by which they have undertaken to try to achieve roughly equal numbers of men and women among their members in the Parliament. The SNP is likely to adopt a similar view. These topics are discussed further in Chapter 8.

The critics of the Convention argue that these radical strands have been outweighed by the caution of entrenched interests, and that these will therefore shape the style of policy-making in the new Parliament. They point to three main places in which this appears. The Convention did not propose to reduce the number of Scottish MPs at Westminster, even though the need for extra MPs will vanish when the Scottish Parliament is set up. The critics allege that the greater numbers were retained in the Convention's scheme only because Labour sometimes depends on its Scottish support to form a majority at Westminster. Despite this partisan accusation, the Labour Government acknowledged their concern in the legislation establishing the Parliament, so that the number of Scottish MPs at Westmninster is likely to fall to about 58 shortly after the Parliament is set up. One consequence will be that the size of the Scottish Parliament will fall too, both in its directly elected section and in the section coming from party lists.

The second criticism of the caution of the Convention's plans concerns the post of Secretary of State for Scotland. Under the terms of the legislation setting up the Parliament the post will be retained, but most people expect that in due course it and its Welsh counterpart will be replaced by the post of Westminster Minister for Constitutional Affairs, whose holder will be responsible for liaising with the Scottish Parliament, the Welsh Assembly and any other elected regional bodies that might be established.

But the most controversial issue in connection with how the Parliament will operate is how it will be financed (see Chapter 4). Under the present system the Scottish Office receives a block grant from the UK Government; this will continue for the Parliament, but be supplemented by the power to raise or lower income tax by a small amount. The controversy arises because Scotland receives more than its population share of that part of public expenditure which can be 'identified' – that is, attributed to particular areas. Conservative politicians have warned that this apparent subsidy will be removed after the Scottish Parliament is set up. Representatives of business interests in Scotland have also expressed their fear that the Scottish Parliament will lead to increased taxation or economic instability (see Chapter 4). The Labour Party has responded to this by emphasising the lack of economic powers that the domestic Parliament will possess, a reaction that somewhat contradicts its claim (when arguing with the SNP) that the Parliament will have the capacity to regenerate the Scottish economy.

So the Parliament that will take power in 2000 will have a conservative as well as a radical inheritance. The conservatism will be reinforced by those features of policy-making that are unlikely to be substantially changed by the new governing body. Most of the pluralism that was outlined earlier in this chapter will continue; indeed it will probably be reinforced if the Parliament does adopt a consensual style of working. One of the fears that has been expressed by radical critics of the Scottish Office is that the proposed open committee system and so on might simply give unprecedented opportunities for pressure groups to lobby, rather than genuinely opening up the policy process to groups that have never previously been involved.

It is likely, too, that Scottish policy-making will continue to be somewhat corporatist. The Parliament will find it convenient to assemble a national coalition to try to negotiate with the UK Government or to try to attract inward investment. For the same reason the system will continue to be tinged with a sense of nationalism, all the more apparently legitimate because expressed by a popularly elected body.

Most fascinating of all to watch, however, will be what happens to dissent. The Scots have learned how to object to policies over the last couple of decades, or even longer. For example it is unlikely that local government, individual schools or groups of medical practitioners based in communities will be any happier at attempts by the Parliament to centralise power than they were at similar attempts by the Conservative Government. Like all systems of national policy making, the parliament will continue to depend on local agents to put policies into practice, and so its intentions will continue to be modified by professional cultures, by a wariness of change, and by a scepticism about politicians. In any confrontation with Scottish civil society the Parliament will be the loser, because – like all modern Governments (even Margaret Thatcher's) – it will find it impossible to circumvent civil society completely.

Conclusions

So the new era on which Scottish policy-making will embark in the
new millennium will add to its complexity and diversity. The
Parliament will inherit a predilection for corporatist consensus that
was remarkably unscathed by the years of Thatcherism. It will also
inherit a deep conservatism – a tendency to fall in behind the leaders
of that consensus for fear of harming the Scottish national interest in
dealings with the outside world. In these senses, despite a great deal
of the rhetoric of constitutional reformers, the Parliament will not
mark a clean break, but an evolution.

But the civil society over which it will preside will continue to be
sceptical of the Government, and will probably cause the new
Parliament some trouble. Some of the pressure might be in a
direction that is more politically radical than the Parliament might
want (for example, through the Scottish Civic Assembly). Other
sections of civil society might exert a conservative influence, because
they are the governing establishment of Scottish society within the
Union. Whatever the outcome of these tensions, the most important
change will be that the shape of Scottish policy will increasingly be
influenced by an internal dynamic, between the national Scottish
Government on the one hand and the wider Scottish society on the
other. No longer will these tensions be hidden in discrete negotiations between national and local elites. Even the ways in which
Scotland reacts to outside pressures will change as a result. When
the national Government is democratically elected, the borrowing of
ideas for policy from elsewhere will slowly become more acceptable
than at present, having to be sanctioned by Scottish popular
preferences. So the sources of policy will become more diverse,
both because there will be new ways in which civil society will be
able to influence it, and because Scottish policy-makers will be more
relaxed about seeking inspiration from other places.

6

Party Politics in Scotland

Is Scotland different? How we choose to answer this question will colour our analysis of party politics in Scotland. The conventional wisdom is that Scottish politics only differs from its British counterpart by having a nationalist party, the SNP. Otherwise, the 'British' parties – Labour, Conservative and Liberal-Democrat – are dominant, taking almost 80 per cent of the vote in the 1997 general election. The assumption that these are essentially parties with a Westminster agenda is shared by the SNP, which labels them as 'unionist', just as the nationalists in turn are labelled as 'separatist' by their opponents. Such epithets, however, may make good rhetoric but poor analysis. In this chapter, as well as the next one, which focuses on electoral change in the modern period, we will argue that the party labels may be similar but their histories and agendas are quite different, and increasingly so. In other words the political parties in Scotland cannot be taken as British parties writ small.

This chapter will focus on the origins and development of Scotland's political parties, and charts their rise and, where relevant, fall. We will argue that much of their success (or lack of it) depends on their ability to translate Scotland to Britain and *vice versa*. Hence, as a relatively autonomous civil society, Scotland has relied on its political parties to act as a bridge across which there is a traffic of influence. Parties are successful when they are able to shape Westminster concerns to Scottish interests, and to maximise Scottish influence. Hence we can understand the success of the Liberal Party in the nineteenth century, the Conservatives in the first half of the twentieth century, Labour in its third quarter, and even the SNP's relative success since the 1960s as a reflection of this 'bridge-building' process. In other words the Scottish electorate has been quick to spot the political vehicle which will carry them to maximum influence within a state in which they are a small minority of between one sixth and one tenth over the last 150 years.

Broadly put, there are four key dates in modern Scottish political history, each reflecting the turning fortunes of new political movements. These are: 1832, the date of the Reform Act which ushered in the long hegemony of Liberal Party rule in Scotland; 1886, when that party broke its back on the issue of Irish Home Rule, and a new political force – Unionism – came to dominate right-wing politics in Scotland for the next 50 years; 1922, when the Labour Party formally supplanted the Liberals as the alternative force to Unionism, and began its long march to Scottish supremacy; and, finally, 1974, when the SNP achieved 30 per cent of the popular vote, its highest in a general election, which both reflected and helped to create a new nationalist agenda in Scotland. These major shifts in Scottish politics were not abrupt. Rather, we should see the rise and fall of political parties in Scotland as counterpoint, a process whereby minor and major themes are played out in a complex interaction of movements. The fact that these dates are roughly 50 to 60 years apart is probably fortuitous, although there is a sense of political lifespans involved in this history of party fortunes.

British homogeneity?

Before sketching out the narrative of Scottish politics, let us assess the argument for the unity of the British political system. Most obviously, the UK is technically a unitary state centred on the Westminster Parliament with its monopoly of power centred on the royal prerogative. It would seem quite appropriate that the political parties which mattered (with the exception of Northern Ireland) were British. This has been a cherished assumption in British political and social science. Hence the assumption that politics in the UK is ultimately about social class interests operating in a standardised way across the UK takes a long time in dying. Political science seems very unwilling to let go of its cherished model of the integrity of the UK.

Often, the assumption of homogeneity rests on a fairly straightforward reading. For example McAllister and Rose, in their analysis of the 1983 election, *The Nationwide Competition for Votes* (note, incidentally, the use of the term 'nationwide'), argue that 'Scotland is no exception to the proposition that the predominant influences upon party competition are Britainwide, and that differences of degree should not be treated as differences of kind' (1984, p. 123). On closer inspection, their indicator of British homogeneity is fairly crude: 'The election outcome showed that Scotland was British – but British with a difference. It was British because 88% of the total vote went to parties contesting the election Britainwide' (1984, p. 136). This assumed, of course, that the parties meant the same thing to the voters on both sides of the border, and this, as we shall see, is very doubtful.

The homogeneity thesis is also founded on the straightforward notion that the British political system is simply the English one writ large:

- because of the presumed continuity of the English Parliament at Westminster after 1707;
- because the English are 85 per cent of the electorate of the UK, and so the political and constitutional systems are English (for confirmation of that assumption, one only has to read Bagehot and other writers on the 'British' constitution);
- because the unitary state system and the doctrine of Parliamentary sovereignty prevent the emergence and survival of smaller parties based on regional, religious and ethnic factors as elsewhere.

Hence, it is assumed, the electoral system has been based on the supremacy of the two-party system: in the nineteenth century, Conservatives versus Liberals, and in the twentieth, Conservatives versus Labour. Other parties, it is argued, simply reflect the particular electoral difficulties which one or other of the main parties has got themselves into at the time.

In the last few decades this thesis has become harder to sustain. Since the early 1980s, books on politics and sociology have been published with titles such as *The End of British Politics?* (Miller, 1981), or *A Nation Dividing* (Johnson, Pattie and Allsopp, 1988); again note the common confusing of 'nation' and 'state' in Johnson's title, much the same as in McAllister and Rose. Articles are written and reputations made concerning the north–south divide, the process of class de-alignment, the growing importance of 'sectoral cleavages' and 'neighbourhood effects'. All in their different ways reflect a loss of faith in the traditional models of political behaviour in the UK and indicate an unhappiness with traditional models of explanation, coupled with a realisation that territory matters.

It seems, then, that social and political scientists are recognising that the old certainties are decaying. 'Regional' political geographies emerge, such as the north–south divide. John Curtice, for example, concluded that by 1992 'whereas the North–South gap on economic evaluations appears almost to have disappeared, the ideological gap still seems to be clearly in evidence' (1992, p. 81). In other words, the short-term trends in economic fortunes between the two parts of Britain could not explain why deeper social attitudes and values were divergent.

Our argument in this chapter is that social and political scientists are slowly coming to terms with a more fundamental reality, that the UK is not and never has been a unitary and homogeneous political system other than in rhetorical terms. As regards the fortunes of the political parties in Scotland, most obviously since the mid-1950s, Scotland and England have diverged from each other in support for the two main parties, and, second, the parties only succeed in Scotland when they address Scottish issues. When they are perceived no longer to do so, they suffer accordingly at the polls. The most obvious example is the Conservative Party in the last 30 years or so. As a corollary, when parties do embed themselves in the Scottish agenda, they benefit electorally. The Labour Party, for example, began to do much better in Scotland in the 1980s than south of the border, in large part because it took over a proto-nationalist mantle, mainly from the SNP.

We have been arguing that Scottish civil society has remained relatively autonomous within the British state. Consequently, political parties in Scotland have acted as a bridge between these two spheres of power. For example the success of the Conservative Party in the first half of this century reflected its capacity to speak for Scotland in the south, as well as its ability to interpret British needs to Scotland. Similarly Labour was able to capture the Scottish agenda in the post-war period in its championing of the welfare state, and with it the reforming capacity of the British state. The present crisis of the Scottish political system in the 1990s lies in the fact that neither of these parties is able to act as the medium of change between the Scottish and British levels; both have lost their bridge-building capacities to a large degree.

The political parties in Scotland

The story of modern Scottish politics begins in 1832, the date of the first Reform Act. Sidney and Olive Checkland comment: 'The Whig victory of 1832 proved a lasting one in Scotland. Those who had carried it obtained power in the parliamentary seats and in the town councils' (1984, p. 70).

It is easy to assume that Scotland's divergence from England in terms of electoral behaviour dates only from the second half of the twentieth century. In fact the nineteenth century showed a pattern of Liberal–Conservative difference between the two parts of the UK much more divergent than anything in the twentieth. Between 1832 and the turn of the century, electoral support for the Liberal Party at no point dropped below 50 per cent, and was as high as 85 per cent (in 1865), levels of support unmatched by any party in the twentieth century (see Table 1.1) . Indeed the Liberals took over 80 per cent of the vote four times in nineteenth century Scotland, in 1847, 1857, 1865 and 1868. While it is true that Britain was ruled by the Liberals virtually from 1846 until 1874, the party's hegemony in Scotland was much more extensive than south of the border.

Why was this? Plainly it was not because the Liberals were Scottish separatists. As the historian Michael Fry points out: 'The Whig view was Unionist. It regarded the Union as an act of far-sighted statesmanship which could be logically consummated in Scotland's more or less full assimilation to the rest of Britain' (1987, p. 3).

The Whigs had seized their chance of reforming Scotland in 1832 from under Tory domination, and promoted political and social reform. Scottish Liberalism had three distinct faces, as the Check-lands point out. There were those who believed in a mixture of paternalism and mild franchise reform, those who wanted to promote franchise extension solely, and those, later in the century, who wanted franchise reform and a working-class programme.

If Liberalism was complex as well as Unionist, it grew quite naturally in Scottish soil. Here Liberalism drew on the Scottish Presbyterian tradition with its focus on the democratic tradition of church government and its stress on 'respectability'. The Checklands comment: 'Presbyterianism had at its historical basis a powerful democratic element, whereby the equality of men before God was asserted, and which held that every man was entitled to his voice, and that wisdom might be found in anyone' (1984, p. 83). Despite the male language here, this would have been as true for women too.

In these respects, Scottish Liberalism appealed to radical senti-ment, drawing on as well as providing a 'common sense', a set of taken-for-granted social values, which helped to translate Liberal into Labour values at the turn of the century (Smith, 1984). Smith's argument is that Glasgow at the turn of the century, in contrast with Liverpool, was able to contain religious divisions because of the hegemonic tradition of Liberal 'common sense'. This is a term she borrows from the Italian Marxist writer, Antonio Gramsci, to describe the social values and institutional bedrock of a community, be it city or nation, which underpin individual and collective views of the world. So dominant had Liberalism been in the city (and the country) for much of the nineteenth century that its values became 'common sense'. Hence she argues that 'Most Glasgow working men believed in Free Trade, the iniquities of the House of Lords and all other hereditary positions, loathed landlordism, believed in fairness and the rights of small nations and in democracy and the will of the people' (1984, p. 34). This, of course, does not imply that all were under its spell, but it did have the effect of seeding this common sense in both Scottish socialism and Unionism alike. It made the task of Labour and Unionists easier but also more difficult.

At the same time, Liberal common sense helped to create right-wing Unionism in the form of Liberal Unionism which split from the party and provided a bridge for Scotland's bourgeoisie to cross from Liberalism to Conservatism after 1886. Fry's comment that Scottish Liberalism was 'remarkably nebulous' (1987, p. 74) shows both its strength and its weakness as a political force in nineteenth-century Scotland. While it could set itself up in juxtaposition to (landed) aristocratic Conservatism, it could appeal to capitalists and workers alike.

As the century progressed the differences between Whigs and Radicals within the Liberal Party grew more obvious. In the burghs the Radicals were dominant, while Whig lairds were not without influence in the party (Kellas, 1994). Nevertheless, at the height of its powers the party was supreme in Scotland. In Fry's words: 'The

Scots remained overwhelmingly loyal to the Liberal party and especially to its radical wing. Its programme – the destruction of privilege, the limitation of government power, the extension of civil liberty, and the improvement of popular education – represented public opinion in Scotland much more faithfully' (1987, p. 98).

Paradoxically, the extension of the franchise helped to undermine this support. The party had benefited from the second Reform Act of 1868 (in that year winning 82 per cent of the vote, and 51 of the 58 Scottish seats), but not from the third Reform Act of 1884, which raised the size of the Scottish electorate to over 500 000: that is, to all male householders. The following year the Liberals could manage only 53 per cent of the vote in Scotland, and 51 out of its 70 seats. Gladstone's Midlothian campaign of 1879–80 had provided cover for a party in which internal differences were becoming more obvious and difficult. The rise of the crofting issue in the Highlands had placed Liberal lairds on the defensive, but two other factors helped to destroy their hegemony in Scotland. On the one hand, the split over Irish Home Rule led to a breakaway to the right in the form of the Liberal Unionists, while to the left the growing salience of social and economic issues undermined Liberal support for *laissez-faire* among the working classes.

In electoral terms, the Liberals were still taking the majority of the votes in Scotland and the bulk of the seats. Only in 1900 did the Liberals fail to provide more than half of Scotland's MPs, in taking 34 of Scotland's 70 seats. In this respect the writing was on the wall. Land reform was highlighted by the Land Wars of the 1880s, and it was a key political issue not only in Scotland generally but in the Highlands in particular. Fry comments: 'The attraction of the land question for the Scots was that it could par excellence be presented as the people's struggle against privilege' (1987, p. 103). The trouble for the Liberals was that it highlighted the tension between Whiggish *laissez-faire* and reformism among the crofting MPs who were elected in the Highlands in the 1880s.

Also on the radical side, strains began to show in class terms. Unlike south of the border, there was no Lib-Lab pact in Scotland, largely because of Liberal dominance and early Labour weakness. Keir Hardie had found himself squeezed out of winnable seats by the Liberal ascendancy, and went on to found his Scottish Labour Party before taking himself off to England where winning a seat was easier.

It was, however, the Home Rule issue which broke the back of the Liberals as the dominant party in Scotland. The schism over Gladstone's Home Rule bill divided pro- and anti-Home Rule factions, especially as Gladstone insisted that Irish Home-Rule take precedence over a Scottish demand for the same. On the face of it the Home Rule split did not much affect Liberal strength in Scotland, as it won 43 out of 70 seats in 1886, with 54 per cent of the vote. It was not to lose its majority of the popular vote until 1918, but problems could be detected 30 years earlier in the 1880s. By 1900 the Liberal Party lost its hold on the majority of MPs it had had since 1832, and this was particularly noticeable in the Highlands (to the crofting MPs), and in the west of Scotland where the Liberal Unionist dissidents were strong. Even its surge in 1906, when it won 58 of Scotland's 70 seats on 56 per cent of the vote, failed to destroy its Unionist and Labour opposition.

In essence, the Liberal Party was caught, as Fry points out, between Unionist paternalism and interventionist socialism: 'In [the] mid-19th century, the Liberal national consensus was the fairly passive expression of a society where there was little disagreement on fundamental aims and not much call for policy' (1987, p. 147). By 1929 the Liberals were down to 13 seats and a mere 18 per cent of the popular vote. They had become Scotland's third party.

The Liberal Party was, after 1832, Scotland's first mass political party with an electoral strength which was never attained by any party in the twentieth century. It had managed to capture a variety of social and political platforms. It was radical, and yet elitist. It appealed to both urban and rural interests. It could claim to be a party of the left as well as the right. It was committed to *laissez-faire*, and also to social reform. Its broad appeal was both its strength and its weakness. It was attacked from the right by Unionists in defence of imperial Britain with its economic interests, and so alienated the west of Scotland bourgeoisie thirled to Empire and to Union. It was attacked from the left for being unable to translate itself into a working-class party, while at the same time its underlying social values – its Liberal common sense – allowed a relatively easy birth for parties on the left. It lost its capacity to translate Scotland to London, and vice versa. This process of translation, Scots were to judge by the late nineteenth century, was better served by outright Unionists on the right and Labour to the left. The historic role of the Liberal Party had passed.

The rise of Unionism

If 1832 had ushered in modern party politics in embryonic form, 1886 was no less of a turning point in Scottish political history. As Fry comments:

> The Scots opposition grew from a tiny, landed coterie to a true political party containing some of the leading citizens, grounded on a popular base in the West and espousing a patriotic, Protestant ideology. The official Liberal Party also developed in consequence, becoming more united, radical and proletarian. Scotland started to change from a one-party state, where politics were conducted by individuals and cliques, to a country with a modern, formally pluralistic political system of organised interest groups. (1987, p. 109)

The Conservative Party in Scotland did not do particularly badly in the nineteenth century, at least in comparison with its electoral performance in the latter part of the twentieth century. At general elections between 1832 and 1886 it reached a high of 46 per cent (and 20 seats) in 1837, and a low of 14.6 per cent (and 11 seats) in 1865 (see Table 1.1). Its problem was that its social base was too narrow. In the Checklands' words: 'the incubus of the landlord connection was too great for the Scottish Tory party' (1984, p. 77). Lairds were mainly Tories, with strong political bases in the north-east where the Duke of Gordon ruled, and in the south where the Duke of Buccleuch did likewise. The party's association with the Kirk, the established Church of Scotland, gave it a base, but a restricted one associated with power and patronage.

The party had attempted to reform itself in 1867 when a political organisation was set up for the whole of Scotland. In 1874, when its English counterpart swept the board at the general election, it took 31.6 per cent of the vote and 18 seats; and, significantly, votes were won in the urban areas rather than the counties. It even broke the Liberal monopoly in Glasgow where it won a seat. Nevertheless it found it difficult to attract a working-class following, a Scottish version of (in Disraeli's phrase) 'angels in marble', a proletariat which deferred to its social betters.

Fortunes turned in 1886. The Liberals split down the middle over Irish Home Rule, and the key newspapers of the Scottish middle classes, *The Scotsman* and the *Glasgow Herald*, also defected to the Conservative cause. In the general election of that year, the Liberals lost eight seats nationally, but especially in the west. The Conservatives strengthened to 10 seats. Hutchison observes that: 'whereas Conservatism in the 1880s had appeared reactionary and largely indifferent to the urban-industrial social order, by the mid 1890s a positive Unionism had emerged' (1986, p. 199).

It was clear, however, that Conservatism narrowly defined would not have made the breakthrough without its new Liberal Unionist partners. Here was a party of business rather than of land. Hutchison's analysis of the occupational base of the two parties indicates their differential appeal (1986, p. 207). In 1886, for example, six out of 10 Conservative MPs had landed interests, and four came from business or the professions. A similar picture emerged from its 1895 intake. Nine of its MPs were landowners, out of a total of 17. On the other hand, eight Liberal Unionists in 1886 were businessmen, four were professionals and only five were landowners. Similarly, in 1895 only three of 14 Liberal Unionists were landowners, while nine were businessmen and two were professionals. In other words, Liberal Unionism was the vehicle whereby the right broke out of its narrow landed base.

The effects on the political system of the resurgent right after 1886 was considerable. The Liberal Party as such, of course, did not wither away after 1886. In formal terms it retained its hold on the Scottish electorate until the Great War, at no time falling below 50 per cent of the vote, but the damage was done; there was no way back.

The real strength of the new Unionism lay in the west of Scotland, despite the Liberals' hold on Glasgow. Its 'common sense' was based on the industrial bourgeoisie with its triple icons of Unionism, Imperialism and Protestantism, and this ushered in a new hegemony which reached down into the working class. Bourgeois politics were straightforward. As Fry says, 'it was Unionist because imperialist; it was imperialist because its prosperity was bound up with Empire' (1987, p. 110). Unionism did not dispense with the old Liberal common sense; it fused economic individualism with a collectivist intent to make the city worthy of civic pride. Glasgow became a business city with a social conscience of sorts.

It would be easy, but misleading, to think that the advance of the right stemmed from a revived Conservative Party. If anything it was a junior partner to the new Unionism, and was absorbed into it. It is a measure of this absorption that in 1912 the now-amalgamated party changed its name from Conservative to the Scottish Unionist Party, which it remained until 1965, when it reinstalled part of its original title and became the Scottish Conservative and Unionist Party. The importance of the Liberal Unionist dimension can be seen in Table 6.1, reproduced from James Kellas's analysis (1994) of the party in Scotland.

We may find the proliferation of titles confusing, but Kellas points out that 'National Liberal', 'Liberal Unionist', 'National Liberal and Conservative' and 'Liberal and Conservative' were in practice synonymous with 'Conservative' as the twentieth century wore on. Nevertheless, with its fusion of commitment to free trade and social interventionism, Scottish Unionism was distinctive because of, not despite, its Liberal origins. At key points the Scottish Unionists broke ranks on the issue of protectionism: in 1903, 1923 and 1932. Liberal Unionists, especially in the west of Scotland, made free (imperial) trade an article of faith. These industrialists also were the officer corps of which the Scottish Protestant working class, faced with immigration from Ireland both north and south, were the willing foot-soldiers. As late as the 1960s the Protestant working-class areas were more likely to vote Conservative than their Catholic counterparts who were by then thirled to the Labour Party.

Table 6.1   *The strength of Liberal Unionism in Scotland*

Year	Conservative		Liberal Unionist/Coalition Liberal/National Liberal/ Liberal and Conservative	
	% of vote	*Seats*	*% of vote*	*Seats*
1900	18.4	19	30.6	17
1906	24.3	5	13.9	5
1910 (Jan.)	27.6	7	12.0	2
1910 (Dec.)	31.7	6	10.9	3
1918	30.8	28	19.1	25
1922	25.1	13	17.7	12

Source: Kellas (1994), p. 676, by permission of Oxford University Press.

Despite its proletarian appeal, the new Unionism was first and foremost a way of enticing the Scottish bourgeoisie away from its Liberal roots. As the Checklands comment: 'The Liberal Unionist Party could never hope to become the government; its principal role seen in retrospect was to provide a bridge over which middle class man could pass from Liberalism to Toryism without suffering any sense of betrayal' (1984, p. 85). The key conflict, often overshadowed by the rise of Labour in the early years of the century, was actually between Liberalism and Unionism. It was an ideological struggle which the Liberals, with their attempts to keep open the door to the emerging working class, were ill-suited to win. So it proved.

The electoral strength of Unionism was never at the level of nineteenth-century Liberalism. By the early years of this century Scotland had, to all intents and purposes, universal suffrage, although women, as south of the border, were not to become equal voting partners until much later than men. The Unionists had to confront a Liberal Party still able to take around 20 per cent of the vote in the inter-war period, as well as a rising Labour Party, but by 1924 (on 41 per cent of the vote) it won a majority – 36 – of the Scottish seats. The Unionists were to dip below 40 per cent of the popular vote at general elections only once, in 1929, until the long slide began in the 1960s.

In government, either national or on its own, it developed a distinctive interventionist style, reflected in the role of Walter Elliot who was to be Scottish Secretary between 1936 and 1940, but whose book *Toryism and the Twentieth Century* (1927) laid out the corporatist model which served the party until the Thatcherite experiment began in 1979. Traces could be found in Scottish Office policy long after that.

Like the Liberals before them, the Unionists derived their success from capturing the 'common sense' of Scotland, but like them it was also to be their downfall. Their style of government is described by Michael Fry as 'paternalistic and gently progressive' before and after the Second World War. Its problem was that corporatism could also be a weapon better wielded by a Labour Government. By 1959, despite (or perhaps because of) its interventionist project to restructure Scottish industry, it was losing out to Labour. Fry comments: 'The unionist part of the experiment was not for a moment called into question. But henceforth it was to be conducted under Labour leadership' (1987, p. 199).

By the 1960s Unionism was on the political wane. Largely as a reflection of its financial and ideological dependency on its English equivalent, it inserted 'Conservative' back into its title. The Unionist epithet was rarely used, and in party political broadcasts it was referred to simply as the Scottish Conservative Party. The 1960s saw the resurgence of non-socialist radicalism in the Liberal Party, an extended dominance in the central belt by Labour, and a challenge to come in its rural and small-town heartland from the SNP which it was in no position to withstand. The Unionists had lost their capacity to build bridges across which the middle class as well as the working class could pass except in an outward journey to other parties. Their fall from electoral grace reflected a loss of a Scottish project which would translate Scotland to the British state and vice versa. Thatcherism was to be a poisoned chalice to Scottish Unionism. The final word is Fry's: 'Till 1974 they [the Tories] never got much less than 40% of the vote, and often rather more; afterwards they never got much more than 30%, and often rather less. In the turmoil of the 1970s, they seemed to have forfeited a quarter of their support' (1987, p. 252).

The political future belonged to other parties. In the first instance it was Labour's.

Labour in the ascendant

The interesting feature about the rise of Labour in Scotland was not that it became dominant, but that it took so long to do so. In the last election before the Great War – December 1910 – Labour took only 4 per cent of the vote and three seats (see Table 1.1). By 1918 it had achieved 23 per cent of the vote and won six seats. Why so little and so few, especially given the political and industrial agitation known as 'Red Clydeside'? It was not until the 1922 election that the real breakthrough in Scotland occurred when Labour won 29 seats and became the largest party in Scotland, albeit with 32 per cent of the popular vote. In the following year Labour consolidated its hold in Scotland by winning 34 seats on 36 per cent of the vote, a performance which it was to maintain and improve on over the following 70 years.

Why, then, did Labour take so long in becoming Scotland's largest party? Above all, it was faced with a dominant Liberal Party which took an unconscionable time in dying, and a resurgent Unionist right which appealed to large swathes of the Protestant working class, especially in Glasgow, its largest city. Joan Smith comments that:

> Glasgow was a town with strong, radical Liberal politics. The radical Liberalism of many of the Glasgow working men was not just an ideology that had to be defeated if socialism was to lead the Glasgow working class movement – it was also a rock-like foundation for the development of that socialism. Many attitudes were shared with Liberalism which made it possible, in a town with high Irish immigration, for the Protestant-Catholic divide to be contained. (1984, p. 33)

For socialists, Liberal strength was especially a problem. As James Kellas has pointed out, a strong Liberal Party made alliance with puny Labour less likely north of the border. It also relates to the fissiparous tendencies among the left in Scotland at the turn of the century. Keir Hardie's experiences with the Liberals led him to found his own Scottish Labour Party (SLP) in 1888, in Fry's words 'the first party in British history to aim specifically at promoting the workers' interests' (1987, p. 154). It was not electorally successful, for it fought five seats in 1892 and lost all of them badly. The following year the SLP affiliated to the ILP, which had been founded in Bradford in that year. It is worthy of note that the ILP was a (northern) English creation, despite its subsequent disproportionate success in Scotland. Nevertheless it was no more successful initially than the SLP, and it too lost all seven seats it contested in the 1895 election.

That year the STUC was formed as a separate organisation following the refusal of the (British) TUC to accept Trades Councils into its membership rather than individual unions. The STUC had important links with the ILP, as well as the Social Democratic Federation (SDF), and the cooperative societies. In 1900, and before the Labour Representation Committee (LRC) was formed in the south, it was instrumental, along with the ILP, in helping to form the Scottish Workers' Representation Committee (SWRC). It was not until 1908 that it disbanded in favour of the British organisation.

Scotland at this time had diverse forms of socialist parties. Apart from Hardie's SLP, and the better known ILP which came to be associated with James Maxton, Tom Johnston and John Wheatley, and 'Red Clydeside', there existed the important support for the British-based SDF (later the Social Democratic Party), the Socialist Labour Party founded by James Connolly in 1902 some years before his involvement with the Irish Republican Movement, and the British Socialist Party founded in 1911 by John MacLean. Slightly earlier, there was also the Highland Land League, which followed the Irish Land League in advocating the redistribution of land to the people who worked on it.

Above all there was the Communist Party, which had been formed in Scotland in the 1920s out of the British Socialist Party, the SLP and the left wing of the ILP. The Communists proved to be especially strong in Clydeside and in industrial Fife. Although the party was particularly strong among organised labour, its electoral appeal was limited, its best Scottish performance coming in 1922 when it won 2.6 per cent of the vote. The Communist Party (CP) of Great Britain always relied disproportionately on Scotland and Wales, mainly in mining areas. Hence in 1931 48 per cent of Communist votes in Britain came from Scotland, and in 1951 it rose to 51 per cent, five times what one would have expected on a population basis. By the 1980s around one fifth of the CP vote came from Scotland, whereas in England the party underperformed by as much as 50 per cent. As late as 1995 the Communists had two local councillors in Fife (the Conservatives had none). In Scotland generally, the proliferation of leftist parties was both a sign of the strength of socialist ideology, and a reflection of its electoral failure to mobilise behind one single form.

All of these forces fed into what was the most famous episode in early labour history: Red Clydeside. It was judgements about this event (or, more accurately, sequence of events) which generated hope among radicals and fear among conservatives. Damer's assessment is probably fair: 'Glasgow in 1915 was not St Petersburg in 1917 – although Glasgow in 1919 was probably the nearest that any British city came to it' (1980, p. 75). The key to understanding Red Clydeside lies in appreciating the diverse forces within it, the sectional interests it mobilised, and above all the significance of the time sequences involved.

Put simply, unrest in the west of Scotland at this time may have looked like an organised and contemporaneous set of events, but this is not the case. In the first place, the crisis of working-class housing – its shortage, restrictive letting conditions and high rents – came to a head in 1915 in the form of a series of rent strikes mobilised in large part by the Glasgow Labour Party Housing Committee. It is clear that this episode was in essence a women's struggle, for it was they who were responsible for managing the household budget and negotiating with the landlord in most working-class families. Their centrality in grassroots organisation in mobilising support cannot be overestimated. These included ward committees, labour representation committees, tenants' defence committees and protective societies. Their victory was quick and overwhelming. By 1915 the Rent Restrictions Act had been passed which sounded the death-knell of privately rented housing in Scotland, and with it a major defeat for small capitalists who dominated the housing market at this time (McCrone and Elliott, 1989).

A second major issue began to run in 1915 concerning the 'dilution' of labour, notably in the engineering works and shipyards on the Clyde. In February of that year the Central Labour Withholding Committee was formed ('labour withholding' got round the banned use of 'strikes'). The issue related to an increase in war-time production in key industries by using cheap labour, including women. The skilled manual craft unions, notably the engineers, saw this as a device for reducing their economic and industrial power, and resisted, culminating in 1916 in a series of strikes and lockouts. The issue simmered on until 1919, when the Committee called a 40-hour strike which led to the belief that the Government had mobilised tanks in the city's George Square for fear of an uprising. Much of the iconography of Red Clyde relates to these episodes.

Running alongside housing and industrial disputes was the much more 'political' issue of anti-war protest. The Defence of the Realm Act (DORA) had taken a heavy hand to public protest, and when the state introduced conscription in 1916, protesters had a real issue to mobilise around. With hindsight it is likely that the anti-war movement was restricted in popular appeal (after all, the Unionist and Liberal parties were much stronger electorally than Labour at this time). Nevertheless anti-conscription threw up its most famous martyr in John MacLean, who later in his foreshortened life tried to fuse socialism and nationalism, making him a remembered icon for both political movements.

How are we to assess the significance of this undoubtedly important set of events which have so coloured socialist politics in Scotland, and especially Glasgow? Some (McLean, 1983) consider the events 'much exaggerated', and define it simply as a form of craft conservatism with fear of labour dilution among well-paid engineers at its core. While McLean is probably correct to counsel caution, it is important not to underestimate the real and symbolic significance of Red Clyde. It did bring together a series of disputes – over housing, wages and conscription – which radicalised a substantial and diverse working class. These struggles also helped to forge a common set of interests for men and women, skilled and unskilled, Protestants and Catholics. It provided an infrastructure of socialism in the form of organisations like socialist Sunday Schools, ILP branches, cooperative movements and trades councils, as well as political parties, all of which in turn helped to provide an organisation network for different strikes and struggles.

The protest also had a direct payoff in the form of the destruction of the free market in urban housing rents, not only in Glasgow and in Scotland, but in the UK generally. The state was compelled to meet working-class demands for state housing (which was the main legacy of the first Labour Government in 1924 of which, significantly, John Wheatley was the housing minister). In its attempts to handle the dilution disputes, it also had to get accustomed to treating labour as 'an estate of the realm' in Middlemas's phrase (1979). The bourgeoisie had to adapt to these new angles of power, but this proved not too difficult. In the case of rent legislation, the small capitalists rather than the large had to pay a disproportionate price, while employers learned to live with the new accommodations. In Scotland the new Unionism was not averse to a more interventionist stance; witness its espousal of corporatistic forms of economic relations.

We are now in a position to answer our earlier question: if Labour in its different forms had achieved such heights of radicalisation, why then did they not sweep the board in the 1918 election? The answer is not, as McLean (1983) argues, that it gives the lie to the view that there was revolutionary potential on the Clyde, but that small but significant extensions of support for Labour were not made until the 1922 election. By this time, and following a settlement of sorts to the Irish Question, Glasgow's sizeable Irish working class had transferred their allegiances from Irish nationalism to their 'class' party, Labour (Hutchison, 1986, p. 287). This was enough to translate into a modest but strategic increase in electoral support for Labour (from 23 per cent in 1918 to 32 per cent in 1922). For this increase of less than 10 percentage points, Labour was rewarded under the electoral system with 23 extra seats (increasing from six to 29). Crucially, in this new tranche of Labour MPs as many as 18 out of the 29 came from the west of Scotland.

Glasgow politics has played a disproportionate part in the politics of Labour in Scotland, just as Scotland played a crucial role in British Labourism. In its early days Labour did better outwith Glasgow, notably in Edinburgh and Aberdeen, and later in Dundee once it had captured the Catholic vote there too. Nevertheless the events on the Clyde helped to give Labour politics a heroic resonance in the later years of municipal dominance in Glasgow after 1933 (it took that long to win control from a right-wing 'moderate' party). Thereafter Labour politics had much more to do with building and managing large council housing schemes in which significant amounts of human and political capital were invested. It is important to remember that there is more to politics than Westminster elections, and notably in the day-to-day running of Scotland's towns and cities, without which, as the Unionists discovered to their cost, victories at general elections came much harder.

After Red Clydeside, Labour politics became more mundane. The Labour machine began to roll over and absorb the smaller socialist sects. The ILP, however, maintained their distance and popularity, returning four of its 11 candidates in 1935 and getting all three elected in 1945. By then the ILP had to all intents and purposes become a Scottish party as its MPs were all from north of the border. Fry comments that for the ILP socialism was a crusade, and this was its legacy to Scottish politics, although not one which machine Labourism had much time for. Ultimately, ILP failure to translate that crusade into practical politics led to its demise. Even its commitment to (Scottish) Home Rule, which was greater than Labour's, ended up much reduced as the ILP tradition was taken over by Labour in the post-war period. The result was, in Fry's words, that 'Labour turned into the most unionist and rigidly disciplined of all the parties' (1987, p. 173).

The conversion of ILP into Labour, of crusade into machine politics, are no better expressed by the fact that Tom Johnston, one of its leaders, ended up as Scottish Secretary during the Second World War, and established Labour hegemony until 1951, by which time it had put in place its own version of corporate machine politics in Scotland. That was both its strength and its weakness. Curiously enough, Labour never managed to achieve 50 per cent support at general elections in Scotland, unlike the Unionists who did so in 1955 (Labour that year won 47 per cent: see Table 1.1). Nevertheless Labour took a majority of Scottish seats in 1950 and in every general election up to and including 1997, albeit on a minority of the vote (from a high of nearly 50 per cent in 1966 to a post-war low of 35 per cent in 1983). Its 1997 share of the vote (45.6 per cent) was its highest for 30 years. And the left as a whole – Labour, ILP and the Communist Party – won a clear-cut majority of votes in 1945 and 1966.

Labour's strength lay in its grip of all levels of Scottish politics, and in its capacity to translate British politics to Scottish politics and back again. In its quest for post-war economic planning, it quietly downgraded its traditional commitment to a Scottish Parliament which it had inherited from the Liberals and the ILP. This was to be its Achilles' heel in the 1970s when a new form of populist politics emerged, Scottish nationalism. Not only did that aspire to speak for the Scottish people in a more untrammelled way than Labour; it also sought to use its challenge to the Union to win more resources for Scotland. The final stage was set for the main battle of the final quarter of the twentieth century: that between socialism and nationalism.

A nation once again?

The rise of an explicitly nationalist party in Scotland is perhaps the most distinctive feature of its political system. It is, indeed, often assumed to be the only distinctive feature, as the 'unionist' parties – Labour, Conservative and Liberal – are thought to be the same as those south of the border. This chapter has tried to disabuse the reader of such a notion. Nevertheless the rise of the SNP to become the second party in Scotland behind Labour requires explanation. Of course it lies in nationalism and Scotland's relationship with England, but there is more to it than that. After 1959 it was becoming clear that Unionism – the dominant political creed of the right – was in decline. That decline was even more noticeable as its Conservative counterpart in England did not suffer anything like the same fate. Indeed the divergence in electoral behaviour which we will discuss in the next chapter was largely due to the differential decline of the Scottish Unionist Party.

Labour began to have Scotland to itself, and as such an older pattern of one-party rule re-emerged. Fry puts it this way:

> Scotland thus broke with her recent conformity to the general pattern of politics in the United Kingdom and recurred to her own of former days, likened . . . to a one-party state. True, Labour never emulated the absolute majorities habitually won by the old Liberal Party, and twice even by the Unionists. But it established a decisive lead in votes and, more important, an unshakeable hold over at least forty seats capable of surviving large swings against it in the rest of Britain. Through that alone it set the agenda for Scottish politics, and to some extent all other parties imitated its programme. (1987, p. 223)

The SNP became the main challenger to Labour in the final quarter of this century by fighting on both nationalist and socialist/social democratic battlegrounds. It has drawn Labour on to its claim to be the 'national' party of Scotland, while the SNP has sought to show that it is in a better position than Labour to win resources not only from Britain, but ultimately from Europe. It has not found it easy to square this particular circle. The reasons for that lie in its roots.

In formal terms the SNP was founded in 1934. Nevertheless, its origins and predecessors give vital clues to what kind of party it was to become. The Scottish Home Rule Association (SHRA) had been formed in 1886 having grown out of the Liberals' programme first for Irish Home Rule, and then for 'Home Rule all round'. As its creature, the SHRA was tied to Liberal fortunes, and as these declined, so did the SHRA. It was reconstituted in 1918 by Roland Muirhead, a businessman and socialist, who had been a Liberal and then an ILP member. The SHRA saw itself as non-party, and included in its ranks members from all parties. SHRA adherents now expected the Labour Party to become the vehicle for achieving Home Rule given that party's historic commitment. It is important to stress that the SHRA was 'devolutionist' rather than 'separatist'. In Richard Finlay's words: 'Home Rule, it was claimed, would benefit the government of the United Kingdom and the running of the British Empire, by introducing a more efficient and manageable form of administration' (1994, p. 4).

By 1919 the SHRA had over 700 individual members and over 100 organisations affiliated to it. By 1922 it reckoned to have the support of 44 MPs, and at the general election of that year 26 of the 29 Labour MPs gave explicit support to self-government, together with nine out of 14 Liberals, seven out of 14 National Liberals, but only one Tory out of 15. The problems of the SHRA were two-fold. On the one hand, the collapse of the Liberals in 1924 removed substantial support from the Home Rule lobby and, on the other, Home Rule in the Labour Party took second place to centralist UK concerns. When Labour came to power in 1924 it failed to support a Home Rule bill in Parliament. The inter-war period with its concern for rising unemployment and world depression was not especially conducive to persuading the Labour Party to devote time to Scottish self-government. In 1928 supporters such as Muirhead took the bull by the horns, announced that they would stand against the Labour Party at elections, and formed the National Party of Scotland. The fragile coalition which had sustained the SHRA across the party divide had come to an end.

Alongside the left-leaning NPS, the Scots National League (SNL) was undoubtedly the most important nationalist grouping in the inter-war period. It drew on celtic romanticism and what it called 'celtic communism', giving it an appeal to those on the left as well as the right. It had an appeal to old Highland Land Leaguers, and gave support to Irish Independence after 1916. Partly reflecting the mood of its time as well as its own predilections, it tried to draw a racial characterisation between Scottish and Irish 'Celts' and (English) Teutons, juxtaposing the democratic and progressive nature of Celts with authoritarian and imperialist impulses of the Anglo-Saxon teutons. This form of racial politics focused on English immigration to Scotland, and was a forerunner to the wilder fringe movements in the 1990s such as Scotland Watch and Settler Watch.

The SNL was also responsible for founding the newssheet *Scots Independent*, which was to become a central organ of the wider Scottish national movement and its distinctive newspaper. One of its first campaigns was to propose the creation of a 'National Party' out of the SHRA and SNL, recognising the need for a single distinctive voice for Scottish nationalism. This was not to happen until much later. By 1928 the SNL had over 1000 members in 15 local branches, but it was to be overshadowed in that same year by the new, more leftist party, the NPS.

The most influential group to help create the NPS was the Glasgow University Scottish Nationalist Association, led by John MacCormick who had been a member of the ILP (the nationalists were always to do much better at student and university elections than in the wider society). He made common cause with Roland Muirhead of the SHRA, and the romantic essayist, poet and anarchist R. B. Cunninghame Graham was adopted as the first president of the NPS. By 1929 it had seven parliamentary candidates, including C. M. Grieve, the poet Hugh MacDiarmid. The NPS tried to steer a line between the fundamentalists who wanted no truck with other parties, and the moderates, including MacCormick, who sought a new direction for Home Rule in collaboration with them. The party was not particularly successful in electoral terms, although in the 1930s it was taking more than 10 per cent at by-elections and was accused of preventing Labour winning by taking working-class votes. Both Muirhead and MacCormick retained their ILP and Labour connections in the belief that the latter might raise the profile of Home Rule.

The NPS also found itself challenged by a new formation, the Scottish Party, which sought 'moderate' opinion. It began as a right-wing pressure group seeking a synthesis of Toryism and nationalism, and was opposed to both separatism and to socialism. Somewhat oddly to late-twentieth-century eyes, it sought to strengthen the British Empire by means of Home Rule, thereby echoing earlier SHRA sentiments which wanted Scotland to have dominion status like Canada, New Zealand and Australia.

This new challenge from the right led to a redoubling of efforts by MacCormick and others to capture the middle ground, and in particular MacCormick pushed for amalgamation between the NPS and the Scottish Party, something opposed by fundamentalists in the NPS who saw the latter as a bulwark of British imperialism, and who distrusted devolution as opposed to outright independence. MacCormick and his allies got their way, and a new party was formed in 1934, calling itself the SNP. Under their leadership separation was ruled out. The historian Richard Finlay has commented that 'In the last analysis, it has to be said that in terms of fighting for "national independence" in the normal sense of the word, the creation of the SNP was undoubtedly a regressive step'

(1994, p. 154). Furthermore, in order to accommodate the Scottish Party, the new SNP had to abandon most of the left-of-centre policies of the NPS, and its fuzzy stance on independence reflected this accommodation. What it meant by Scottish self-government was unclear.

Although the new party was well organised because of MacCormick's skills as an organiser, its failure to achieve an electoral breakthrough in the 1930s was its, and his, undoing. It had an ambivalent attitude towards dual party membership, with the effect that, as Finlay points out, 'the SNP had become more of a movement rather than a political party' (1994, p. 183). Home Rule still had enough supporters in other parties, notably Labour and the Liberals, to make this appear a feasible strategy in the hope that a common front – a popular device in 1930s politics generally – on self-government might emerge. It did not, and the party leaders were under pressure from the fundamentalists.

On the issue of the Second World War, the SNP was divided. Its leadership was officially pro-war, but its opposition mobilised against conscription on the grounds that this was a British and therefore Imperialist war, not a Scottish one. The opposition won, and MacCormick left the party taking many delegates with him (most returned later). By the 1940s the SNP, under fundamentalists such as Robert McIntyre and Arthur Donaldson, developed a more coherent electoral strategy which began to pay off in the rather curious by-elections of the war period. McIntyre's victory at the Motherwell by-election, where he achieved 50 per cent of the votes, gave a major boost to the credibility of the SNP as a political party. McIntyre was to lose the seat six weeks later at the 1945 general election, but the damage (to the opposition inside and outside the party) was done. The modern philosophy and strategy of the SNP was set for the second half of the century.

Electoral success was a long time in coming. In 1945, it contested only eight seats in Scotland, and won 30 000 votes, little more than in 1935 under the old, discredited, leadership. Even as late as 1959 it was winning a mere 20 000 votes, about the same as in 1931. Its break-through came at by-elections, first in Glasgow Bridgeton in 1961, and then in West Lothian the following year where it came second to Labour. By 1964 the SNP was fighting 15 seats, three times the 1959 figure, and was taking 65 000 votes. Two years later it had doubled this to 130 000, some 5 per cent of the vote. The key year was 1967. First, it prevented Labour from holding the Glasgow Pollock seat, which went to the Tories, and then, more famously, Winnie Ewing won the Hamilton by-election (from Labour) in November of that year. In the 1970 general election the SNP lost Hamilton but won the Western Isles, the first time the party had won a seat at a general election. That year it took 300 000 votes, 11 per cent, which it duly doubled in the February 1974 election, when it won seven seats. But it achieved its highest share of votes at the general election in October of that year with 30 per cent of the vote and 11 seats.

Unlike the other Scottish parties which had established their organisations and structures at the turn of the century, the SNP was, in a crucial sense, a modern party. That is, it was able to take advantage of the media, notably television, at the key moment in its formation. Whereas the others were 'mass' parties of an earlier age which used the channels of persuasion open to them at the time – rallies, pamphlets and associations – the SNP was able to use the new media to make a direct appeal to those sections of the population, notably (as we will see in the next chapter) the socially and geographically mobile sections of the working class. Just as the anti-Labour parties, the Conservatives (by then they had changed their name from simply Unionist in 1965) and the Liberals, had settled into second place, so the SNP offered a new challenge on a nationalist agenda. It was not simply that the SNP pushed for separation: it found the ambiguity of 'self-government' to its electoral liking. It also claimed, as Winnie Ewing did in her acceptance speech after winning the Hamilton by-election in 1967, that it would make a better job than Labour of winning resources from and influence at Westminster.

Why, we might ask, did it take so long for the SNP to break through into the mainstream of politics in Scotland? At this stage of our argument we might offer three reasons. First of all, other institutions and movements served the purpose, such as the Scottish Office. Nationalism was deemed cultural and at the service of all the political parties, who appealed to it when it suited them. The Liberals in particular were able to mobilise it especially through what Fry called Scots' 'ethical liberalism which had kept them distinct' (1987, p. 210). Second, the collapse of the Liberal coalition after the Great War diminished Scottish influence at Westminster. The point here is that there had to be a political vehicle which Scots could use to maximise advantage. In other words there was a kind of instrumental nationalism which voters would bestow on a party it thought might deliver. In much the same way, Labour's failure to deliver the goods in the late 1960s and early 1970s led to the search for a new political vehicle, and this time it was an explicitly nationalist party, the SNP.

Finally, we must recognise that even the nationalist party contained people who believed that it was a movement, not a party. Home Rule could be encouraged in all parties (what Michael Fry refers to as John MacCormick's 'latitudinarian policies'). The SNP had always contained those who believed that the party's role was to stimulate other parties rather than to win power for itself. Only after independence would it disband, its aim having been achieved, the argument went. The tension between gradualists and fundamentalists which is associated with this division had long been, and continues to be, evident in the party. As proof that there was more to nationalism than the SNP, we need only recall that John MacCormick resigned from the SNP in 1942 to form the Scottish Convention, which achieved two million signatures to a mass petition for Home Rule in 1949, reflecting a more general commitment to a Scottish Parliament than to SNP voting.

What are the implications of the results of the May 1997 general election and the referendum on a Scottish Parliament the following September? In this chapter we have argued that the main political parties in Scotland have histories and agendas that make them quite different political formations from their English counterparts, even although their titles – Liberal, Conservative, Labour – may suggest the opposite. What difference is a devolved Scottish Parliament likely to make to their capacity to act as bridge-builders between the Scottish and British political systems?

The Scottish Parliament will clearly be a much more solid structure from which to negotiate with Westminster. Labour's stunning success in the 1997 election gave it the largest number of Scottish seats in its history, based on a bigger share of the vote than at any general election since 1966 (albeit less than 50 per cent). It took considerable credit from the decisive result of the referendum vote in September 1997, confirming the late John Smith's opinion that a devolved Parliament was the settled will of the Scottish people. How could Labour fail in the light of these two triumphs? Its bridge-building skills will depend on it balancing itself between

being a Scottish and a British party, between speaking for Scotland
and having an inside track to the Westminster Government. Its risks
are that, despite its change of name in 1994 to the Scottish Labour
Party (previously it was called the Labour Party in Scotland), it will
be unable to pursue policies and an agenda different from those
operating south of the border. The issue of Scottish autonomy will
be a concern of the party as well as the Parliament.

The Scottish National Party seems well-placed to benefit from
likely Labour mishaps. It is undoubtedly Scotland's second party in
terms of share of the vote, and it is hopeful that it can push its share
up from around a quarter to over 30 per cent of the vote in Scottish
elections, thereby giving it sight of power. The dilemma for the SNP
is how to capture a devolved Parliament and then persuade the
voters that it is a stepping stone to full political independence. Under
the leadership of Alex Salmond, the party has moved away from its
hostility to a home rule Parliament, and it shared the political
honours to be had from the referendum victory. Nevertheless,
fundamentalist critics within the SNP are biding their time in the
expectation that the contradiction of a separatist party supporting
devolution will become increasingly apparent.

As regards the Tories, we have to go back to 1868 to find a
comparable share of the vote in a general election, and even then the
Conservatives won seven seats as opposed to none in 1997. While it
is true that half a million people in Scotland voted for them in 1997,
the party seems to have entered its wilderness years. Its political
leverage is also low as it was on the losing side on the referendum,
and it is unlikely to be the sought-after coalition partner for any
other party in the Scottish Parliament in the short-to-medium term.

The Scottish Liberal Democrats surprised many by increasing
their net number of seats by one (to 10), while remaining at 13 per
cent of the popular vote. Their work in the Scottish Constitutional
Convention and their long commitment to home rule gave them
considerable reflected glory in the outcome of the referendum vote.
The party's problem is that its likely coalition with Labour, should
the latter fail to win a majority of seats in a Scottish parliament, will
give it access to power but without necessarily increasing its electoral
support. Ironically for a party committed to ending the first-past-
the-post electoral system, its lack of electoral strength throughout
Scotland makes it an unlikely beneficiary from proportional
representation.

Essentially, politics in Scotland have been about translating the Scottish and the British political agendas into each other. Given Scotland's relative autonomy within the UK, defending and extending its civil society while maintaining the advantages of the Union, parties have been electorally successful when they have succeed in this translation process. The Liberals did this in the nineteenth century, the Tories in the early twentieth century, and Labour in the second half of the twentieth century. When the three UK parties began to falter, the way was open from the 1970s for a more explicitly nationalist party. The SNP, however, found it difficult to maintain its balancing act as Scotland's party in Westminster, the bridge across which political resources and influence flowed. It did not matter that the SNP was not in power in London; it could claim to be able to pressurise the Westminster system to act under the fear of separation. Many of its tensions – gradualists versus fundamentalists, left versus right – can be traced to its dilemma as to whether it is or is not a 'British' party in this sense.

This chapter has tried to show that the jibes that Labour, Tories and Liberal-Democrats are 'unionists', while the SNP is 'separatist', miss the point that the parties are faced with problems that are quite different from those experienced by parties in England. Who captures the agenda for the rest of this century and into the next will depend on who is best at translating Scotland into Britain, and *vice versa*.

7

Electoral Change and Political Attitudes

So far in the book we have looked mainly at institutions and political parties. In this chapter we pay more systematic attention to the political behaviour and attitudes of the Scottish population as a whole. To do this, we rely mainly on the evidence of statistical surveys and opinion polls. These have become available only in the last 30 years, and so our attention is on the recent past. Four broad questions are addressed.

- To what extent is Scotland an anti-Conservative country? If it is, can the apparent hostility to the Conservative Party be explained by Scotland's being more 'working class' than the rest of Britain?
- What support has there been for a Scottish Parliament? And what support is there for the SNP?
- Is Scotland different from the rest of Britain in its political attitudes (as opposed to the support it gives the parties)?
- How large are regional differences within Scotland?

The chapter is concerned with broad trends over time, from the 1970s to the 1990s, rather than with the kinds of immediate assessment of political changes that a newspaper might attempt through opinion polls. A book cannot be up to date in that way. As in other chapters, we are interested here in the underlying processes that can help us to understand the shape of Scottish politics at the end of the twentieth century.

The data we use comes from three sources: the *Scottish Election Surveys* and *British Election Surveys* of 1974, 1979, 1992 and 1997; the *British Social Attitudes Surveys* of the 1980s and 1990s; and opinion polls conducted for newspapers between the 1970s and the 1990s. The precise sources are given in the tables; when other figures

151

are mentioned in the text, they come from the *Scottish Election Survey* unless we state otherwise.

As the analysis is from surveys, the percentages we quote are subject to sampling error. As a rough rule of thumb, this means that where the sample size is about 1000, a percentage is accurate only to within about plus or minus 3 per cent of the true figure. Where the sample size is only 100, the percentage is accurate only to within plus or minus 10 per cent of the true figure. For example if a survey shows that support for the Conservative Party is at 20 per cent in a group of 1000 respondents, then we can be sure only that the true support for that party probably lies somewhere between about 17 per cent and about 23 per cent. If the sample figure of 20 per cent is obtained in a group of 100, then the true figure probably lies between 10 per cent and 30 per cent.

Is Scotland an anti-Conservative country?

Part of the answer to this first question is historical, and was discussed in the last chapter. In one sense there is no straightforward answer. In the nineteenth century, Scotland was more strongly Liberal than England, but after the Liberal–Unionist split at the end of the century Scotland gave substantial support to the conservative Unionist party. So from that historical experience, Scotland is neither left wing nor right wing.

On the other hand, probably one of the reasons why Scotland acquired the reputation of being left-wing is that the country has contained strong socialist traditions. From the Highland Land League of the 1880s, through Red Clydeside in 1917 and the Upper Clyde Shipbuilders in 1971, to the opposition to the poll tax in the 1980s, it is possible to trace a fairly unbroken tradition of Scottish radicalism. As detailed in Chapter 6, the firmly left-wing parties of the first part of the twentieth century – mainly the ILP and the Communist Party – did better in some parts of Scotland than anywhere else in the UK (with the partial exception of South Wales and parts of London). More lastingly significant was the dominant centrist tone of Scottish Conservatism, drawing on the nineteenth-century tradition of Protestant paternalism. When the Scottish Unionist Party famously won over half of the vote in 1955, it did so only in alliance with the National Liberal Party. The subsequent electoral history of the north of Scotland – where the Liberal Party took over from the National Liberals in the 1960s – suggests that the Unionists would not have won their victory without the patina of moderation acquired by that alliance.

So there is enough in Scottish political history to lend credibility to the idea that the country is, at least, left of centre. But the dominant source for that belief in the 1980s and 1990s has been the decline of the Conservative Party since its high point in 1955, in contrast to Conservative strength in England. The details for all the general elections between 1945 and 1997 are shown in Table 7.1. The explanations for the decline have been discussed in Chapters 3 and 6.

The weakness of the Conservative Party is exaggerated by the first-past-the-post electoral system. For example, in the 1987 and 1992 general elections it received around a quarter of the vote but only about 15 per cent of the seats; in the 1997 election it received 18 per cent of the vote but no seats at all. Nevertheless, the reason why the party has done so badly in terms of seats reveals something about its deep unpopularity. It has become the victim of a tendency by Scottish voters to see the non-Conservative parties as inter-changeable: people who do not want the Conservative candidate to win in a constituency are willing to switch to the best-placed challenger. That has been most obvious in by-elections. For example, it benefited the Liberal Democrats when they won the Kincardine and Deeside by-election in the autumn of 1991, and it helped the SNP to defeat the Conservatives in the Perth and Kinross by-election in 1995. But there is evidence that this anti-Conservative voting happened even in general elections. In 1987, when the Conservatives lost 11 of their previous 21 seats, each of the other three parties benefited, even in adjacent constituencies that resemble each other in many ways. For example, across southern Scotland in the 1987, 1992 and 1997 elections the main challengers to the Conservatives were the Liberal Democrats in the two eastern constituencies, Labour in Dumfries, and the SNP in Galloway.

In the 1997 Scottish Election Survey, the 882 respondents were asked about their second choice if their preferred candidate could not win. The results showed the Conservatives to have markedly fewer second choices than any of the others: they had 7 per cent of second choices, whereas Labour had 21 per cent, the Liberal Democrats 24 per cent and the SNP 34 per cent.

Table 7.1 *Shares of the vote in Scotland and England, general elections, 1945–97*

Year	Conservative		Labour		Liberal etc.		SNP
	England	Scotland	England	Scotland	England	Scotland	Scotland
1945	40.2	41.1	48.5	47.6	9.4	5.0	1.2
1950	43.8	44.8	46.2	46.2	9.4	6.6	0.4
1951	48.8	48.6	48.8	47.9	2.3	2.7	0.3
1955	50.4	50.1	46.8	46.7	2.6	1.9	0.5
1959	49.9	47.2	43.6	46.7	6.3	4.1	0.5
1964	44.1	40.6	43.5	48.7	12.1	7.6	2.4
1966	42.7	37.7	48.0	49.9	9.0	6.8	5.0
1970	48.3	38.0	43.4	44.5	7.9	5.5	11.4
1974(Feb)	40.2	32.9	37.6	36.6	21.3	8.0	21.9
1974(Oct)	38.9	24.7	40.1	36.3	20.2	8.3	30.4
1979	47.2	31.4	36.7	41.6	14.9	9.0	17.3
1983	46.0	28.4	26.9	35.1	26.4	24.5	11.8
1987	46.2	24.0	29.8	42.4	23.9	19.3	14.0
1992	46.7	25.6	34.7	39.0	19.8	13.1	21.5
1997	33.7	17.5	43.6	45.6	17.9	13.0	22.1

* 'Liberal etc.' includes Liberal, Liberal/SDP Alliance, and Liberal Democrat. It does not include National Liberal, the vote for which is included with the Conservatives between 1945 and 1964.

This fall in Conservative support in the 1980s and 1990s was spread across all social groups, even those which had traditionally been their main supporters.

• First, all social classes – defined in terms of occupation – figured in the decline. By the early 1990s, the Conservatives were attracting only about one third of even middle-class support. This is shown in Table 7.2.
• Second, the previous advantage the Conservatives had enjoyed among female voters vanished as shown in the first two rows of Table 7.3 (the remainder of this table is discussed later).
• Third, Conservative support dropped among all age groups, from about 35 per cent among people aged over 55 in 1979 to about 18 per cent in that group in 1997, and from about 25 per cent in the 18–34 age group in 1979 to only about 8 per cent in 1997.
• Fourth, the Conservatives lost support in all religious groups, most significantly among Protestant working-class people, as Table 7.4 shows.

Table 7.2 *Conservative support, by social class, 1974–97*

Class*	1974	1979	1984	1989	1992	1997
Professional and managerial	36 (114)	46 (114)	56 (109)	41 (115)	35 (204)	23 (185)
Skilled non-manual	29 (278)	46 (135)	38 (156)	31 (202)	33 (202)	17 (167)
Skilled manual	14 (203)	17 (132)	27 (251)	17 (292)	18 (165)	7 (123)
Semi-skilled and unskilled manual	12 (185)	21 (92)	13 (313)	14 (312)	15 (223)	3 (184)

* Social class is defined here by the market-research social grades in 1974–89, and by the Registrar General's scheme in 1992 and 1997.
The figures shown are the percentages supporting the Conservative Party among people who voted (1974, 1979, 1992 and 1997) or who gave their intention to vote (1984 and 1989). Sample sizes are in brackets.

Table 7.3 *Party support, by sex, 1974–97*

Percentage supporting party	Sex	1974	1979	1984	1989	1992	1997
Conservative	Male	21	31	25	22	24	14
	Female	27	38	29	22	28	14
Labour	Male	38	40	52	50	35	52
	Female	36	36	46	43	39	52
Liberal etc.*	Male	5	8	12	4	13	11
	Female	10	10	15	9	9	16
SNP	Male	33	18	10	22	26	21
	Female	22	13	10	25	21	17

* 'Liberal etc.' includes Liberal, Liberal/SDP Alliance, and Liberal Democrat.

The figures shown are the percentages supporting each party among people who voted (1974, 1979, 1992 and 1997) or who gave their intention to vote (1984 and 1989). Sample sizes are:

	1974	1979	1984	1989	1992	1997
Male	550	306	373	464	377	322
Female	488	332	456	457	439	376

Sources for Tables 7.2 and 7.3: 1974, 1979, 1992 and 1997 *Scottish Election Surveys*; MORI February/March 1984 and June 1989.

Table 7.4   *Conservative support, by religion and social class, 1974–97*

Class* and religion	1974	1979	1992	1997
Non-manual				
Protestant	37 (251)	50 (163)	45 (224)	26 (179)
Catholic	16 (38)	19 (26)	12 (51)	9 (40)
Other	20 (103)	45 (60)	24 (131)	15 (134)
Manual				
Protestant	27 (387)	39 (205)	24 (226)	12 (155)
Catholic	8 (88)	8 (51)	4 (71)	2 (59)
Other	12 (171)	19 (136)	16 (113)	5 (131)

* Class is as defined in the footnote to Table 7.2; non-manual groups 'professional and managerial' with 'skilled non-manual', and manual consists of the other two categories.
The figures shown are the percentages supporting the Conservative Party among people who voted (1974, 1979, 1992 and 1997). Sample sizes are in brackets.
Sources: 1974, 1979, 1992 and 1997 *Scottish Election Surveys.*

   This decline in Conservative support across a wide spectrum of social groups suggests that the party had become alienated from Scottish society as a whole, not just from some segments within it. In other words, it suggests that there was a national dimension to Conservative unpopularity in Scotland. That idea is supported when we compare Conservative support in Scotland with that in England. Table 7.5 shows Conservative support in the rest of Britain, separately for the different social class groups. Comparing this table with Table 7.2 we can see that, in each social group in each year, Scotland was less supportive of the Conservative Party than the rest of Britain. For example in 1997, Conservative support in the professional group was 23 per cent in Scotland and 37 per cent in the rest of Britain; in the semi-skilled and unskilled group, Conservative support was 3 per cent in Scotland and 22 per cent in the rest of Britain. Thus the party's weakness in Scotland cannot be explained by there being more social groups in Scotland that tended to be anti-Conservative – for example, more working class.
   In fact the crucial class difference between Scotland and England concerns the skilled working class, a group which was particularly enthusiastic about Margaret Thatcher's policies in the 1980s. Conservative support in this group in the rest of Britain was around

Table 7.5 *Conservative support in Britain, excluding Scotland, by social class, 1974–97*

Class*	1974	1979	1992	1997
Professional and managerial	51 (251)	59 (252)	53 (682)	37 (685)
Skilled non-manual	43 (613)	53 (342)	56 (535)	37 (487)
Skilled manual	25 (401)	36 (329)	40 (451)	22 (416)
Semi-skilled and unskilled manual	23 (320)	33 (210)	31 (515)	22 (437)

* See footnote to Table 7.2.
The figures shown are the percentages supporting the Conservative Party among people who voted (1974, 1979, 1992 and 1997). Sample sizes are in brackets.
Sources: 1974, 1979, 1992 and 1997 *British Election Surveys*.

40 per cent between 1979 and 1992 and was still over 20 per cent in 1997 (Table 7.5). In Scotland, by contrast, it was usually under 20 per cent and plummeted to under 10 per cent in 1997 (Table 7.2).

Of course, what we have called here 'the rest of Britain' is not homogeneous either, and   as mentioned at the beginning of Chapter 6 – a great deal of political science has looked at the increasing regional divergence in England. In the three general elections before 1997 the Conservative Party attracted a majority of the vote only in the southern regions of England outside London, and even in these regions they had only just over 50 per cent. But in the 1997 general election, when Conservative support in Scotland was 18 per cent, the party's lowest share in an English region was 22 per cent in the north-east; in Wales it was 20 per cent (Butler and Kavanagh, 1997, pp. 256–7). The differences between Scotland and the north of England and Wales can only be explained by there being a national Scottish dimension to the unpopularity of the Conservative Party in Scotland, because the social class structure of these two places should, if anything, make them less supportive of the Conservatives than Scotland.

Support for the SNP and for a Scottish Parliament

The unpopularity of the Conservatives has benefited all three of the other parties at different times (see Table 7.1 again). As argued in the previous chapter, the Scottish electorate has used whatever instrument is to hand to put pressure on UK Governments. The problem for the Conservatives is that they have not been that instrument since the 1950s. The Liberals (and their successors) gained from this in the early 1960s and the early 1980s, the Labour Party in the 1980s and 1990s, and the SNP in the late 1960s, the mid-1970s, and possibly again in the mid-1990s.

When the SNP first rose to prominence in the 1960s, the readiest explanation was that they were attracting the votes of people who no longer had strong class loyalties. Several surveys found that they were most popular among people who had moved from working-class backgrounds into white-collar, middle-class jobs (the upwardly socially mobile). This pattern persisted into the 1970s: Table 7.6

Table 7.6 *Party support, by social class, 1974–97*

Percentage supporting party	Class[†]	1974	1979	1984	1989	1992	1997
Conservative	Non-manual	31	46	45	34	34	20
	Manual	20	28	19	15	18	8
Labour	Non-manual	26	24	22	32	29	43
	Manual	44	47	61	54	46	62
Liberal etc.*	Non-manual	9	11	23	9	14	18
	Manual	7	8	9	5	8	9
SNP	Non-manual	29	18	9	22	21	17
	Manual	26	14	10	24	26	21

[†] See footnote to Table 7.4.
* 'Liberal, etc.' includes Liberal, Liberal/SDP Alliance and Liberal Democrat
Figures shown are the percentages supporting the parties among people who voted (1974, 1979, 1992 and 1997) or who gave their intention to vote (1984 and 1989). Sample sizes are:

	1974	1979	1984	1989	1992	1997
Non-manual	392	249	265	317	406	352
Manual	646	392	564	604	410	246

Sources: 1974, 1979, 1992 and 1997 *Scottish Election Surveys*; MORI February/March 1984 and June 1989.

shows that the SNP vote in the 1974 election was higher in the middle-class social groups than in the others. In England, such people were voting Liberal or (by the 1980s) Conservative. The SNP was also strong in the new towns (the places which were built from the 1950s onwards first of all to rehouse people who had been displaced by the clearing of slum tenements in the cities, and then to act as focal points for new hi-tech industries).

By the 1980s, however, the nature of SNP support had changed, and it was now more working class. In the 1997 election the SNP attracted 21 per cent of working-class votes, and 17 per cent of middle-class ones. This change was probably a result of two interrelated trends. One was the shift by the SNP to the left, in competition with Labour, and the other was the emerging anti-Conservative leanings of Scottish politics in general. The SNP both followed this shift and also helped to lead it. The result by the 1990s was that the main battle in Scottish politics was between the SNP and Labour for the working-class vote: their class profile looks similar in the sense that both Labour and the SNP drew the majority of their voters from the manual occupational group. In 1997, 59 per cent of all Labour supporters were in that group, as were 54 per cent of SNP supporters. By contrast, only 27 per cent of Conservative supporters were in the manual group, and 33 per cent of Liberal Democrat supporters. Labour and the SNP have similar policies on everything apart from the constitution, and so the conflict has become very bitter.

Table 7.3 shows that the SNP has remained relatively less popular among women than men. The anti-Conservatism of Scottish women has tended (although not in 1992) to favour the Liberals rather than the SNP or Labour. This sex difference was the same in both the manual and the non-manual social classes.

In contrast to the volatility of support for the political parties, we find a great deal of stability in preferences for constitutional change. The main developments have been a slight growth in overall support since the early 1970s, and a more marked growth in support for independence since the late 1970s, especially in middle-class social groups. Table 7.7 shows the broad pattern of the fall in support for 'no change'.

Support for a Scottish Parliament has been higher in working-class than in middle-class groups in every survey that has ever asked the question: see Table 7.8. There is little sex difference in the overall

Table 7.7   *Support for constitutional options, 1974–97*

Percentage in favour of:*	1974	1979	1984	1989	1992	1997
Independence	21	7	25	34	23	26
Home rule	44	54	45	49	50	51
No change	34	26	27	15	24	17
Sample size	1175	729	962	1054	957	882

* 'Independence' refers to options which mentioned that word or 'separation'. 'Home rule' refers to any other type of directly elected assembly or Parliament.
Sources: 1974, 1979, 1992 and 1997 *Scottish Election Surveys*; MORI February/March 1984, June 1989.

Table 7.8   *Support for Scottish Parliament by social class, 1974–97*

Percentage in favour of:*	Class†	1974	1979	1984	1989	1992	1997
Independence	Non-manual	18	7	17	25	18	23
	Manual	27	7	29	38	27	30
Home rule	Non-manual	48	56	49	53	51	51
	Manual	39	53	43	47	48	51

* See footnote to Table 7.7.
† See footnote to Table 7.4.
The figures are the percentages supporting the options. Sample sizes are:

	1974	1979	1984	1989	1992	1997
Non-manual	427	277	315	317	455	428
Manual	445	452	647	604	502	454

Sources: 1974, 1979, 1992 and 1997 *Scottish Election Surveys*; MORI February/March 1984 and June 1989.

level of support for a Parliament, but women are somewhat less likely to favour independence than men (Table 7.9).

Support for a Scottish Parliament has also been strongest among younger age groups, and it is among them too that independence is most popular, approaching 50 per cent in some polls in the early 1990s. Support has also been influenced by religion, although to a declining extent. Among Protestants as a whole, opposition is

Table 7.9   *Support for Scottish Parliament by sex, 1974–97*

Percentage in favour of:*	Sex	1974	1979	1984	1989	1992	1997
Independence	Male	25	8	29	40	28	29
	Female	19	6	22	28	18	24
Home rule	Male	47	55	41	45	46	51
	Female	42	53	47	53	53	51

* See footnote to Table 7.7.
The figures are the percentages supporting the options. Sample sizes are:

	1974	1979	1984	1989	1992	1997
Male	554	350	422	509	445	352
Female	621	375	540	545	512	346

Sources: 1974, 1979, 1992 and 1997 *Scottish Election Surveys*; MORI February/March 1984, June 1989.

greater than among Catholics, but – as with Conservative voting – that is partly because Protestants are more likely than Catholics to belong to those social classes that are less likely to support a Parliament. But in the middle class we find that Catholics have been slightly more likely to support a Parliament than Protestants. In 1997, for example, among people in non-manual jobs, 82 per cent of Catholics and 67 per cent of Protestants supported some kind of Scottish Parliament. Among those in manual jobs, the figures were 79 per cent Catholic and 80 per cent Protestant.

These broad patterns of support were also found in attitudes towards the specific proposals for a Scottish Parliament produced by the Labour Government in the summer of 1997 and endorsed by the referendum in September 1997. The groups campaigning for a Parliament were very successful in capturing the votes of nearly all those who supported independence or home rule in general surveys: according to the Scottish Election Survey, 91 per cent of those who favoured independence intended to vote in favour of a Scottish Parliament in the referendum, as did 82 per cent of those who favoured home rule.

The translation of support for a Scottish Parliament into political action was complicated by two further points. First, the support cut across party loyalties, as Table 7.10 shows. Each party had a

Table 7.10   *Support for constitutional options, by party allegiance, 1997**

	Party allegiance			
Percentage in favour of:	*Con.*	*Lab.*	*Lib. Dem.*	*SNP*
Scottish independence outwith the EU	6	5	2	23
Scottish independence within the EU	2	18	9	37
Scottish assembly in the UK	30	60	65	34
No change	58	12	19	5
Sample size	96	363	96	132

*Restricted to people who voted.
Source: *Scottish Election Survey* (1997).

substantial minority of its supporters favouring an option other than the one that is official party policy. Thus 38 per cent of Conservative supporters wanted a Parliament, 23 per cent of Labour supporters wanted independence (and 12 per cent did not want a Parliament at all), and 34 per cent of SNP supporters wanted a Parliament that would stop short of full independence. Such figures are one reason why votes for the SNP could not be easily interpreted as votes for independence, any more than voting for the Conservatives implied opposition to any change. As we will see in Chapter 9, Conservative supporters are almost as likely to feel Scottish as supporters of any other party. The small number of SNP supporters who did not appear to want any change from the present constitutional system were not being self-contradictory: they might simply have been using a vote for the SNP in the instrumental ways that we have discussed several times in earlier chapters, as a means of putting pressure on the Government to deliver more resources to Scotland. Thus no party was able to claim to lead the movement for self-government, and all parties could claim that their rivals' supporters were divided.

    The second problem in organising popular support for a Parliament is that voters did not give it a high priority. In September 1997, just before the referendum on the Scottish Parliment, an ICM poll of 1809 people found that only 16 per cent rated 'a Scottish Parliament/independence/devolution' among the two or three most important issues influencing their vote. This came sixth in the list of influential issues, after education (46 per cent), the National Health Service (45 per cent), unemployment (25 per cent), taxes (24 per cent) and welfare (21 per cent). If people wanted a Parliament, it was as a means to secure economic and social reform (a point that was discussed more fully in Chapter 1). In that sense, a Scottish Parliament was not an 'issue' but a way of resolving issues. Only when other routes to these goals seemed to be blocked did a Scottish Parliament rise in voters' priorities. For example, in the six months after the 1992 general election the issue of a Parliament rose in prominence, around one third of respondents saying that it was an important issue in a succession of monthly MORI polls; only the issue of unemployment was more influential. This temporary rise to prominence was almost certainly because the election of a fourth Conservative Government induced its opponents in Scotland to become more sceptical that unreformed constitutional structures could deal with the issues that normally came at the top of such lists.

Indeed, it is probable that the main reason why the referendum did lead to a clear endorsement of a Scottish Parliament was that people were persuaded that a Parliament would be a means of achieving better welfare and so on. Thus 62 per cent of respondents expected education to get better under a Parliament, 60 per cent expected the health service to get better, 54 per cent expected the economy to strengthen and 48 per cent expected social welfare to improve; moreover, for each of these categories, only around one in seven respondents or fewer expected matters to get worse with a Parliament.

Scottish political attitudes

The statistics we have looked at so far show that Scotland has a distinctive pattern of voting compared with the rest of Britain, and that this probably helped to encourage support for a Scottish Parliament. It might be reasonable to conclude from this that people in Scotland want different things from those in the rest of Britain. But despite the popularity of the Conservative Party in large parts of England, English preferences on policy matters are in fact not vastly different from those in Scotland. It appears that the difference is simply that, until the early 1990s at least, voters in the south of

England trusted the Conservative Party to continue to deliver a reasonably fair welfare state.

This fairly uniform pattern throughout Britain can be seen in Table 7.11. Although Scotland, the north of England and to some extent Wales were more in favour of state involvement than the south of England and Midlands, the differences were not great. In particular, there was no clear separation of Scotland from England as a whole. Such conclusions are similar to those reached by Curtice (1992, 1996) using the *British Social Attitudes Surveys*.

On social policy, the rest of Britain was not generally less in favour of the public provision of services than was Scotland. For example, in repeated *British Social Attitudes Surveys*, around three quarters of people in every area of Britain have said that health and education should have greater priority in government spending.

In some areas of policy, Scotland is not as radically left wing as opposition politicians claim. On defence – where the SNP proposed that an independent Scotland could pursue a distinctively non-nuclear policy – the *British Social Attitudes Surveys* of 1985–91 showed 33 per cent favouring unilateral nuclear disarmament in Scotland and 28 per cent in the rest of Britain, not much of a difference, and not anywhere near a majority in Scotland. In general

Table 7.11   *Political attitudes, by area of Britain, 1997*

	Scotland	Wales	North of England	Midlands of England	London	South of England
Percentage saying:						
Private enterprise is the best way to solve British economic problems	21	25	25	27	33	32
Public services and industry should be state owned	43	44	43	37	45	38
Government should provide jobs for all	67	67	59	61	52	53
Working people should get a fare share of wealth	13	9	14	15	17	18
Sample size	756	150	611	448	249	871

Source: *British Election Survey* (1997).

Table 7.12   *Attitudes towards civil liberties, by area of Britain, 1997*

Percentage taking libertarian view	Scotland	Wales	North of England	Midlands	London	South of England
Homosexual relations are always wrong	36	35	38	36	50	38
People should be tolerant of those who lead unconventional lives	18	11	15	15	17	16
Censorship is necessary to uphold moral standards	49	48	47	44	59	46
Sample size	756	150	611	448	249	87

Source: British Election Survey (1997).

fewer people in Scotland are concerned with environmental problems than is the case in the south of England. And on civil liberties, Scots are not noticeably more libertarian, and in some respects are less so than Londoners: see Table 7.12 (and also Curtice, 1988).

In summary, we can say that the people of Scotland are probably somewhat more collectivist in outlook than people in the south of England, but no more so than those in the north of England or Wales. Certainly, the differences in attitude towards policy are not as large as the differences in party votes. The distinctiveness of Scottish voting is not really a social conflict with England but a political one. Scottish voters dislike the Conservative Party, which until 1997 the majority of people in the south of England chose to further much the same social and economic goals as the Scots entrust to the parties of the left and centre.

Regional differences within Scotland

If we should not treat England as homogeneous, then we also should be cautious of doing so with Scotland. The regional divergence in Scotland that haunted the Scottish majority from 1979 to 1997 concerned the outcome of the 1979 referendum on devolution. With the exception of the Western Isles – which in fact had the largest percentage voting for a Scottish assembly – the only regions with fairly clear majorities in favour were in the central belt: Strathclyde,

Central and Fife. Lothian and the Highlands had small majorities in favour, and Tayside and Grampian were marginally against. Dumfries and Galloway, the Borders and the Northern Isles were far more strongly against an assembly than even the Western Isles were in favour. Although the referendum in 1997 showed clear support for a Scottish Parliament in all regions, those which were hostile in 1979 remained lukewarm in 1997 (Pattie *et al.*, 1998).

Throughout the last twenty years the argument that has commanded some support in areas away from the central belt can be summed up in a neat slogan: any assembly, it is claimed, will be dominated by Glasgow Labour councillors and Edinburgh lawyers. For the analysis in this section, we have had to group the regions into four broad categories in order to have obtain a large enough sample from the *Scottish Election Survey* to give reliable estimates. The broad regions are west central (the whole of the former Strathclyde), east central (Lothian, Fife and Central), the north east (Grampian and Tayside), and the outlying rural regions (Highlands and Islands in the north, and Borders and Dumfries and Galloway in the south).

Table 7.13 shows the support for a Scottish Parliament in the four regions in 1997. Although all showed majority support, the opposition to a Parliament of any sort was strongest in the outlying

Table 7.13 *Attitudes to a Scottish Parliament, by broad region of Scotland, 1997*

Percentage in favour of:*	Region[†]			
	West central	*East central*	*North-east*	*Outlying rural*
Independence	26	24	26	32
Home rule	50	55	53	42
No change	16	17	16	23
Sample size	362	268	127	124

[†] West central consists of Strathclyde, east central of Lothian, Central and Fife, north-east of Tayside and Grampian, and outlying rural of Highlands, Islands, Borders, and Dumfries and Galloway.
* See footnote to Table 7.7.
Source: *Scottish Election Survey* (1997).

Table 7.14   *Party support, by broad region of Scotland, 1997*

Percentage supporting:	Region*			
	West central	East central	North-east	Outlying rural
Conservative	10	16	23	12
Labour	64	55	27	37
Liberal Democrat	7	14	27	19
SNP	17	16	22	29
Sample size	286	216	101	95

* See footnote to Table 7.13.
The figures show the percentages supporting each party among those people who voted.
Source: *Scottish Election Survey* (1997).

rural areas. The north east had the highest level of support for the Conservative Party, as can be seen from Table 7.14. There was also a great deal of variation in support for the other parties, although this partly reflects the anti-Conservative coalition discussed earlier: in the Highlands and the Borders, for example, the Liberal Democrats are the main home for non-Conservative voters, in the urban areas it is Labour, and in large parts of the rural north-east it is the SNP.

Political attitudes vary among the regions too (see Table 7.15). In 1997 the north-east was the most opposed to Government action. It was also somewhat more optimistic about equality of income. The north-east is also quite hostile towards the European Union, 23 per cent saying that it was bad for Scotland (compared with 17 per cent in the west central region and 19 per cent in east central, although 28 per cent in the outlying rural areas also expressed hostility towards the EU).

Nevertheless, these differences – especially the distinctiveness of the north east – should not be allowed to conceal the general agreement in all regions on an essentially left-of-centre political programme, one which is to the left of most of the rest of Britain. Thus in 1997 even the most conservative region of Scotland – the north-east – gave less support to the Conservative Party than most of the standard regions of England: the 23 per cent there was much the same as in the north-east of England (22 per cent), and higher than in all the other regions. By comparing Tables 7.15 and 7.11 we

Table 7.15   *Political attitudes, by broad region of Scotland, 1997*

	Region*			
Percentage saying:	*West central*	*East central*	*North-east*	*Outlying rural*
Private enterprise is the best way to solve British economic problems	16	26	17	26
Public services and industry should be state owned	51	39	34	38
Government should provide jobs for all	74	62	51	68
Working people should get a fair share of wealth	8	13	20	10
Sample size	295	230	124	110

* See footnote to Table 7.13.
Source: *Scottish Election Survey* (1997).

Table 7.16   *Attitudes towards powers of the European Union, by broad region of Scotland, 1997*

	Region*			
Percentage saying:	*West central*	*East central*	*North east*	*Outlying rural*
Britain should leave EU or EU powers should be reduced	53	54	49	62
Powers of EU should not be changed	13	18	21	10
EU powers should be increased, or there should be a single EU government	22	20	18	18
Sample size	362	268	127	124

* See footnote to Table 7.13.
Source: *Scottish Election Survey* (1997).

Table 7.17   *Attitudes towards powers of European Union, by area of Britain, 1992*

Percentage saying:	Scotland	Wales	North of England	Midlands	London	South of England
Britain should leave EU or EU powers should be reduced	52	53	61	60	59	64
Powers of EU should not be changed	15	19	13	15	16	14
EU powers should be increased, or there should be a single EU government	20	19	18	15	18	15
Sample size	882	182	716	520	314	1001

Source: *British Election Survey* (1997).

can see that the north-east of Scotland has been more hostile to private enterprise than most of the regions of England, but also more sceptical of state action. On attitudes towards the European Union, Tables 7.16 and 7.17 show that the Scottish regions are slightly more in favour of increasing the EU's powers than most of the regions of England, and that all but the outlying rural areas are less in favour of reducing the EU's influence than most of the regions of England. This difference between Scotland and the rest of Britain in attitudes to the European Union has persisted since 1992, although all parts of Britain (including Scotland) have shifted markedly towards a more hostile attitude towards the EU: for example in 1992 the proportions wanting an increase in EU powers were above 30 per cent everywhere, in contrast to the 20 per cent or less in Table 7.17.

Thus no region of Scotland can be accurately described as a Conservative heartland. The Conservative Party is in a minority in all regions, Government action to further social reform commands majority support everywhere, and the constitutional framework that is favoured in all regions for tackling these matters involves a Scottish Parliament and the European Union.

Conclusions

Scotland is an anti-Conservative country in the sense that it has generally not voted for that party at any time since the beginning of mass democracy in 1832. The one significant exception was the relatively brief period between the 1930s and 1950s. Anti-Conservative voting has intensified since 1979. On the other hand, Scottish policy preferences are not markedly different from some regions of England or from Wales. The British regions that are out of line are the prosperous parts of southern England outside London. Although Scotland is somewhat more disposed towards the EU than most other parts of Britain, the differences are not enormous.

However, perceptions matter in politics as much as reality (as we shall discuss in Chapter 9). The very obvious weakness of the Conservative Party in Scotland has fuelled the belief that Scotland is a firmly left-wing place, and has been influential on the growing European orientation of Scottish politicians. We saw in Chapter 4 that beliefs about the best way of solving the problems of the Scottish economy matter more than some aspects of the reality: if there is political consensus that the economy will benefit from the leadership that the Scottish Parliament might provide, then the Parliament's economic task will be easier. Similarly it could be that the strength of the debate and campaigning about women in politics in Scotland since the late 1980s – a topic that is discussed in more detail in the next chapter – will help to shape a belief that Scottish politics is fertile ground for women's influence (however ironic that may sound to feminists who know Scottish misogyny only too well). These beliefs are not just fictions. As in any other country, they could greatly influence the style and ideals of the politicians who will dominate the Scottish Parliament. Believing that Scotland is in the mainstream of modernising European social democracy might be the first step towards placing it there.

8

Women and Scottish Politics

The 1997 general election will be remembered as record-breaking in many respects. One of the features that attracted media headlines was the significant rise in the number of women MPs in the House of Commons, increasing from the 1992 figure of 60 to a total of 120. In Scotland, the number of women MPs rose from the five elected in 1992 to an all-time high of 12, a representation rate of just under 17 per cent. Nevertheless, in spite of the increase in women's representation, there is still a long way to go before women have parity with men in terms of their participation in the House of Commons.

The unequal representation of women in conventional politics is mirrored by their exclusion from top positions in other key decision-making bodies in Scotland, including business, the legal profession, the police force, the media, the arts, public bodies and the trade unions. To illustrate this point, Scotland has just one woman judge and her appointment is on a temporary basis, and there are no women editors in the Scottish national press. Furthermore, although legislation which provides for equal pay between women and men, and laws against discrimination on the grounds of sex, have existed since the 1970s, women in Scotland still experience economic and social disadvantage compared with men. In 1996, women full-time workers in Scotland on average earned less than 73 per cent of the earnings of men in full-time employment. Women are concentrated in low-paid, low-grade jobs in the service sector of the economy, and they make up the majority of those living in poverty in Scotland.

The 1980s witnessed a growing pressure for change from women activists in Scotland. Their campaigns were fuelled by economic, social and political developments in Britain and particularly in Scotland, and more generally as part of a wider campaign by women in European and other countries for greater equality and autonomy. The demand for fair political representation was linked to broader aims and objectives to improve the lives of women in Scottish society. The development of the constitutional debate in Scotland in the 1980s and 1990s provided a particular opportunity for women to articulate their desire for more equal representation in the political sphere and beyond. In addition their vision of a new legislature that would encourage the participation of women and would have procedures and ways of operating that were fundamentally different from the Westminster Parliament acted as a politically mobilising force.

Historical background

The representation of women as MPs from Scottish constituencies has a somewhat unusual history compared with trends in other West European countries. The extension of the franchise in 1918 to women over the age of 30 (and to women over the age of 21 in 1928) and the opening up of the party competition to women candidates, when women were given the right to stand for Parliament, had an immediate impact on the attitudes of political parties towards women. This interest did not relate to questions of equal representation; rather it focused on what Catriona Levy (1991) describes as the battle between the parties for power and for votes. That is, given the expansion of the electorate to include women for the first time, the political parties were primarily concerned with winning the support of this new body of voters rather than fielding them as Parliamentary candidates.

Consolidating the attitude of political parties, the few women who were successful in obtaining Parliamentary seats did not see themselves as campaigners for the advancement of women, and they resisted attempts by others to label them as 'women MPs' who were in Parliament to raise issues of importance to women. The Scottish women MPs rarely declared their support for, and were rarely prepared to take up what are traditionally defined as, women's issues at Westminster (Levy, 1991, 1992).

Thus the main reason the political parties were interested in women stemmed from their aim to secure women's votes, and even those women who were elected to Parliament did not see their role as including the advocacy of equal representation for women or advancing women's interests. This lack of commitment on behalf of the parties and the successful women no doubt contributed to the erratic pattern of women's representation in Scotland from 1918. In contrast to other West European countries, where there has been a steady increase in the participation of women in the post-war period – to levels as high as 40 per cent in Scandinavian countries – the Scottish experience shows a rise and fall around a low level of representation. In the general elections of 1959 and 1964, a record five Scottish women MPs were elected from a total of 71. However this number then dropped to as low as one woman MP in 1979 (the general election in which Margaret Thatcher was elected as Britain's first woman Prime Minister), before rising again to three women in the 1987 general election, and returning to five out of 72 MPs in the 1992 general election.

The pattern of women's representation in Scotland has been one of fluctuation around a low level. From 1918, when women received the franchise and the right to stand for election, until the general election of 1992, just 24 women were elected to represent Scottish constituencies: 14 Labour MPs, six Conservatives, three Nationalists and one Liberal Democrat. There is no evidence of women in Scotland attempting to build up a tradition of retaining Parliamentary seats as 'women's seats' in the constituencies they represent. Furthermore, in spite of evidence that voters do not discriminate against women candidates, very few women have been put forward for selection. For example only 33 women in total were selected by the political parties as potential Parliamentary candidates in the period between 1918 and 1945 (Levy, 1991).

Current position

Notwithstanding the increase in the number of women MPs after the 1997 general election, compared with other European countries, the representation of women in Scotland, as in other parts of the UK, is still relatively low (see Table 8.1). As well as the record number of 120 women MPs entering the House of Commons in 1997 (18.2 per cent) a record number of women also received Cabinet appointments and ministerial posts, some in areas not traditionally held by women, such as Mo Mowlam as Secretary of State for Northern Ireland and Margaret Beckett as President of the Board of Trade. Women in the Labour Party in particular experienced a

Table 8.1   *Percentage and number of women Parliamentarians in West European legislatures (1997*)*

State	Date of election	% women	No. of women MPs: total membership
Austria	Dec. 1995	26.8	49:183
Belgium	May 1995	12.0	18:150
Denmark	Sept. 1994	33.0	59:179
Finland	Mar. 1995	33.5	67.200
France	Mar. 1993	6.4	37:577
Germany	Oct. 1994	26.2	176:672
Greece	Sept. 1996	6.3	19:300
Ireland	Nov. 1992	13.9	23:166
Italy	April 1996	11.1	70:630
Luxembourg	June 1994	20.0	12:60
Netherlands	May 1994	31.3	47:150
Norway	Sept. 1993	39.4	65:165
Portugal	Oct. 1995	13.0	30:230
Spain	Mar. 1996	24.6	86:350
Sweden	Sept. 1994	40.4	141:349
Switzerland	Oct. 1995	21.0	42:200
UK	May 1997	18.2	120:659

*The figures shown are as they stood at 1 January 1997, with the exception of those for the UK, which have been updated to include the May 1997 election.
Source: Inter-parliamentary Union (1994).

substantial breakthrough, increasing their number to 102 and around one quarter of the Parliamentary party. The introduction of all-women shortlists in the selection process of the Labour Party played a significant part in explaining this rise of women MPs (Lovenduski, 1997). Only the Conservatives returned fewer women in 1997, reflecting, to some extent, the overall fall in the number of seats won.

In Scotland, nine of the 12 new women MPs came from the Labour Party. Two of these new women defeated former Conservative Secretaries of State for Scotland (Anne McGuire won Stirling from Michael Forsyth and Lynda Clark won Edinburgh Pentlands from Malcolm Rifkind). Ray Michie continued to represent the Liberal Democrats in Argyll and Bute, and both Margaret Ewing (Moray) and Roseanna Cunningham (Perth) were successful in retaining their seats for the SNP (see Table 8.2)

Table 8.2   *Elected women MPs in House of Commons*

Party	1987 UK	1992 UK	1997 UK	1997 Scotland
Conservative	17	20	13	0
Labour	21	37	102	9
Liberal Democrats	2	2	3	1
Others (SNP)	1	1	2	2
Total	41 (6.7%)	60 (9.2%)	120 (18.2%)	12 (16.6%)

At the local government level, women's representation has been higher, with 22 per cent of women elected in the 1992 district elections and 17 per cent in the 1994 regional elections in Scotland. There was a small decrease of around 1 per cent in the percentage of women candidates standing at the elections for the new shadow unitary authorities in April 1995 compared with the 1992 district elections, but a marginal rise in their representation rate, which increased by about 0.5 per cent over the 1992 results to 22.3 per cent. Finally, Scotland had two women as Members of the European Parliament (MEPs) from a total of eight MEPs, but this figure dropped to just one after the 1994 European elections. This reduction was the trend in most other European countries.

Table 8.3   *Percentage of women candidates and elected councillors, by political party (elections for shadow unitary authorities in Scotland, 1995)*

Party	Candidates	Elected councillors
Labour	26.9	23.7
Liberal Democrats	33.3	28.5
Conservative	26.3	26.8
SNP	24.1	19.9
Independent/Other	17.5	13.0
Total	25.7	22.3

Source: Scottish Local Government Information Unit.

Why so few women?

The above figures lead to an obvious question: why has the representation of women in Scotland remained so low? Unfortunately there is no straightforward answer. The explanations are, in part, linked to the more general reasons cited for the poor representation of women in other legislatures throughout the world. In reviewing the literature on women's political participation, Monique Leijenaar and Evelyn Mahon (1992) argue that the empirical research in Western European democracies has revealed that there is no significant gender gap in turnout figures for elections; there is no significant gender difference in voting preferences; and in countries where the option is available there are indications that women voters vote more often for women candidates. Yet although the number of women in Parliaments has gradually increased, there is still a worldwide underrepresentation of women in political bodies. The authors divide the key explanations for this underrepresentation into two categories, namely 'individual characteristics' and 'institutional factors'. The individual character-istics include the educational level and professional experience of women candidates, as well as their ability to apportion their time. It is acknowledged that, because of their role as carers for others, women may not have the same control over their time as men. Also, one consequence of women giving priority to their role as mothers is that they may enter politics at a later stage than most men, or return to a political career after rearing their children, when their age may count against their selection. The other broad category of institutional factors encompasses the organisation of society, the political system, selection procedures and criteria, barriers such as lack of appropriate childcare, and other impediments placed on women as a result of their disadvantaged position in the labour market.

At the UK level, the most comprehensive summary of the potential reasons for the poor recruitment of women and others at the political elite level can be found in the work of Norris and Lovenduski (1995). The main focus of this study is a questionnaire survey of Parlimentary candidates in the British general election in 1992 and a survey of party members, supplemented by a survey of applicants who failed to become candidates and some interviews with MPs, prospective Parliamentary candidates and applicants. The study covers the perspectives of gender, race and class in political recruitment. The authors also place their understanding of political recruitment in Britain within a wider cross-national context, and draw on evidence comparing the recruitment to the lower house of national legislatures in 25 established liberal democracies. They analyse the influences on participation and recruitment at three different levels. The first level, or 'systematic factors', relates to the broad context in which the recruitment of political candidates takes place in a country, and includes the legal system, the electoral system, the party system and the structure of opportunities. The second context in which recruitment takes place involves 'political party factors' such as party organisation, rules and ideology. The third influence on selection – 'individual recruitment factors' – includes factors determining the supply of candidates (for example the resources and motivation of aspirants), and demand factors such as the attitudes and practices of 'gatekeepers'.

In seeking to explain how and why the recruitment process produces a legislative elite which does not reflect the diversity of British society, Norris and Lovenduski (1995, p. 247) conclude that 'the primary results from this study suggest that on balance supply-side factors are the most persuasive explanation for this social bias' and that 'adopted candidates usually reflect the pool of applicants who come forward'. In identifying lack of motivation or available resources as key factors influencing supply, they argue that 'policy options directed at changing the resources and motivation of potential applicants . . . will probably prove most effective' (1995, p. 248). Furthermore, they state that evidence from their survey 'reveals little discrimination against women applicants' and that 'gatekeeper attitudes are not the main reason for the lack of women in Parliament' (1995, pp. 141–2).

To some extent, these findings are at odds with the results of earlier research which locates one of the key explanations for the poor representation of women in the direct or indirect discrimination in the selection process of political parties; that is, the demand side (see, for example, Rasmussen, 1983; Vallance, 1979; Adonis, 1990). However Norris and Lovenduski's findings are based largely on a questionnaire survey of candidates and party members involved in the selection process. In that sense the candidates are already a 'successful' group of potential MPs in that they have overcome the many hurdles of selection. Their perspective is therefore one which is based on a group of people who have 'made it' through all the difficulties involved. But what about those who have put themselves forward and 'failed', or those who have excluded themselves long before the selection process? The former are given some attention by Norris and Lovenduski, but not the latter. It is the process of exclusion before the selection stage which needs to be explored in more detail. For example, when the Women's Issues Group of the Scottish Constitutional Convention consulted widely on the reasons for women's poor representation, the submissions received focused on the practical barriers faced by women, their lack of confidence and experience in operating in formal power structures, and their disenchantment with what they perceived as the aggressive nature and style of political debate at Westminster. The underlying assumption was also that 'women were ruled out of consideration a long way short of the selection meetings' (Levy, 1992, p. 66).

A 1994 interview survey of women political activists in the main political parties in Scotland revealed that the reasons for women's poor participation are interrelated in a complex way, and operate on all three levels identified by Norris and Lovenduski (Brown, 1995a).

At the 'systematic' level, the Scottish women interviewees high-lighted the particular practical difficulties imposed by the location of Parliament in London, and the unsocial hours and times of Parliamentary sittings and meetings. A Parliament located in Scotland will provide a political opportunity structure allowing for radical change and a way of removing at least some of the practical and logistical barriers currently faced by women, making it more possible to be both a full-time politician and a mother. Added to this, the first-past-the-post electoral system has been perceived by some to disadvantage women. Proportional representation in the Scottish Parliament is expected to be a positive step forward for women's participation.

Barriers to women's involvement in politics have also been identified at the 'political party' level. Party rules and organisation, the timing of meetings, the ways of conducting political business and the method of political appointments within the party are not viewed as conducive to the equal participation of women. Some women, particularly those in the Scottish Liberal Democrats and the

SNP, feel their party is doing more to involve women actively. In contrast, women in the Scottish Labour Party (SLP) are most critical of the rate of change within their party, while women in the Conservative Party are inclined to the view that able women will succeed in spite of the obstacles they face.

Both supply and demand factors were specified as influencing 'individual recruitment'.

Women's role in the family is considered to be a key factor limiting the supply or participation of women in Scottish political life. Even when women do manage to combine paid work with family responsibilities, or indeed do not have a family of their own, the traditional attitude that women are 'home-makers' and men are 'decision-makers' continues to prevail and influences the expectations of both women and men with regard to political participation. Responsibility for the family comes first – before political ambition – for most women in the different parties, but some of the survey interviewees argued that women who have raised their children bring an added dimension and understanding to politics and have more to offer.

However, some women acknowledge that family responsibility is too 'easy' an explanation for the low representation of women and avoids analysing potentially more contentious reasons such as discrimination against women. If women in modern Scotland are expected to combine a full-time paid job with looking after a family, then the question remains as to why a parliamentary career should be relatively closed to women.

Contrary to the findings of Norris and Lovenduski that the lack of resources is a key determinant, few women in the Scottish study cited finance as a serious barrier for women. It is interesting to note that the financial assistance offered to women in the Labour Party through Emily's List, a scheme designed to promote more women candidates for Parliament by providing financial and other support, was not taken up by women in Scotland (see the report in *The Herald*, 6 February 1995). This does not necessarily mean that the amount of available resources is not important to women, but rather that other barriers are seen as more pressing. For example, women's lack of confidence, including inexperience in public speaking or a fear of making a fool of themselves, were cited as important factors which prevented women from putting themselves forward for senior posts within the party or for selection to local or central government. In arguing that men are 'more likely to put themselves forward', a number of women have noted the importance of being asked to consider a candidacy.

The individual factors relating to the supply of women available for political positions are accompanied by identification of demand-side factors and party variables which also play a role in deciding the level of women's political participation. Some of the women interviewees who had stood for office had been encouraged to do so by a male colleague. Indeed, somewhat ironically, some women, particularly those in the Conservative Party, identified other women in their parties as more biased against promoting and selecting women candidates. However, women within the SLP were much more likely to explain the exclusion of women from selection to safe seats in terms of the reluctance of men in the party to give up power.

With regard to the actual selection process, the responses of the Scottish activists varied across the parties. Women in the Scottish Liberal Democrats and SNP did not identify any specific problems for women at the selection stage, although they saw it as more of a problem for women in the Conservative Party in Scotland and particularly for women in the SLP, firstly because they considered that men and women in the Conservative Party were more inclined to hold traditional views on the role of women in society, and secondly because they were of the view that the SLP is very dominated by men and the trade unions.

Some of the Conservative Party interviewees agreed that women often face problems at the selection stage in their party because of the attitudes of both male and female selectors. Although at national level the policy of the party had changed, they considered that women continued to be disadvantaged because of the power still resting in the hands of the local party.

Women in the SLP considered there were great difficulties for women in being selected, partly as a result of Labour's dominance in Scottish politics. That is, as the party with 56 of the 72 Parliamentary seats in Scotland following the 1997 election, Labour holds a considerable degree of power; also, within the first-past-the-post electoral system, the incumbency of sitting MPs is an important factor. When Labour seats do become available, the competition for them is fierce. This in part explains why the party adopted a policy of all-women shortlists in 50 per cent of the vacant winnable seats in preparation for the 1997 general election. Some women activists in the SLP put forward a proposal that there should be all-women shortlists in every vacant seat in Scotland because of the low turnover levels. This proposal was defeated at the 1994 party conference in Scotland. Furthermore the Labour Party dropped its policy of all-women shortlists in 1996 following a successful challenge to the policy in an industrial tribunal by two male aspirants, who argued they had been disadvantaged in the selection process (Lovenduski, 1997).

The Labour Party women interviewees gave specific examples where they or other strong women candidates had not been short-listed for the selection interview, or had been disadvantaged at the selection meeting. For them it was clearly an issue of power and the refusal of many men to share power with women in the party. There is still a strong sense of injustice that often very able and high-profile women, who have worked in the party for 20 or more years and have considerable experience, are not being selected for Parliamentary seats. Thus, although men in the Labour Party employ the rhetoric of women's equality, it is felt that these principles are not always practised within the party.

Finally, an important influence operating at all levels – systematic, political party, individual – is the political culture in Scotland, and more specifically in the House of Commons. The predominantly male culture in which politics is conducted was cited by women interviewees across the party divide as a key inhibiting factor for women. Some women made the link between women's apparent lack of confidence and their reluctance to participate in what many women described as the macho, adversarial style and ethos of politics which they saw as dominating political parties and the operation of Parliament in Britain. Thus the whole political culture and the way in which politics is conducted is perceived as a disincentive to women's participation and a subtle way of excluding women from the political process. The women who do reach high office, therefore, are said to be those who are most able to fit in with the predominant male culture. Studies conducted mainly in Scandinavian countries demonstrate that the male political culture is unlikely to change until there is a 'critical mass' of women of around 30 per cent or more. It would appear that women are discouraged from taking part in a game in which many of the unwritten rules are defined by and favour men. Others interpret it as the deployment of exclusionary tactics by men.

Women activists in Scotland, therefore, have highlighted factors operating at the systematic, political party and individual recruitment level. The many and varied explanations discussed demonstrate that there is a complex interplay between the three levels and also between the supply of and demand for potential women candidates. This complex relationship currently acts to discourage women, both directly and indirectly, from participating in conventional politics. If women think they will be discriminated against at the selection stage, or will be treated as inferior because of their sex, or if they are simply not encouraged to see themselves as potential candidates, it is not surprising that they are less inclined to put themselves forward.

Policies to improve women's representation

In the light of the picture of women's representation described above, it is not surprising that there has been pressure for change, in the main from women themselves within political parties in Scotland but also from women active in women's groups and other organisations and institutions. There is a strong consensus that women's representation in politics is far too low and that something has to be done to bring about change. There is less agreement, however, on what precisely should be done and the policies required to effect significant change.

Public opinion in Scotland would also appear to favour the involement of more women in political life. In an opinion poll conducted in 1994 by ICM, 85 per cent of those questioned were of the view that not enough women were involved in politics, and 76 per cent thought that political parties should make special efforts to involve more women. Seventy-two per cent considered that governments would make better decisions if more women took part in politics, and 75 per cent disagreed with the statement that men are better at politics than women (*The Scotsman*, 11 March 1994).

The approach of the political parties and, for the most part, of women activists within them tends to be influenced by the party's ideology. Lovenduski and Norris (1993) describe three broad strategies which parties have pursued to increase the proportion of women in decision-making positions. These are rhetorical strategies 'whereby women's claims are accepted in campaign platforms and party spokespersons make frequent reference to the importance of getting more women into office'; strategies of positive or affirmative action 'in which special training is offered to aspirant women, targets are set for the inclusion of women and considerable encouragement, including sometimes financial assistance, is given to enable women to put themselves forward to be considered'; and positive discrimination strategies 'in which places are reserved for women on decision-making bodies, on candidate slates, on short-lists. In addition, special women's committees with significant powers may be set up parallel to or within existing party decision-making structures and institutions' (p. 8). In general terms, parties on the political left are prepared to adopt all three strategies, including positive discrimination measures such as quotas. In contrast, parties more associated with the right and free-market ideology reject the use of any positive discrimination or intervention in the recruitment process. The policy approach of the parties within the specific context of a Scottish Parliament is discussed below.

Given the different perspectives of the women party activists in Scotland who were interviewed (in the 1994 study referred to above) on the reasons for women's poor representation in politics and within the House of Commons, and their different experiences of the selection process, it is not surprising that their proposed solutions to the problem also varied. These women activists, with the exception of the women from the SLP, were generally against quotas or any form of positive discrimination. Instead they favoured changing the electoral system, improving training and support mechanisms for women, the payment of childcare and other carer allowances, changing the timing of parliamentary sittings and meetings, and other ways of encouraging women to put themselves forward. The problem from the point of view of the Labour women is that they have undergone the training and have put themselves forward only to find that the door to Westminster is still firmly shut against them.

The constitutional question: a catalyst for change?

As discussed in Chapter 3, the election of a third Conservative Government under the leadership of Margaret Thatcher in 1987 had an immediate impact on the constitutional question in Scotland. The return of only 10 Conservatives from a total of 72 MPs representing Scottish constituencies at Westminster added strength to the argument that the Conservative Government did not have a mandate to rule in Scotland and that Scotland was suffering from a 'democratic deficit'. Some women activists in Scotland were of the view that they were on the receiving end of a 'double democratic deficit', first on the ground that they supported political parties which campaigned for an independent or devolved Scottish Parliament, and second because as women they were grossly underrepresented as MPs. Following publication of the document *A Claim of Right for Scotland* in 1988 and the establishment of the Scottish Constitutional Convention in 1989, working groups were set up by the Convention to prepare options for the future government of Scotland. One of these groups was the Women's Issues Group, chaired by the Labour MP, Maria Fyfe. The agreement to have a group looking specifically at the issue of women's representation in a Scottish Parliament was an achievement in itself. It was made possible because of pressure from women representing political parties, the trade union movement and women's groups, together with the support of some men within the Convention.

It was at this early stage that other women activists in Scotland entered the debate and formed the Woman's Claim of Right Group. The group comprised women from different political parties, but predominantly the Scottish Green Party, in addition to women who were not formally involved in party politics. They came together mainly as a reaction to the small percentage of women, some 10 per cent, who had been nominated for membership of the newly established Scottish Constitutional Convention: 'Once again, major proposals and decisions affecting the life and well-being of Scottish people would be made with women being significantly under-represented' (*Woman's Claim of Right Group*, 1991, p. 1). The group monitored the work of the Convention, and submitted a separate document entitled *A Woman's Claim of Right in Scotland* to the Women's Issues Group, later publishing a book of the same title. As a group they recognised the opportunity and the need to make a specific claim for women.

The Women's Issues Group invited submissions from women in Scotland, and the question of women's representation within a new Scottish Parliament was discussed amongst women in political parties, trade unions, local government, women's organisations and community groups. The reaction of women to the constitutional debate in the 1980s can be contrasted with their involvement in the 1970s. Both Esther Breitenbach (1990) and Catriona Levy (1992) discuss the role of women in the devolution debate in the 1970s and the division between women on the issue. While some women took an active part in the campaigns for a Scottish Assembly, others felt that such a body could be more reactionary in its attitudes and policies towards women than the Westminster Parliament. Catriona Levy quotes the feminist journal, *MsPrint*, as going so far as to comment, 'On the whole the women's movement ignored the referendum or saw it as irrelevant' (1992, p. 63). An attempt by the Scottish Convention of Women (SCOW) to raise the issue of women's representation by distributing a questionnaire to the political parties met with little success.

By the late 1980s the political situation had changed in Scotland. Women activists across the party divide and outside party politics became increasingly aware that women's representation was extremely low and that it compared unfavourably with most other European countries (Brown and Galligan, 1993). They immediately began to ask why. The possibility of a new Scottish Parliament, which was to be run on a radically different basis from the Westminster Parliament, gave added impetus to the demands for change and provided a common focus for political action. In contrast to the 1970s, there was broad agreement that such a Parliament could act as a progressive force for women, and the campaign to ensure more equal representation gathered steam.

This active involvement of women in the constitutional debate in the 1980s prompts the question: why did women in Scotland change their minds on the issue? A number of factors can be advanced to provide an explanation.

The first factor relates broadly to the impact of Thatcherism in Scotland. It can be argued that one of the unintended consequences of the Conservative Government's policies in Scotland from 1979 was to force a reappraisal by women of their political alliances and strategies. To some extent a division existed in the women's movement in the 1970s on appropriate strategies for change. On the one hand, some women activists believed it was necessary to get access to, and equal representation in, the formal political arena. Other feminists considered that such an approach was irrelevant to the lives of most women and ran the risk of deradicalising women's demands. Instead they argued for autonomous political activity by women in their own organisations. However the experience of government cutbacks in the 1980s demonstrated that, without resources, the scope for autonomous activity is limited. In this respect, organisations such as Women's Aid have found it difficult to operate effectively in a climate of decreasing resources. It is rather ironic that during the period when Britain had its first woman Prime Minister, women as a group suffered disproportionately from the most adverse effects of Thatcherite economic and social policies such as deregulation of the labour market and cuts in public services (Brown, 1991). As Breitenbach (1989) has argued: 'If we are to ask the question whether women in Scotland have made progress towards equality in the decade since Mrs Thatcher came to power, then the short answer is that they have not.'

Faced with cutbacks in resources and policies which were seen to disadvantage women, there was a growing recognition of the value of having women, and particularly women with a feminist perspective, in decision-making bodies, including Parliament. As a result the polarisation between the so-called liberal demands for equal representation and the more radical autonomous action approach has been narrowed. There was a growing awareness that these strategies were not necessarily contradictory, and an acceptance that, through the support and election of women who did want to become involved in the formal arena of party politics, the needs of women outside this process could be articulated. This coming together of different approaches provides an illustration of Valerie Bryson's discussion of feminist theory and strategies and her recommendation that: 'there must be flexibility and a plurality of forms of feminist political activity, which should be seen as complementary rather than rival feminist strategies' (Bryson, 1992, p. 267).

A second explanation is that, during the 1980s, there was an increase in women's political activity around issues of representation within political bodies, including the political parties, trade unions and local government. Women in the political parties kept up their pressure for more equal representation in key posts, as delegates to party conferences and as candidates selected to represent the parties at local and central government elections. In the trade union movement also, women worked to gain access to key decision-making positions and were successful in their campaigns to achieve more equal representation and to get their interests high on the agenda of the unions. Another form of women's activity took place at the local government level through the establishment of women's committees and equal opportunities committees. It was possible within these forums to articulate the needs of women and to initiate policies for change. Sue Lieberman (1989) argued that the creation of committees fulfilled a broader role in raising awareness of both men and women regarding the inequalities that women faced in society and in putting issues of concern to women on the political agenda.

It should be stressed that the increase in women's involvement in the different political arenas should not be seen in isolation. There was a relatively small political network in Scotland and those who were active in one political arena may also have been involved in at least one other. This activity was likely also to extend to the participation of women in the workplace, in major institutions in Scotland, in community groups and in the voluntary sector. There may have been few women MPs and few women in decision-making positions. Nevertheless, it should not be assumed that there were no women of influence. The appointment of a few key women to bodies dealing with important policy issues such as education, health or housing, to organisations including the Equal Opportunities Commission in Scotland, and within the trade union movement, meant that women had some say in policy-making and implementation.

A third reason relates to the growing frustration amongst women activists with the British political system and the Westminster model of government. The process of getting more women elected to the Westminster Parliament had been long and slow and was producing only modest results. Within the current political system the problem of incumbency was acting as a serious barrier to the selection and election of women MPs. However it was recognised by women that the incumbency problem would not exist in a new Scottish Parliment and the election of women would not require the removal of the sitting male MP. As a result it was considered that male activists would be less likely to oppose policies for equal representation of women in a Scottish Parliament. The establishment of a completely new Parliament, therefore, offered the opportunity for radical change in the distribution of seats between women and men, a change which could be achieved in the immediate future and without necessarily having to wait for changes in the recruitment to the House of Commons.

Related to the frustration with the failure of the Westminster Parliament to give fair representation to women was a dislike for the way in which business was conducted in the House of Commons, as borne out by the 1994 interview survey of women activists. It can be argued that women in particular were being alienated from the Westminster Parliament because it was seen as male dominated, hostile to women, run in a confrontational and aggressive style, and with procedures and times of conducting business which acted as unnecessary barriers for women's participation. The interview evidence with women activists suggests that women, particularly those with young children, were discouraged from putting themselves forward for selection as a result. In planning a new legislature in Scotland, the possibility of a different political culture, codes of behaviour and proceedings was opened up, and women began to consider ways in which the new Parliament could be more accessible to them.

Lastly, there was a growing realisation by women that they had to be involved in the preliminary stages of the discussions surrounding the proposed Scottish Parliament; otherwise the key decisions would be taken by men and the needs and priorities of women would be marginalised yet again. This factor clearly influenced the women involved in the Woman's Claim of Right Group and was reinforced by the late Maidie Hart of SCOW, a lifelong campaigner for women's equality, in her statement that 'Women had got in at the ground floor for once' (quoted in Levy, 1992, p. 65). Unlike the Westminster Parliament, where women MPs still have to operate within the ruling ethos established by men in the political parties, a new Scottish Parliament was seen as providing the opportunity to make a fresh start and establish different rules of the game which would encourage rather than discourage the participation of women.

In summary, the 'constitutional question' opened up issues of democracy and representation and provided a unique chance for women to voice the related question of women's participation in the political process and helped push the issue up the political agenda. Thus the opportunity to challenge the status quo regarding women's representation came in the form of a wider challenge to the constitution. The political debate and activity surrounding the issue of equal representation continued within the Scottish Constitutional Convention, but was also taken forward by women activists in Scotland by other means.

Response of the political parties

The initial response of the political parties in Scotland on the gender question varied across ideological lines, as predicted by Lovenduski and Norris (1993), and can be classified in terms of three main styles of political management: 'promotional' strategies to encourage women's participation, 'active intervention' through the adoption of quotas and the use of the legal system to effect change, or adherence to the '*status quo*' (Brown and Galligan, 1993).

Between 1989 and 1995, the two main parties within the Scottish Constitutional Convention put forward different proposals in relation to elections for a Scottish Parliament. The SLP adopted an 'active intervention' strategy with a policy of 50:50 representation of men and women, to be achieved by means of a statutory requirement for the parties to select a male and a female candidate for each constituency in Scotland. The policy was first proposed by the STUC Women's Committee and later adopted by the Labour Partys and the STUC. The 50:50 representation would operate within a reformed electoral system based on the Additional Member System. The Scottish Liberal Democrats opposed a statutory obligation on the parties because it interfered both with the freedom of parties to select candidates and the freedom of voters to elect politicians. Instead they advocated a 'promotional' strategy of supporting and encouraging women candidates, and reforming the electoral system. Their preference was for 'STV plus' – a form of Single Transferable Vote plus elements of the Additional Member System to redress any gender imbalance.

The SNP was not a member of the Convention and developed its own policy for elections in an independent Scotland. On similar grounds to the Scottish Liberal Democrats, the SNP was also against positive action measures, favouring a 'promotional' strategy and a proportional electoral system to improve the gender balance. As the Conservative Party was against constitutional change and supported the *status quo*, the Conservative Party in Scotland had no specific proposals for increasing women's participation in a Scottish

Parliament. However the party declared its desire to have more Conservative women elected to the House of Commons.

The different policy positions of the two main parties within the Convention caused some problems with respect to reaching a consensus on a scheme for a Scottish Parliament. The submissions to the Women's Issues Group drew attention to the many barriers facing women when participating in politics and standing for selection; this led to recommendations by the group for changes in the procedures and timing of Parliament, the payment of carer allowances, the establishment of a Scottish Equal Opportunities Commission and a Ministry for Women, and the publication of an equality audit (Levy, 1992). After the consultation process was completed, the Convention issued its report, *Towards Scotland's Parliament,* in November 1990, in which it acknowledged the failure of the first-past-the-post electoral system and the Westminster model of government to foster the participation of women. The Convention (1990) then stated its commitment to the principle of equal representation:

> The new Parliament provides the opportunity for a new start and the Convention is determined that positive action will be taken to allow women to play their full and equal part in the political process. The principle of equal representation for women in a Scottish Parliament has been agreed. The Convention is committed to securing the mechanism to achieve this in further consultation and discussion about the electoral system.

Following the publication of its report, the Convention established two new groups to take the issues forward, one to discuss the procedures and preparations for a Scottish Parliament, and the other to examine the electoral system for a Scottish Parliament. It was at this stage that the conflicts between Labour and the Liberal Democrats on how best to achieve equal representation surfaced and threatened to destabilise the consensus between them. Early in 1992, with the general election fast approaching, the Convention was finally able to announce an agreed scheme. The proposals included electoral reform based on the Additional Member System, an obligation on parties to select an equal number of men and women candidates, and measures to achieve gender balance if this was not achieved through the constituency elections. This policy did not represent full endorsement of the 50:50 proposal supported by the SLP, or acceptance of the STV-plus electoral system advocated by the Scottish Liberal Democrats. However it demonstrated an important compromise on the part of the political parties involved and a significant move towards more equal representation for women in a Scottish Parliament. In the run-up to the 1992 general election, expectations were high amongst opponents of the Government that the Conservative Party would not achieve sufficient seats to govern the country. With a Labour victory or a Labour–Liberal coalition government, many looked forward to the establishment of a Scottish Parliament with equal representation in the near future.

The 1992 general election: no Scottish Parliament, no gender equality

The return of the Conservative Party to power in 1992 meant that the expectations of those in the Scottish Constitutional Convention and others supporting constitutional change were dashed. It was expected by some that the demands for constitutional change and with it the campaign for equal representation would be shelved, at least until the run-up to the next general election. However, as 75 per cent of the electorate in Scotland voted for parties who supported either a devolved or an independent Parliament for Scotland, it was unlikely that the pressure for constitutional change would evaporate until the next opportunity to challenge the Government in a general election. Opinion polls and elections in Scotland continued to show that support for the Government was falling to as low as 11 per cent (see Chapter 7).

After the general election, campaign groups were formed to pursue the demand for a Scottish Parliament, including groups such as Common Cause, Scotland United and Democracy for Scotland. The Scottish Constitutional Convention continued its work, and established a Scottish Constitutional Commission in 1993 to examine issues left unresolved before the general election. Also in 1993 the Coalition for Scottish Democracy was formed, bringing together political activists from the different pressure groups and political parties. The Coalition was successful in setting up a Scottish Civic Assembly, which held its first meeting in March 1995 (see Chapter 3).

The women's movement in Scotland also continued to work for change and to maintain pressure on the political parties and trade unions. The Women's Co-ordination Group was formed in 1992, with representatives from the main women's groups in Scotland. The aim of the group was to act as a means of communication and support, and to co-ordinate efforts in the campaign for improving the position of women in all aspects of Scottish society and politics. The group lobbied the Scottish Office and the political parties in Scotland on the issue of women's representation. In addition it organised informal discussions between women from the political parties on strategies for improving the representation of women both within party structures and in a Scottish Parliament. At the same time women sustained their campaign for gender balance within their own workplaces and organisations, and sought to strengthen campaigns for a new legislature in Scotland. Illustrations of these ongoing demands for improved representation can be found in the activities of women in the SLP and the STUC.

The Scottish Labour Women's Caucus was formed in 1993 in response to the perceived failure of the Labour Party to attract women's votes in Scotland, a perception that was in fact out of date or based on data referring to Britain as a whole (and therefore reflecting mainly the position in England). As Table 7.3 (Chapter 7) shows, in the 1992 general election the Labour Party in Scotland attracted a greater proportion of female votes than of male. One of the key aims of the Caucus was to campaign for greater representation for Labour women at all levels of the party, and it was this group that advocated the policy of all-women shortlists in all vacant, safe and winnable seats in Scotland. In spite of their defeat on this particular issue, the Caucus maintained its campaign for change and still monitors the party's policies and appointments.

Another example of the ongoing activity of women can be found in the trade union movement in Scotland. As well as arguing for 50:50 representation in a Scottish Parliament, women trade unionists extended this principle into their own organisations when articulating their demands for change. Thus the concepts of democracy, accountability and equal representation were also applied to trade union structures. The STUC reviewed its structure and organisation and produced a consultative document to forward the debate (STUC, 1994). One of the key objectives of the review process was to find ways of improving the representation and participation of women. The General Council put forward its own suggestions, which included positive action measures to empower women and the specific proposal that the Council itself should be based on the principle of 50:50 representation. The women within the trade union movement were, of course, in a relatively strong position in the political climate of the early 1990s. With declining union membership, mainly in areas of traditional male employment, the trade unions were anxious to recruit new members. One area of potential recruitment was amongst women newly entering or returning to the labour force. This factor undoubtedly helped the women activists in their pressure for change.

At the end of 1994 the Scottish Constitutional Commission delivered its report to the Scottish Constitutional Convention. The Commission's task was to make recommendations on electoral systems, including gender balance provisions, for the new Scottish Parliament, and on the wider constitutional implications involved in its establishment. The Commission recommended a Scottish Parliament consisting of 112 members elected on the Additional Member System with 72 constituency Members of the Scottish Parliament (MSPs) elected on a first-past-the-post basis using the existing Westminster Parliamentary constituencies, and an additional 40 MSPs elected on a proportional basis from party lists using the eight European constituencies. In order to achieve greater gender balance, the Commission recommended that parties be asked to achieve a target of 40 per cent-plus representation of women within five years of the setting up of a Scottish Parliament, in addition to targets for the fair representation of minority ethnic groups. The Commission added proposals to remove social, economic and other barriers to women's political participation. These included changing working hours, meeting times, facilities for caring, and the location of the Parliament; providing adequate allowances for carers; changing the adversarial style and ethos of Parliamentary behaviour; and encouraging the participation of women and women's groups in Parliamentary Committees. Finally, a Parliamentary Equal Opportunities Commission was recommended, together with the establishment of a Public Appointments Commission, to ensure the full participation of women in public bodies.

In making these recommendations, the Commission rejected the adoption of a statutory scheme for the equal representation of women, but it acknowledged that a 'dual ballot' system which gave political parties the opportunity to put forward an equal number of female and male candidates was 'the most straightforward way of ensuring equal representation of men and women in the Scottish Parliament'. It also noted that in the event of voluntary targets not being reached in the five-year period, the Parliamentary Equal Opportunities Commission should be empowered to re-examine statutory means of ensuring gender balance and the fair representation of minorities. In making this recommendation the Commission referred to the UN Charter on the Rights of Women, which includes a provision for 'temporary special measures' to redress the inequality experienced by women (Scottish Constitutional Commission, 1994).

The Commission's report was met with disappointment by women activists who had campaigned long and hard for a firm commitment to gender equality for the first Scottish Parliament. However, it had one, perhaps unintended, consequence: it prompted women to come together to put forward an alternative scheme of their own. Talks between women within the two main political parties in the Convention and the Women's Co-ordination Group took place to see if there was a way of resolving the differences and finding an alternative solution.

It was accepted by all the women involved that it was vital to begin with a Parliament of equal representation as it would be very difficult to reform the institution once it was established and the Parliamentary seats were occupied. As a group of women, they were concerned to find a way forward which built on their shared objectives and principles for equal representation. They therefore sought a mechanism for the first Scottish Parliament that would satisfy the different perspectives of all those involved, and drew up an Electoral Contract for consideration by the executives of both parties. On the understanding that the Electoral Contract would pertain only to the first elections of the Scottish Parliament, the parties were asked to endorse the principle that there should be an equal number of men and women members of the first Scottish Parliament. This aim was to be achieved by the selection and fielding of an equal number of male and female candidates, the fair distribution of female candidates in winnable seats, the use of the Additional Member System, and the setting-up of a Parliament large enough to facilitate effective democratic and representative government. This marked a historic development in the debate and broke the deadlock which had been reached on this contentious issue. The proposal for the Electoral Contract was put to the conferences of the Scottish Labour Party and the Liberal Democrats in the spring of 1995 (A. Brown, 1995b). The Electoral Contract (or Agreement) was subsequently signed by George Robertson, leader of the Scottish Labour Party, and Jim Wallace, leader of the Scottish Liberal Democrats. It was also endorsed by the members of the Scottish Constitutional Convention and incorporated into their final document, *Scotland's Parliament Scotland's Right,* published in November 1995.

The 1997 general election and beyond

In the period leading up to the 1997 general election, the Women's Co-ordination Group used different opportunities to keep the issue of equal representation on the political agenda. They also entered into discussions with women activists in the different political parties to consider ways in which the Electoral Contract might be implemented. It was left to the political parties to agree the precise mechanism to be used to achieve gender balance within their own selection procedures.

After the 1997 general election the Women's Co-ordination Group decided to play an active part in the referendum campaign and to lend their support to Scotland FORward (the organisation campaigning for Yes votes). They organised a conference and invited the newly appointed Minister for Women at the Scottish Office, Henry McLeish, to give the keynote address. The minister reaffirmed the Government's commitment to establish a Scottish Parliament with more equal representation, and later in the year announced the Scottish Office's intention to establish a Scottish Women's Consultative Forum. However there was some disappointment for the women political activists. The Government's White Paper, *Scotland's Parliament*, published in July 1997, listed equality legislation as a power to be reserved to Westminster. Furthermore, the Scotland Bill, published in December of the same year, did not contain a clause exempting political parties from the full scope of the Sex Discrimination Act. Women activists had argued for this in order to allow the political parties the maximum freedom to draw up mechanisms to ensure gender balance in the Parliament without fear of the legal challenge that had thwarted the Labour Party's policy of all-women shortlists.

In spite of these setbacks, the commitment to equal opportunities in selection was articulated in the White Paper. The Government stated that it attached 'great importance to equal opportunities for all – including women, members of ethnic minorities and disabled people' and urged 'all political parties offering candidates for election to the Scottish parliament to have this in mind in their internal candidate selection processes'. After the referendum the political parties considered ways in which their selection procedures could meet the stated aim. Given that the first elections to the Parliament are to be held in May 1999, decisions on selection procedures and the selections themselves will have to take place during 1998. However in, January 1998 the full details of the procedures and methods of increasing the representation of women had still not been decided by all the parties. It is likely that the Labour Party will adopt a 'twinning' arrangement whereby both female and male candidates can be selected for a pair of 'twinned' constituencies. The women with the highest number of votes in the party's selection process will be nominated for one of the seats, while the man with the highest number of votes will be nominated for the other. In addition, the party has agreed to endorse further changes to its selection procedures. Those interested in representing the Labour Party in the Scottish Parliament will be invited to complete an application form. The applications will be considered by a selection panel (comprising members of the British National Execeutive Committee, five members of the Scottish Executive, an additional five active Labour Party members, and five 'independents'). The panel will be responsible for considering the applications, interviewing candidates and compiling a list of around 200 people from which constituencies can draw. For their part, by the end of 1997 the Scottish Liberal Democrats had already begun the process of interviewing potential candidates. Their mechanism for involving more women is to have two men and two women for each constituency election, using the top-up list to help redress any gender imbalance resulting from the first-past-the-post elections. The order of names on the list will alternate between male and female candidates (so-called 'zipping'). The SNP has not as yet announced its method of bringing more women into the Parliament, and it is unlikely that the Conservative Party will take any positive measures to meet the objective.

It is unlikely that the outcome of all these processes will result in the 50:50 male–female balance advocated by many women political activists. It is likely, however, that Scotland's first Parliament since 1707 will have a significant percentage of women MSPs. The Scottish Parliament will also have responsibility for equal opportunities policy in all areas for which it has legislative responsibility, including health, education, training, local government, social work, housing, economic development, transport, law and home affairs and the environment. Thus although equality legislation is reserved, the Scottish Parliament will have power over equality matters in a broad range of policy areas. There is additional scope for wider involvement in the democratic process if the planned changes are made to Parliamentary arrangements (as discussed in Chapter 5). The hours and workings of the Parliament will make it more feasible to combine family responsibilities with political office. In addition there will be opportunities for women's organisations to influence policy if the committee structure is designed to take on board the views of legitimate interests and has the power to initiate, scrutinise, amend and monitor legislation.

Conclusions

The expectation that a Scottish Parliament will be established in which women will be able to play an equal part has continued to energise women activists involved in the constitutional debate in Scotland. Through their various activities in the political parties, trade unions, local government and, significantly, Scottish civil society, women have begun to exert their political influence and to challenge the myth that women are not political. There is a strong consensus that the Scottish Parliament must be a different type of legislature, one which is accessible to women and others traditionally excluded from formal arenas of politics.

Reviewing the experience of contemporary feminism in Britain, Lovenduski and Randall (1993, pp. 364–5) state that 'we believe the arguments for a widespread "depoliticization" under Mrs Thatcher are convincing and relevant to the fortunes of feminism', and that 'Thatcherism surely contributed both to the deradicalization of feminism and to fragmentation within it.' This may be true for the parts of England surveyed by the authors, but such a conclusion would be difficult to sustain in relation to Scottish politics and the Scottish women's movement in the 1980s and 1990s. During this period, women activists have demonstrated that they are highly political, if not represented in great numbers within the political elite. There has also been a broad coalition around a common agenda between women within the formal political institutions and other women who do not belong to a political party or are instead active in women's groups and other organisations. Women activists have supported wider campaigns for constitutional change and worked to defend Scottish education, health and other services in the wake of sustained cutbacks and reform, but they have also put the issue of women's representation high up on the political agenda. They have used the prospect of a new Scottish Parliament to attempt to change the rules of the game. In reviewing the widespread demand by women for greater political representation, Anne Phillips (1983, p. 204) recalls the opposition of those who fought against women's right to vote at the beginning of the century because they feared that women would vote in a block and differently from men, and would upset established political alignments: 'Those who resist an increase in women's representation no doubt harbour similar fears, anticipating that the women elected will alter the game.' In one sense, men have a right to be fearful because the women involved in the campaign want to do precisely that. However they wish to do so not in order to impose another kind of inequality, of female dominance and overrepresentation, but because a new legislature with more women and sensible working practices will be more conducive for men as well as women and will ultimately provide a more effective and participatory democracy making better decisions for the whole of Scottish society. In the words of one woman activist:

> With more women the whole political ethos would change absolutely. We would have a fundamentally different approach to how politics are put into operation. Particularly in terms of looking at economic policies and how they impact on women. What we would deliver for men as well as women is a completely better quality of life. (Brown and Galligan, 1995)

This statement echoes the hopes and aspirations of many women political activists in Scotland. By 1999 it will be possible to evaluate whether the campaign has been successful in substantially improving the representation of women in Scottish politics. The difference that these new women will make to the Parliament and the influence they will have on policy outcomes will take somewhat longer to assess.

9

Ethnicity, Culture and Identity

As the twentieth century draws to a close, so the issue of national identities becomes more salient. In the modern world, we have become used to conflicts over forms of political identity. We can find examples of disputed identities in many Western countries. The peoples of Quebec, Catalonia and Euskadi (the Basque Country), Scotland and Wales are among the most obvious groupings who, to a greater or lesser extent, dispute the political identities conferred on them by the states to which they belong. In many respects this is a remarkable occurrence because, for most of the century (indeed for most of the period we now call 'modern'), it seemed as if the problem of national identity had been solved once and for all.

The modern state requires the commitment of its citizens in exchange for the provision of services which can only be delivered at the national level. The state, in other words, requires the citizen to be loyal to it, to obey its rules, and, when required, to fight on its behalf. National identity is a necessary device for exacting the obedience of the citizen to the state. This does not need not be an oppressive feature, because people want to belong to the 'national community' from which they derive psychological, cultural and social benefits.

There is no question about who they are. Their 'national' identity is bestowed by the state, and citizens appear happy to accept it. What we might call 'identity politics' – disputes about to whom people should give their loyalty – have little or no place on the political agenda. Politics is deemed to be about material matters; issues of social class and the distribution of resources are the substance of politics. Identity politics are confined, or so it was thought, to the periphery of the modern political process, to the less developed world, and to those parts of Europe – for example Northern Ireland and the Balkans – which have somehow been left out of the processes of 'real' politics and succumbed to ancient, ethnic rivalries. Modern societies worthy of the name are deemed to have 'civic', not 'ethnic', politics.

The crisis of identity

Life in the late twentieth century, however, has not turned out to be so simple. Challenges to existing states have grown more, not less, common. Political identities have been emerging that are different from those laid down by existing state structures. Late twentieth-century challenges to the social, economic and cultural jurisdiction of the modern state – what we might call processes of state reformation – have begun to have implications for national identity. Suddenly identity issues are back on the political agenda. In Mercer's words: 'Identity only becomes an issue when it is in crisis, when something assumed to be fixed, coherent and stable is displaced by the experience of doubt and uncertainty' (Mercer, 1990, p. 43). From this angle, the eagerness to talk about identity is symptomatic of the post-modern predicament of contemporary politics.

What help can we find in the academic literature to explain this crisis of identity? It is a remarkable feature of this literature that until recently identity had virtually dropped out of the vocabulary of sociologists and political scientists. Simply by scanning the indexes of central texts in these subjects, we find little to guide us. In politics, for example, as Mackenzie pointed out in his useful review 'Political Identity', 'the victim was the word "identity", an ancient word, which once had a certain dignity' (1978, p. 11). In sociology, it seems that the term had become so much part of the central structures of the discipline that it had ceased to be contentious and researchable.

How are we to explain this lack of interest in identity? It is important to recognise at the outset that the term has largely migrated into the reserve of micro-sociology, where it is inextricably bound up with social psychological notions of 'self'. In the rest of sociology, it is quite unproblematic. As Stuart Hall (1992) has pointed out, the implicit model of modernity which underpins contemporary sociology assumes that the key social identities in the modern world were formed long ago by the process of modernisation. Political, social, occupational, class and even gender identities were assumed to have been formed in this process, and nothing new needed to be said.

The sociological concept of identity, he argues, was shaped as a reaction to the orthodox notion that identity was an individual characteristic, that 'the essential centre of the self was a person's identity' (Hall, 1992, p. 275). Sociology, in dispute with this orthodoxy, argued that identity was formed in relation to significant others, in the interactions between self and society. Using Hall's metaphor, identity 'sutures' the subject into relevant social structures, thereby making social interaction unified and predictable. Once this orthodoxy took hold, identity became uncontentious, the product of processes of primary and secondary socialisation. There was little need to ask who we were, because the social structures we lived in allowed us to read off our identities in an unproblematic way.

This notion of identity, however, has in recent times begun to come apart. The 'crisis' of self has entered the discourse, not simply as a theme of social psychology, but in response to radical change in the social structures which maintained a fairly consistent sense of self: family, marriage, occupation. Self appears to have become more fragmented, composed of several competing identities, and the generic process of identification has become more problematic and contentious. Increasing rates of social change are destabilising traditional social structures, opening up new anxieties as well as new possibilities.

It is this fairly recent mode of analysis which has restored the concept of identity to problematic status. Simply put, we can no longer assume that there is much that is fixed, essential or immutable about identity, but rather that individuals assume different identities at different times which may not even be centred around a coherent sense of self. The sociologist who insinuated this new perspective back into sociology was Erving Goffman, whose concern with the 'presentation' of self implied that identity is basically a badge with little real substance (Goffman, 1973).

Although Goffman was writing about self in the 1950s and 1960s, his thesis was the precursor of what became the post-modern concept of identity. Post-modernism argues that late or post-modern societies are impelled by constant and rapid social change which makes a fixed and immutable sense of self redundant. The result of this discontinuity and fragmentation is that social life is increasingly 'open', to use Giddens' term, offering opportunities and choices for individuals in a rapidly changing world. His formulation of the issue (Giddens, 1991) is that lifestyle choice becomes more important in the constitution of identity, and as a result a new kind of 'lifestyle' politics emerges from the shadow of 'emancipatory politics'.

In parallel to this, no 'master identity' is possible, and, in particular, people can no longer identify their social interests mainly or entirely in terms of social class, the classical mode of emancipatory politics in 'modernist' society. In Hall's words, 'Class cannot serve as a discursive device or mobilising category through which all the diverse social interests and identities of people can be reconciled and represented' (1992, p. 280). What occurs, Hall argues, is a politics of 'difference' – defined by new social movements such as feminism, black struggles, nationalist and ecological movements – which supersedes a politics of class identity.

The other manifestation of this collapse of 'modernist' social identities is the reassertion of individualism in both philosophical and economic forms. We might interpret the political success of New Right liberalism in Western countries as one version of this process of deconstruction. After all, saying that there is no such thing as society is to assert that individuals are free to construct their identities as they please. Its economic expression is the supremacy of the consumer, as Bauman observes:

> it is the consumer attitude which makes my life into my individual affair; and it is the consumer activity which makes me into the individual . . . It seems in the end as if I were made up of the many things I buy and own: tell me what you buy and in what shops you buy it, and I'll tell you who you are. It seems that with the help of carefully selected purchases, I can make of myself anything I may wish, anything I believe it is worth becoming. Just as dealing with my personal problems is my duty and my responsibility, so the shaping of my personal identity, my self-assertion, making myself into a concrete someone, is my task and mine alone. (1992a, p. 205)

Bauman is articulating here the post-modern, even the post-sociological construction of identity. Just as sociology in its modernist form reacted against methodological individualism by asserting the ways in which individuals were social beings whether they realised it or not, so lifestyle and consumerist conceptions of identity have returned to a highly individuated and economically liberating sense of identity. The demise of overarching or meta-identities appears to have allowed a plurality of new ones to emerge from under the corpse. These are not simply individualist *tout court*, but reflect the possibility of playing out what one wants to be, selecting from an array of choices, and with greater control over the messages and signals given off. Essentially, the politics which emanate from this process is indeed personal, a feature recognised by feminism, for example, which adopted the slogan that 'the personal is political'.

The discussion about national identity, then, properly belongs to a much broader debate about identity generally, which will be flagged here but not discussed in full. Rapidly changing social structures have had an effect on all forms of social identity, including the ones which interest us here (national and political identity). By the 1990s, the old agenda had changed. New political structures, and the concomitant decline of older ones, seem to have forefronted the issue of identity. The discontinuity, fragmentation and dislocation of social arrangements mean that no meta-identity seems possible, and that how different identities relate to each other is quite unpredictable. In Giddens' words, 'The more tradition loses its hold, the more daily life is reconstituted in terms of the dialectical interplay of the local and the global, the more individuals are forced to negotiate lifestyle choices among a diversity of options.'

National identities become more problematic as conventional state identities are corroded by forces of globalisation which shift the classical sociological focus away from the assumption that 'societies' are well-bounded social, economic and cultural systems. What replaces conventional state identities is not 'cultural homo-genisation', in which everyone shares in the same global post-modern identity because they consume the same material and cultural products; rather, in Hall's words, 'We are confronted by a range of different identities, each appealing to us, or rather to different parts of ourselves, from which it seems possible to choose' (1992, p. 303).

Hence, globalisation may lead to the creation or strengthening of local identities, as well as to the emergence of strong counter-ethnicities. These may simply be the reproduction of traditional ones, devoted to defending and restoring the purity of the original, or 'translating' new identities into the spaces created by new social forces. That these may employ the rhetoric of tradition might mask their novelty and adaptability to new social circumstances. These 'cultures of hybridity', as Hall calls them, are more likely to try to assimilate different identities without asserting the primacy of one in particular. The examples he gives are derived from the experiences of people with Afro-Caribbean and Asian backgrounds in Britain today, who produce new identities which 'translate' between different cultures.

Identity and ethnicity

Before examining national identities in this context, it is necessary to focus more closely on the assumptions which underlie identity construction. The conventional assumption, as Fredrick Barth pointed out, is that discrete groups of people – ethnic groups – generate their own distinctive cultures in geographical and social isolation before encountering alternative and competing ones. In his words:

> We are led to imagine each group developing its critical and social form in relative isolation, mainly in response to local ecologic factors, through a history of adaptation by invention and selective borrowing. This history has produced a world of separate peoples, each with their own culture and each organised in a society which can legitimately be isolated for description as an island to itself. (1969, p. 11)

In this conventional model, ethnicity (and the ethnic identity which ensues) is taken for granted as the basis of common cultures which may or may not come into conflict with each other over issues of territory, power and so on. In this account, Bosnians and Serbs and Croats are representatives of fundamentally embedded cultures which collide with each other as new political formations are made. However, says Barth, we ought to treat ethnicity as something to be explained, not as the explanation for social and identity conflict. In other words, sharing a common culture should be an implication or result of ethnic group organisation, not its primary or definitional characteristic. Barth comments: 'Features that are taken into account are not the sum of "objective" differences, but only those which the actors themselves regard as significant' (1969, p. 14).

What are the implications of this perspective for identity? The conventional wisdom is that identity is the expression of objective (and measurable) differences between social groups, whether they are based on class, gender, age or ethnicity. The task is then to uncover the layers of social reality as these are articulated by people, and to see how conscious they are of them. In essence, identity is embedded in the individual *qua* social being. This suturing of the individual into the relevant social structures ought to make it possible to read off the different identities which he or she has accumulated. In this regard the sociologist acts as a kind of social archaeologist, carefully uncovering the layers of identity. Identity is 'in there somewhere' if only we can get at it with the right tools.

If, on the other hand, we adopt Barth's perspective, identity does not reside in the individual but in the signs and meanings which are given off by the social institutions they inhabit, and crucially the social actor has a considerable amount of leeway in resonating those identities which they find useful in different social settings. Hence, as Barth points out, 'a drastic reduction of cultural differences between ethnic groups does not correlate in any simple way with a reduction in the organisational relevance of ethnic identities, or a breakdown in boundary-maintaining processes' (1969, pp. 32–3).

We have grown used to the common-sense notion that the identity differences which people express are 'real' in an ontological sense. They are, of course, real insofar as people treat them as such, but ethnic identities have to be treated as social and cultural accounts which participants use to make sense of their actions. In essence, ethnicity is a reflection of a relationship, not the property of the group as such. It is sustained in the course of the interaction, and does not exist in isolation. Hence to be Bosnian is not to be Serb; to be Scottish is not to be English; to be English is not to be French; and so on.

While it is true that identities are constructed by participants in the course of social and political action, they are not entirely of their own making. We work within cultural representations, as Stuart Hall points out: 'We only know what it is to be "English" because of the way "Englishness" has come to be represented, as a set of meanings, by English national culture. It follows that a nation is not only a political entity but something which produces meanings – a system of cultural representation' (1992, p. 292).

Hall argues that national culture is a discourse, a way of constructing meanings which influences and organises our actions and our conceptions of ourselves. The idea of the nation is a 'narrative' (Bhabha, 1990) whose origin is obscure, but whose symbolic power to mobilise the sense of identity and allegiance is strong. By looking at national identity in this way, as multifacted and plural, we begin to see that it cannot be taken for granted, that it will reflect social power, and that competing identities will emerge and challenge each other. In Peter Worsley's words: 'Cultural traits are not absolutes or simply intellectual categories, but are invoked to provide identities which legitimise claims to rights. They are strategies or weapons in competitions over scarce resources' (1984, p. 249).

Neither are national cultures and identities fixed and immutable. They are subject to processes of translation and change. Hall's term 'cultures of hybridity' refers to the ways in which identities are subject to the play of history, political representation and difference, and are very unlikely to be pure or unitary. He cites the writer Salman Rushdie's description of his controversial book, *The Satanic Verses*, as 'a love-story to our mongrel selves' (Hall, 1992, p. 311).

Edward Said has also made this point central to his writings on Orientalism, in *Culture and Imperialism*. He points out that imperialism and resistance to it are inextricably linked, defining and competing with each other. There is no meaningful 'us' and 'them'. 'Gone', he says, 'are the binary opposites dear to the nationalist and the imperialist enterprise' (1993, p. xxviii), although each has a vested interest in their defining separateness. He elaborates as follows:

> If you know in advance that the African or Iranian or Chinese or Jewish or German experience is fundamentally integral, coherent, separate, and therefore comprehensible only to Africans, Iranians, Chinese, Jews or Germans, you first of all posit as essential something which . . . is both historically created and the result of interpretation, namely the existence of Africanness, Jewishness or Germanness or for that matter Orientalism and Occidentalism. (1993, pp. 35–6)

The point is that the codification of difference is a vital part of the strategy of identity politics, and ought not be taken for granted by the social scientist and historian. In practical terms, as Said says, today no one is merely one thing. Such stereotypes are part of the polemic batteries of discourse, especially in a rapidly changing world in which state formations are coming under attack from below and above. Here, then, are some of the analytical tools we can use in understanding Scotland and Scottish identity.

Understanding Scottish identity

We have argued in this chapter that identity is not a fixed characteristic of an individual, to be uncovered by peeling back the layers until one finds an immutable self. We are persuaded by the argument that identity is the result of a process of claim and acknowledgement, a process whereby who we are and who we claim to be is dependent on the social and political situation around us, and our participation in it. In the words of the social anthropologist Thomas Eriksen: 'ethnic classifications are . . . social and cultural products related to the requirements of the classifiers. They serve to order the social world and to create standardised cognitive maps over categories of reluctant others' (1993, p. 60).

Exploring how identity is constructed and negotiated is a complex process, and our understanding of how this operates in a Scottish context is rudimentary. However, we have at our disposal survey material which allows us to gauge the extent to which people living in Scotland think of themselves as Scots. These surveys began in 1986 when Luis Moreno devised a question to tap the relationship of Scottish to British national identity, and the survey was carried by the *Glasgow Herald*. Since then, the question: 'We are interested to know how people living in Scotland see themselves in terms of their nationality. Which of these best reflects how you regard yourself?' has been asked in a number of opinion polls and surveys, the results of which are shown in Table 9.1.

Whichever way one looks at these data, it is clear that people living in Scotland give priority to being Scottish. Between six and nine times more people stress their Scottishness than their Britishness. This is a remarkable and consistent finding.

Table 9.1 *National identity (per cent)*

Respondent feels:	July 1986	Sept. 1991	SES 1992	SES 1997
Scottish not British	39	40	19	23
More Scottish than British	30	29	40	38
Equally Scottish and British	19	21	33	27
More British than Scottish	4	3	3	4
British not Scottish	6	4	3	4
None of these	2	3	1	4
Sample size	1021	1042	957	882

Sources: July 1986: Moreno (1988); September 1991: *The Scotsman*; SES 1992: *Scottish Election Survey* (1992); SES 97: Scottish Election Survey (1997).

What are we to make of these data, and what do they tell us about Scottish identity? Certainly, the question is framed in terms of 'nationality' rather than 'identity', but this seems a fairly good proxy for national identity. If anything, it might underestimate identity as such ('nationality' seems closer to political 'citizenship' – formally British – than it is to cultural 'identity'). 'Dual identity' (Scottish as well as British in varying degrees) is a feature in all the surveys, claimed by around half to three quarters of respondents. We do not know, of course, how strongly committed to 'nationality' the respondents in these surveys are, or indeed what it actually evokes in people to answer in these ways. Nevertheless it is quite remarkable that, after nearly 300 years of Union in a large and centralised state with no separate legislature, Scottish identity is so strongly held across a wide spectrum of people living in Scotland.

In recent years national identity has taken on a political colour, particularly with the rise of the SNP, and the Conservative Party playing the Union card. In spite of this, supporters of all the main political parties in Scotland place their Scottish identity before their British one. We will focus here on the *Scottish Election Survey* of 1997 (SES 97) because it asked respondents to recall how they actually voted in the general election rather than to say how they might vote if there were a general election tomorrow. It is important to remember that the Scottish/British distinction might be best thought of as a continuum rather than a set of discrete categories.

Table 9.2   *National identity by vote in 1997 general election (per cent)*

Respondent feels	Con.	Labour	Lib.-Dem.	SNP	All
Scottish not British	10	25	13	32	23
Scottish more than British	26	39	42	44	38
Equally Scottish and British	45	26	28	18	27
British more than Scottish	7	4	6	2	4
British not Scottish	7	3	5	2	4
None of these	4	3	5	1	4
Sample size	96	363	96	132	882

Source: *Scottish Election Survey* (1997).

How does national identity relate to political behaviour? Conservatives were more likely than members of other parties to stress their Britishness, but even among them far more emphasised their Scottish national identity, as Table 9.2 shows. The modal position for the supporters of all parties, including the SNP, was to claim to be Scottish more than British, with the exception of the Conservatives, the largest number of whom said they were Scottish and British. Nevertheless, more than twice as many Conservatives gave priority to being Scottish (36 per cent) as to being British (14 per cent). SNP voters were more likely than those of other parties to highlight their Scottish national identity (76 per cent), while two thirds of Labour voters (64 per cent) and over half of Liberal Democrats (55 per cent) did likewise.

As we might expect, there was a rough relationship between national identity and preferred constitutional option (Table 9.3), those preferring independence being the most likely to claim Scottish national identity. However, the relationship is by no means clear-cut. For example, only one in eight of those preferring the constitutional status quo gave precedence to being British.

Taking Tables 9.1, 9.2 and 9.3 together, and in the light of the data discussed in Chapter 7, we can see that there is no simple relationship between vote, preferred constitutional option and national identity. For example, Conservatives or those preferring the constitutional *status quo* did not see themselves primarily as British. In like manner, a third (32 per cent) of SNP voters, and 40 per cent of those preferring independence, claimed to be Scottish not

Table 9.3 *National identity by preferred constitutional option (per cent)*

Respondent feels:	Independence	Home Rule	No change	All
Scottish not British	40	18	12	23
More Scottish than British	40	43	23	38
Equally Scottish and British	14	27	47	27
More British than Scottish	2	5	7	4
British not Scottish	2	4	5	4
None of these	2	3	6	4
Sample sizes	231	449	150	882

Source: *Scottish Election Survey* (1997).

British, indicating that a majority of each group claimed at least a degree of British national identity, albeit in a weakened form.

The propensity of people living in Scotland to claim a stronger sense of Scottishness over Britishness is also carried across all social classes. As Table 9.4 shows, the former was preferred to the latter among all social classes, from social classes I and II, through to classes IV and V.

Table 9.4 *National identity by social class (Registrar General's categories. per cent)*

Respondent feels:	I and II	IIIn–m	IIIm	IV and V	All
Scottish not British	13	19	32	31	23
More Scottish than British	36	41	40	37	38
Equally Scottish and British	33	26	21	26	27
More British than Scottish	7	4	4	3	4
British not Scottish	8	4	1	1	4
None of these	3	5	2	3	4
Sample sizes	222	206	172	223	882

Source: *Scottish Election Survey* (1997).

The claim for Scottish national identity over being British is reflected not only across social classes, but regionally. Using the same classification of 'regions' as in Chapter 7, we can see that Scottishness is strongest in east central Scotland (ratio of 'Scottish' to 'British' being 9:1), and weakest in north-east Scotland (5:1), with west central and rural Scotland at 8:1. Likewise there is no major gender difference, with men stressing Scottish national identity (first two categories) at 65 per cent compared with 58 per cent of women, and relatively few their Britishness (8 per cent in each case).

As we saw in Chapters 6 and 7, historically in Scotland there was an association between religion and voting patterns, with Catholics more likely to vote Labour than Protestants; but no residual association between religion and claimed national identity can be found in recent data, as Table 9.5 shows.

It is plain from these data that Catholics are somewhat more likely than Protestants to claim Scottish national identity, a reversal of the historic association between Protestantism and Scottishness. Similarly, the claimed link between Catholicism and, for example, Irishness, is not expressed in these data, as fewer than 4 per cent of Catholics claimed to be neither Scottish nor British.

This review clearly indicates that most people living in Scotland (the population of which, according to the 1991 census, includes around 10 per cent of people born outside the country) consider themselves to be Scottish in terms of their 'nationality'. Of course, we can not tell from these survey data how they themselves interpret this term, but it is plain that the Scottish dimension is deemed more

Table 9.5   *National identity by religion (per cent)*

Respondent feels:	Catholic	Protestant	Other	All
Scottish not British	23	19	28	23
Scottish more than British	38	41	35	38
Equally Scottish and British	26	31	23	27
British more than Scottish	5	4	4	4
British not Scottish	5	3	4	4
None of these	4	3	6	4
Sample size	125	345	362	882

Source: *Scottish Election Survey* (1997).

significant than the British one for most people. We can also see that this preference, while it varies from survey to survey, is consistently strong, and that it holds across political party, constitutional preference, gender, social class, religion and region of the country.

National and state identities in Britain

To understand why this should be so (whether, for example, this is a reflection of a strong Scottish identity or a weak British one), it is necessary to introduce comparative data from other parts of Great Britain (no comparable data were collected in Northern Ireland for this purpose, and so the data are not for the UK). Once more, the question asked was: 'We are interested to know how people living in [Scotland/Wales/England] see themselves in terms of their nationality. Which of these best reflects how you regard yourself?' Table 9.6 shows the answers.

These are remarkable findings. They show that 'national' identity (being Scottish, English or Welsh) was felt to be more important than 'state' identity (being British) in all parts of Britain. In no country did Britishness take precedence over nationality. Sixty one per cent of people living in Scotland gave priority to being Scottish rather than British (only 8 per cent considered their British identity more significant). Nearly half of people living in Wales (42 per cent) considered themselves primarily Welsh (only 25 per cent mainly British). Perhaps the most striking feature of all is how few 'English'

Table 9.6 *National identity by country (X = Scottish, Welsh or English)*

Respondent feels:	*Scotland*	*Wales*	*England*
X not British	23	13	8
More X than British	38	29	16
Equally X and British	27	26	46
More British than X	4	10	15
British not X	4	15	9
None of these	4	7	6
Sample sizes	882	182	2551

Source: *British Election Survey* (1997).

people described themselves as primarily British. Whereas 24 per cent gave priority to being English, the same percentage defined themselves primarily as British, with the largest number – 46 per cent – describing themselves as equally English and British.

What we see here is that even the core 'British' people, the English, do not describe themselves as such. The question we must ask is why the sense of being British is so weak? We might observe, of course, that people are simply confused about the distinction between Britain and England. Is it not simply a propensity to call Britain 'England' which is reflected here? Undoubtedly this happens, but that raises a further intriguing question: why is the very identity of the state confused? We are, as commentators have pointed out, citizens with no name. We live in a state without an inclusive name for its citizens. Its formal title is the United Kingdom of Great Britain and Northern Ireland, but there is no easy description for us. If we describe ourselves as 'British' we are taking, as Bernard Crick has pointed out, 'the name of a former Roman province which has no modern legal or precise geographical meaning' (1989, pp. 24–5). The original 'British' were those who were not ethnically Anglo-Saxon. In modern terms, the British are those who inhabit 'Britain' – the main island – and excludes the Northern Irish, whose Protestant community is a central repository of British identity (Ignatieff, 1994). In a survey reported in British Social Attitudes (1990–1 edition), 66 per cent of Protestants described themselves as British compared with only 10 per cent of Catholics in the province.

Being 'British' is a weak form of political identity, and its confusion with 'English' is proof of that. How are we to explain this? The answer is that we are dealing here with a supra-national form of identity. Readers of this book will by now be familiar with Linda Colley's argument that Britishness was created with reference to two related geopolitical phenomena: war with France (for much of the century following the Treaty of Union in 1707), and Protestantism. The wars were largely religious wars, at least in their ideology. The overthrow of the Catholic Stuarts in 1689 and their replacement with the Protestant William of Orange reinforced the political–religious nature of the settlement. Colley concludes:

[Britain] was an invention forged above all by war. Time and again, war with France brought Britons, whether they hailed from Wales or Scotland or England, into confrontation with an obvious hostile Other, and encouraged them to define themselves collectively against it. They defined themselves as Protestants struggling for survival against the world's foremost Catholic power. They defined themselves against the French as they imagined them to be, superstitious, militarist, decadent and unfree. (1992, p. 5)

This struggle against a common enemy – the French – was an integrating mechanism which was essential to the forging of this new identity of being British. (Note, incidentally, Colley's word 'forge'. She uses it to imply the hammering together of different elements on, as it were, a common anvil. However it can also mean a subterfuge, an illicit process of creating a 'forgery' which can be passed off as the real thing.)

There is, however, a tension in Colley's argument. On the one hand, she acknowledges that the new eighteenth-century identity did not wipe out older ones. 'Britishness', she says, 'was superimposed over an array of internal differences in response to contact with the Other, and above all in response to conflict with the Other' (1992, p. 6). Yet on the other hand, she uses the terms 'British nation' and 'British national identity', as if to imply that these were on all fours with other forms of national expression. The political scientist Bernard Crick has commented that Colley is wrong to speak of British 'nationalism' rather than 'patriotism', because 'Britain' was in essence a state not a nation, or rather a multinational state. This is the key. It was precisely the fact that Britishness sat lightly on top of constituent national identities – English, Scottish, Welsh (Ireland presented different problems) – which explains state–society relations in the UK. The plural identity of being Scottish/English/Welsh as well as British has probably been better understood in Scotland and Wales than in England, given its size and dominance in both political and demographic terms.

The key to understanding the relative strength of national identity and the weakness of state identity in these islands relates to the kind of Union which was forged in 1707, and with whose ramifications readers will by now be familiar. The retention of the institutions of civil society – in Scotland, the church, education system, the legal system, burgh politics – reinforced an autonomy and with it an alternative national identity which did not disappear with the unitary state of 1707. Feeling Scottish was not a sentimental left-over of previous independence, but derived from the day-to-day workings of Scottish civil society as it affected people directly.

The Union between the Scottish and English Parliaments which took place in 1707 did not, by all accounts, much affect the lives of ordinary people or their immediate masters. 'High politics' were matters of state dealt with in London; 'low politics' allowed civil life to continue much as before. The middle classes – the lawyers, ministers and teachers – continued to run Scottish institutions, especially the 'holy trinity' of law, religion and education. With hindsight, it seems that the only kind of state which allowed the Scots and other national groups to retain such a high degree of civil autonomy was one in which the links between high and low politics were tenuous. It is also doubtful whether the Scots would have agreed to submerge their institutional autonomy into the British state if it had been a thoroughly 'modern' formation in which civil society and the state were firmly aligned. The British state – a state-nation, certainly not a nation-state – was formed in this rather curious way because no other Union was possible, or at least acceptable.

Why should an event like the Union of 1707 matter so much almost 300 years later? Put simply, it set the institutional infra-structure on to which Scottish national identity was grafted. Not only did such autonomy maintain and develop a high degree of self-governance in Scotland, but it did the same for national identity. Identifying oneself as Scottish was not simply some memory trace of pre-Union independence, but a reflection of the governing structures of Scottish civil society. It both derived from, and laid the basis for, nationhood.

Nationalism and national identity

There is another important dimension to be taken into account in understanding national identity. It is not singular, but several. There is not one national identity, but a plurality. In the late twentieth century the questioning of the historical basis of the 'nation-state' concept has been matched by a growing social-scientific interest in the concepts of nation, national identity and ethnicity, and their constructed and contested character. Nation is an 'imagined community' (B. Anderson, 1983). It is imagined insofar as it carries the image of communion with people one has never met; it implies community, a sense of deep and horizontal comradeship among people; it has limited though elastic boundaries; and it implies that its members have the right to determine their own future.

At the same time, there are different routes to and versions of national identity. The American sociologist Rogers Brubaker, in an important book published in 1992 entitled *Citizenship and Nationhood in France and Germany*, has argued that these two key European states took quite different routes to national citizenship which laid down who could participate in national life. In France, citizenship relates to a territorial community which derives from *Jus Soli*, a territorial jurisidiction which reflects the fact that France was first a state and then a nation. In Germany it was the other way round: nationhood came first, and with it an ethnic definition of national identity. There, citizenship was based on a community of descent, on *Jus Sanguinis*. Anyone with German blood was German, and the nation was defined as an organic, cultural, linguistic and racial community. Hence,

> The state-centred, assimilationist understanding of nationhood in France is embodied and expressed in an expansive definition of citizenship, one that automatically transforms second-generation immigrants into citizens, assimilating them – legally – to other French men and women. The ethnocultural, differentialist understanding of nationhood in Germany is embodied and expressed in a definition of citizenship that is remarkably open to ethnic German immigrants from Eastern Europe and the Soviet Union, but remarkably closed to non-German immigrants. (Brubaker, 1992, p. 3)

In other words, simply living on German soil does not confer national identity. In like manner we are becoming aware that what it means to be Scottish, English, British and so on changes over time. For example, as Graeme Morton's work shows, in early to mid-nineteenth century Scotland there was a strong sense of unionist-nationalism: that Scotland only became a full and equal partner of the British Union in 1707 because of (not despite) its successful wars of independence against England in the thirteenth and fourteenth centuries. It could then take part in a negotiation of constitutional equals, reinforced, as Linda Colley shows, by a common project of

Protestant liberalism and imperial militarism within the British Empire. This Protestant and unionist sense of Scottishness has been waning since at least the middle of this century, and we have grown accustomed in the late twentieth century to an ideological antithesis between unionism and nationalism. This has been reinforced by the cultural politics of Scotland in the 1980s and 1990s: writers, folk singers, rock musicians, painters, and sculptors have all claimed to be creating a new Scotland that is democratic, European, and firmly not English. In other words, a new sense of Scottish national identity has emerged which is distinctly at odds with the old, and which occupies a spot in the political spectrum much more to the left of centre than before.

To paraphrase Stuart Hall, we only know what it is to be Scottish because of the way Scottishness has come to be represented (Hall, 1992, p. 292). As we argued in Chapter 2, 'Nations' as such do not have some external or objective reality. If, then, we treat national identities not as some taken-for-granted categories we inherited at birth but as a culturally constructed category, we raise some interesting questions. How have they come to be formed and reformed? How and by whom are national identities constructed? In whose interests – class, gender, ethnicity – are they formed and mobilised? Who is included and excluded? Are there competing definitions, and whose win out? What, if any, are the political claims which attach to national identities? Are you more of a Scot if you vote SNP? Are you more English if you are a Tory? How and why have some versions of national identity waxed and waned? Why has the Labour Party rarely managed to appear 'English'? Is it simply to do with disproportionate numbers of Scots and Welsh in its leadership? And what is the relationship between national and state identities in these islands? The attempt, largely successful, to manufacture a cultural Irishness for political purposes is well known, as is the debate in the north of Ireland about versions of Irish and British national identities. In strict geographical terms Unionists are not in geographical terms 'British' at all. The point, of course, is that being British is a political aspiration, not a matter of geography.

The debate about national identity in Scotland reflects the constructed and contested nature of nationality. In Scotland's past these have taken a politico-religious form, as Willie Storrar (1990) has pointed out. His argument is that these have taken Catholic,

Protestant and latterly secular forms. Each carries its set of motifs, and rules for inclusion and exclusion. We have referred above to the diminution of the Protestant Unionist version of Scottishness which excluded Catholics in particular. In similar vein, we have seen a shift from right-wing to left-wing versions of Scotland. Nationalism has also migrated from a cultural to an explicitly political form.

What is a Scot?

The emergence of groups seeking to mobilise ethnic versions of Scotland in their quest to combat 'anglicisation' has aroused a broader debate about who is and can become Scottish. Put simply, we can identify criteria which are territorial, natal and ethnic. In other words, are you a Scot because you live in Scotland, because you were born in Scotland, or because your parents and forebears were Scottish, or some combination of these? Are some people more Scottish than others? The political consensus from the mainstream parties is that territoriality is sufficient, and it is interesting that the SNP has indicated that in an independent Scotland, when citizenship would have to be defined legally, this would be the key criterion. In an opinion poll in March 1992 for *The Scotsman* newspaper, when respondents were asked who they thought should qualify as a Scottish national in an independent Scotland, 58 per cent replied that anyone born in Scotland would qualify (a 'natal' definition); 39 per cent that anyone living in Scotland should (territoriality); and 18 per cent that someone with Scottish parents could be counted as Scottish (definition by descent). As regards variation, middle-class people tended to take a more 'territorial' view, as did people under 35, whereas there was no difference between the supporters of the political parties on this matter, the majority of each plumping for a 'natal' definition.

The key point about all social identities, including national ones, is that they are not given once and for all, but are negotiated. People's claims to an identity have to be recognised to be valid and operative. We have to be able to read the signs when claims are made, and treat them not as ready-made and fixed characteristics, but as aspirations made in a social and political context. Hence the claim of Northern Ireland Protestants to be British is not a statement of fact but an assertion made in hope rather than expectation. To be valid it has to be recognised by those on the mainland who hold the key to that identity. In a similar way, we have to be able to 'read' what lies behind the strong and consistent claims of people living in Scotland that they put their national identity above that relating to their current citizenship status. We can see this in comparison with similar ethnic groups within larger state formations. Luis Moreno has gathered data using his nationality question in the nations and regions of the Spanish state. Direct comparison is difficult, given quite different contexts, but the parallels are instructive. If we take 1992 as our benchmark, and focus on the two strongest national identities, that of the Catalans and the Basques, we find, if anything, Scottish national identity to be stronger than either (Table 9.7).

If we compare the ratios of 1 and 2 in each case to those of 4 and 5, we can see that whereas in Catalonia it is approximately 1.5:1, and in Euskadi 2:1, in Scotland it is 10:1, suggesting that in the political and cultural situation of 1992 the Scots were more assertive in terms of their national identity. The ratio in 1997 was almost 8 to 1. The obvious difference between Scotland and the one hand and Catalonia and Euskadi on the other is that far fewer claim 'British' than 'Spanish' nationality. Immigration into Catalonia and Euskadi in recent years partly explanains why substantial minorities in these places think of themselves as 'Spanish' rather than as Catalans or Basques. Furthermore, both Catalonia and Euskadi have autono-

Table 9.7   *National identity in Scotland, Catalonia and Euskadi in 1992 (X = Scottish, Catalan or Basque) (per cent)*

Respondent feels:	Scotland	Catalonia	Euskadi
1. X not British/Spanish	19	20	31
2. More X than British/Spanish	40	16	14
3. Equally X and British/Spanish	33	35	33
4. More British/Spanish than X	3	5	8
5. British/Spanish not X	3	23	14
Sample size	957	1200	1200

Sources: Scotland – data from SES 92; Catalonia and Euskadi – Moreno (1995).

mist Parliaments within the Spanish state, whereas Scotland does not yet have a Parliament in Edinburgh. When this comes about, there might be a decline in the assertion of Scottishness over Britishness because this political goal will have been achieved.

Forging new political identities: the European agenda

The final point to make is to underline the fluidity and contingent nature of national identity. It has to be interpreted as a response to an ongoing set of political and cultural relations rather than a once-and-for-all characteristic. The new parameter in late twentieth-century politics is Europe. Both Scottish and British politics cannot be understood without appreciating this dimension. On the one hand, the three main political oppositional forces in Scotland – Labour, the SNP and the Liberal Democrats – have found the European card an important one to play against an increasingly Eurosceptical Conservative Party, especially south of the border. In many respects the European identity provides an alternative to the British one. Both are Unions which require a trading-off of political decision-making for economic and political benefits. We are able to explore the European dimension of identity. In response to the question, 'Which of the following describes how you feel about your national identity', we obtained the results shown in Table 9.8.

There are different ways of reading this table. Being 'Scottish' and being 'Scottish and British' were the most salient forms of identity

Table 9.8 *National identity: Scottish, British and European*

Respondent feels:	*Con.*	*Lab.*	*Lib. Dem.*	*SNP*	*All*
Scottish only	26	41	31	62	42
Scottish and British	42	37	40	26	36
Scottish and European	4	6	7	8	6
British and European	8	8	15	4	7
Scottish, British and European	4	4	5	4	4
Sample size	96	363	96	132	882

Source: *Scottish Election Survey* (1997).

for most voters. Conservatives were more likely to emphasise their Britishness, while Labour and SNP supporters emphasised their Scottishness. Further calculations from the survey showed that 10 per cent of all voters (and 18 per cent of Liberal Democrats) claimed 'European' identity. The table shows how this Europeanness overlapped the other two types of identity: most people who felt European also felt either Scottish or British, or both.

We would be mistaken if we expected 'European' to become a competing political identity with either national or state ones, at least in their current form. Why cannot the EU become, in Benedict Anderson's phrase, an 'imagined community', a nation like any other? First, the conventional cultural identifiers like language and religion do not line up. You cannot make a national brick without a modicum of cultural straw of this sort. In Schlesinger's words, 'there is no predominant cultural nation that can become the core of the would-be state's nation and hegemonise Euro-culture' (1991, p. 17). Second, we know that nationalism grows best in a medium in which there is an Other: an enemy against which we can measure and develop our own identity. But who, if anyone, is to be that Other? Third, we have to consider a radically different environment for the European state (if that is what develops) from the one in which 'nation-states' emerged in the last two centuries. New state structures now emerge into a world framed by 'globalisation' and the impact of a world economy. The correspondence of the nation with the state, the cultural with the political, was always more of an aspiration rather than a reality, but in the social conditions of globalisation in the late twentieth century, the age of the nation-state (even as a dream) seems past its best.

What kind of Europe is on the agenda? It is significant that 'Europe' is as much defined by the plurality of expectations people have of it as by its reality. In the British context, 'Europe' has become a shorthand for quite diverse processes. To Scottish (and Welsh) nationalists it is a means of bypassing the British state so as to usher in a new political system more sympathetic to small nations. For many on the Liberal and Labour left it provides a viable political project towards federalising both Britain and Europe, and towards developing the social-democratic project which Conservative Governments after 1979 sought to bring to an end. For the radical right it offers enlarged economic markets without the hindrance of political regulation. And, of course, for the Conservative right it represents the most major threat to 'national' sovereignty for at least 500 years. We might conclude that much of Europe, whether negative or positive, lies in the eye of the beholder.

There is little doubt, however, that 'Europe' does not have the wherewithal to become a nation-state. It is far more likely to develop as *demos* than as *ethnos*, as a political rather than a cultural system, much, ironically, as 'Britain' did in the eighteenth century but, one hopes, without the pretensions to be a nation as well as a state. The best plan for the European Union would seem to be to work with rather than against the grain of post-modern, even post-nationalist, times. In this context we are seeing the reconceptualisation of notions of identity and of citizenship. In both cases the 'national' level focused on existing states becomes less salient. As Meehan points out (1993) in a discussion of citizenship and the European Unioin, legal status and the content of citizenship rights are not determined by conventional nationality alone. Instead, a new kind of multiple citizenship appears to be developing which recognises different identities and interests operating at various levels: local, regional, national and transnational.

Europeanness, if it develops beyond the embryonic stage, will have to work as a complement of, rather than a competitor to, rapidly changing state structures. Its future seems to lie in its association with democracy, pluralism and the rule of law, as a means of redressing the democratic deficit at the regional, national and supra-national levels. There seems to be little future in a Europe which translates its Europeanness as a restrictive, ethnically defined and exclusivist identity rather than one which is pluralist, territorial and inclusivist. This is a message not simply for Europe but for national identity in the modern world. In the final chapter we will examine the Scottish question in the context of a more general debate about the future of politics in the late twentieth century and the demand for new and better forms of participatory politics as the next century beckons.

10

The Scottish Question and the Future of Politics

Why look at Scotland? In nations which do not have independent legislatures, it is easy to assume that they do not have 'politics'. Scotland does not figure in conventional textbooks on British politics, which assume the homogeneity of the British state, or, at best, add a chapter on Scotland or 'the Celtic fringe'. Hence one immediate purpose of this book has been to tell Scotland's political story to redress the balance. When we do so, we find a narrative which connects with many of the key events and processes of British politics, but we cannot take for granted that these are the dominant ones, or that they have the same meaning and significance. In party political terms we have seen how, although the names of the parties are by and large the same, their histories, how they operate, their understandings and frameworks have been quite different. To take one example, we cannot explain the decline of the Conservative Party in Scotland simply with reference to social structural differences between Scotland and England. After all, many of the English regions have economic and social structures which are very similar to Scotland's, and yet their politics are different. Similarly, as we showed in Chapter 7, the Conservatives do badly among all social classes in Scotland, and have done for at least 20 years. In 1974 Conservative support in Scotland was between 11 and 15 percentage points lower in each class. By the 1992 election, the differential had grown to 16 percentage points among semi-skilled and unskilled manual workers, and to 23 percentage points among skilled non-manual workers. In 1997, despite the sharp fall in the Conservative vote in England, the differentials either stayed the same or increased slightly again: the difference was 14 percentage points in the professional and managerial class, 20 points among skilled nonmanual workers, 15 points among skilled manual workers, and 19 points among semi-skilled and unskilled manual workers.

The key to explaining this lies in the different agendas and discourses which now operate north and south of the border. To a degree, of course, they always have done. Scotland's civil society was never incorporated into England's, and its institutional autonomy helped to foster social and political systems which were always different. This is not to imply, however, that these systems were entirely different. In the middle of the nineteenth century, as we have seen, it was possible to be a Unionist and a nationalist at the same time. Scotland entered the Union of 1707 as a smaller, but equal, partner, and the argument that the Union was advantageous to Scotland because of, rather than in spite of, its historic independence has remained a key argument of Conservatives and Unionists. The problem for them has been that Unionism and nationalism have steadily diverged in the last 40 years to the point that they no longer seem compatible to much of the electorate.

Showing that Scotland's political history of the last 300 years is interesting and different is only one purpose of this book. We have also gone beyond that to show how, by analysing Scottish politics, we can see the way the wider world is going. Small nations are like corks in the sea. They are the first indicators of the way currents are flowing, and that the tide is turning. We have argued in this book that larger states may have more geo-political power, but they are often poor indicators of political and social change. Large states are also creations and expressions of older certainties which are themselves eroding. The eighteenth-century Enlightenment gave birth to the idea of the 'nation-state' in which political, cultural and economic power coincided, or at least were meant to. The political world was deemed to be made up of sovereign entities speaking and acting on behalf of culturally homogeneous and politically sovereign people. The fact that in reality few countries were like that was neither here nor there. The template on offer was the 'nation-state'. So powerful was this idea that even today 'nation' is treated as a synonym for 'state'.

Nothing has done more to question these old certainties than, ironically, the revival of nationalism in the late twentieth century. The irony lies in the fact that nationalism in its classical form was meant to be the ideological motor for creating nation-states in the eighteenth and nineteenth centuries, not their destruction in the late twentieth. Hence many writers, for example Hobsbawm (1990), have chosen to attack modern forms of nationalism as atavistic throwbacks to ethnic conflict. The word 'ethnic' is the clue: conventional academic wisdom has chosen to distinguish (following Kohn's influential entry in the 1950 edition of the *Encyclopaedia Britannica*) between Western and Eastern forms of nationalism, or civic versus ethnic. Western nationalism was deemed to be 'political' and rational, whereas Eastern forms were 'cultural' and mystical. Ernest Gellner (1983) has called this the 'dark gods' theory of nationalism, and Pi-Sunyer (1985) has argued that it is shared by writers of different political persuasions. He comments that: 'liberal scholarship has tended to look at nationalism, when it has done so at all, as an antique evil bound to give way to progress. Marxist theories generally treat nationalism as an ideological manifestation of some less-evident infrastructure' (1985, p. 254). As a result of this consensus, modern states were deemed to be expressions of civic, western nationalism, whereas developing, pre-modern states were easy prey for ethnic, eastern forms, reinforced by interpretations of modern events such as 'ethnic cleansing'. The optimistic legacy of modernisation theory, that 'progress' would replace ethnic with civic values, gave way to a more pessimistic assessment that some forms of nationalism were good, and others bad.

We have argued in this book that the old models and conventional explanations are losing their force. Not only are modern states less self-sufficient in economic and political terms, but they are not culturally homogeneous. They are increasingly being challenged at the supra-state level by new political formations such as the EU, and nations and regions within these states are becoming more assertive. A new kind of politics is emerging which emphasises the contingent nature of power, and above all the lack of correspondence between statehood and nation-ness. A reassessment has begun of the naturalness of the 'nation-state'. To some (Beetham, 1984) the nation-state is losing its political, economic and cultural integrity in a rapidly changing world. To others (Mann, 1993) the nation-state is adapting to these conditions rather than being destroyed by them, while others share the view of Mommsen that 'the nation-state is still with us as an essential principle of political organisation, but it is to be hoped that it will not resemble too closely its forerunners of the late 19th and early 20th centuries' (1990, p. 226). As a 'stateless' nation within the British state, Scotland provides new ways of understanding economic and political processes in the late twentieth century, and in particular recognition of the limited and shared nature of sovereignty.

Much of the reassessment of ways of explaining political and social change has focused on the changing economic context. 'Globalisation' has a particular resonance in Scotland. As we saw in Chapter 4, the relative openness of its economy is reflected in the substantial amounts of inward investment, and in the phenomenon of the branch-plant economy. This openness is in large part an outcome of the process of industrialisation which Scotland took part in from the eighteenth century as part of the British state and the British Empire. At its height, the Empire afforded Scottish capital opportunities for overseas investment. In the post-imperial age, Scotland's economic decline reflected its over-adaptation to imperial markets, and the need to find new sources of employment and economic enterprise. The evidence does not support the view that Scotland has become a poorly paid and underdeveloped region of the world economy. It is far more clear that economic change has itself been caught up in a constellation of political and social change. The old loyalties to indigenous elites which brought affiliation to Unionist politics have eroded, and been replaced with a set of social and political perspectives which have moved the Scottish electorate away from those of its southern neighbour.

Keynesian economic management was applied to Scotland in the post-war period as a solution to the need for industrial restructuring. Scotland, like other declining areas of the UK, relied more heavily on public initiative than on private enterprise. As the midwife of economic regeneration, the state devolved a considerable part of its administrative resources to the Scottish Office, which provided a powerful administrative apparatus or 'negotiated order' (Moore and Booth, 1989), and in turn fuelled the 'policy communities' in which the values and culture of decision-making elites helped to sustain a distinctive set of institutions and relationships within Scotland. The pattern of policy-making in Scotland, as we saw in Chapter 5, evolved in response both to strong local control over the institutions of civil society, as well as greater involvement by the state than elsewhere in Britain, mainly through the Scottish Office. With the election of right-wing Thatcherite governments from 1979, the state both withdrew from explicit ownership of economic assets and was at the same time shaped into a more interventionist instrument of social and political control. This policy of 'regressive modernisation' (Marquand, 1993) had its social and political base in southern England, and speeded up a process of political decline in the Conservative Party in Scotland which had been going on since 1955.

While the processes of industrial decline and economic restructuring were happening north and south of the border, their political outcomes were different, largely because the political and cultural agendas in Scotland had evolved differently (Chapters 6 and 7). Thus the political parties in Scotland had different histories and appeals, and a broad nationalist agenda was able to develop, fostered not only by the SNP but by the other non-Tory parties as well. In essence, Scotland and England diverged in terms of political behaviour because the agendas were set differently, rather than because economic and social structural processes diverged. The perception of Scotland as a separate unit of political and economic management coincided with the arrival of North Sea oil, which made it easier to imagine an alternative political future to the benefit of nationalists in general, and the SNP in particular. Even British-wide political developments opened up new Scottish political possibilities. The post-war belief in equal citizenship built into the welfare state could be mobilised in terms of Scotland's claim to equal treatment within the UK.

The broadening dimension of 'nationalist' politics in Scotland focused on the 'democratic deficit' whereby political control of the Scottish Office was constitutionally invested in the Westminster system. At a time when the gendering of politics was emerging as a key issue in debate, constitutional questions were mobilised as part of it. The demand for a Scottish Parliament, both within and outwith the British state, drew women who were underrepresented in both Scotland and Britain into the constitutional debate. Gender politics in Scotland, as we saw in Chapter 8, thus took a distinctive direction in its focus on the constitutional question.

The rise of nationalism is one reflection of a new form of identity politics. Issues of nationality and identity forefront the 'personal' dimension, and open up the taken-for-granted assumption of malestream politics. The quest for new forms of autonomy lends itself to challenges from groups relatively excluded from the political process, notably women, in such a way that demands for national and gender power interlock. Similarly, the quest for national identity is a highly personal one. In Cohen's words: 'Individuals "own" the nation; the nation conducts itself as a collective individual' (1994, p. 157). The power of nationalism in the modern world lies in its capacity to reconfigure personal identities and loyalties in a way more in tune with the social, cultural and political realities of the late twentieth century. Conventional nationalism stresses the cultural similarities of its members, and implies that political boundaries should be coterminous with cultural ones. Tamir (1993) observes that this 'thick' nationalism approach assumes that individuals are thereby locked into their cultural identity, and that it will be the paramount form of identity. On the other hand a more pluralistic, or 'thin', approach does not imply that ethnic identity will have priority over other forms of social identity including those of gender and social class. In Edward Said's words: 'No one today is purely one thing. Labels like Indian, or woman, or Muslim, or American are no more than starting points, which if followed into actual experience for only a moment are quickly left behind' (1993, p. 407).

This quest for identity politics does not necessarily imply that independent statehood will automatically follow. In Western politics in particular, there is an ongoing debate about the degree of autonomy required in the interlinked modern world. The issue is more likely to be expressed in terms of degrees of autonomy rather than its presence or absence. Hence there are similarities between Scotland, Catalonia and Quebec, to take notable examples, with regard to negotiated autonomy in the context of existing state and supra-state levels of power. A concomitant language has evolved which speaks of 'Home Rule', 'Autonomy' and 'Sovereignty-Association' respectively.

The terms of debate are increasingly defined by a complex set of reference points. In Scotland's case, these are the British state and the EU (just as for the Catalans they are the Spanish state and the EU and, for the Quebecois, Canada and the North American Free Trade Association). What these new reference points do is highlight the process of contingent negotiation between 'stateless' nations and existing state structures. In Scotland's case, as we saw in Chapter 3, the formal aspects of dependence versus independence are less significant than the actual ongoing processes of negotiation and compromise. To use an analogy, the ancient and formal marriage contract is a relatively poor guide to how partners will behave. If we view the 1707 Treaty of Union as a 'marriage of convenience' which was drawn up to suit the different interests of Scotland and England, we should not expect that the terms and conditions which applied nearly 300 years ago have been unmodified in the intervening period, or that the most recent modification – the post-1945 Scottish Office overseeing the Scottish Welfare State – should continue to work for the twenty-first century. The creation of a formally integrated and unitary state in 1707 sat alongside highly autonomous control of domestic policy in Scotland. The basic contradictions of the British state – centralist but *laissez-faire* – were never resolved, and have called into question the historic relationship between Scotland and the UK.

Only since the election of the Labour Government in 1997 has some resolution been sought, by means of the proposal to set up a Scottish Parliament in 2000. The two-question referendum held prior to the introduction of the Scotland Bill was designed as a legitimacy exercise to ward off expected Parliamentary opposition to what was expected to be a long and complicated piece of legislation. Having a second question on tax-varying powers had the added political value of removing from the electoral agenda the sensitive issue of taxation at a time when the conventional wisdom was that no electorate in the Western world would vote for, even potential, tax increases. In the event, given Labour's majority, there was little need for such caution, but the referendum gave to the Scottish Parliament a strong and independent source of legitimacy, confirming it as the settled will of the Scottish people. While the devolved Parliament is theoretically designed to be subject to the greater sovereignty of Westminster – as 'the crown in Parliament' – its legitimacy derives from this expression of popular will, and gives added force to the belief that in Scotland sovereignty resides in the people and not in the crown. We should remind ourselves at this point that the issue of the sovereignty of the Westminster Parliament has already been raised as a result of the UK's membership of the European Union. The creation of a Scottish Parliament adds another dimension.

The historic relationship between Scotland and the UK has circulated around debates on sovereignty, especially *vis-à-vis* Scotland, the UK and the EU. Defenders of the constitutional *status quo* have laid stress on the indivisibility of sovereignty despite the fact that the relationship between the UK and the EU over the last 20 years has called it into question. New attempts have been made to redefine sovereignty, and to shift it away from absolute and unitary definitions. In Neil MacCormick's words:

> Neither politically nor legally is any member state in possession of ultimate power over its own internal affairs; politically, the Community affects vital interests, and hence exercises political power on some matters over member states; legally, Community legislation binds member states and overrides internal state-law within the respective criteria of validity. (1995, pp. 9–10)

The juxtaposition here is between viewing sovereignty as property which is given up when another gains it, or viewing it more like virginity, which can be lost without another gaining it (MacCormick, 1995). As we pointed out in the last chapter, the EU seems to offer the possibility of new forms of citizenship rights based on *demos*, or civil rights, rather than deriving from *ethnos*, or cultural specificities (Meehan, 1993). In essence, we can transcend the state without dissolving the nation (MacCormick, 1995).

In sum, it is easy as well as misleading to see the Scottish question as deriving from local, specific issues with little wider significance. However the Scottish question is at the confluence of a number of wider key debates in the late twentieth century:

- the future of the 'nation-state' as an integrated political and cultural formation faced with challenges to its power;
- the implications of the EU for relationships between states and nations in the late twentieth century;
- the redefinition of sovereignty in such a way that top-down monolithic democracy breaks down to permit a redistribution of power as new political structures are formed.

The Scottish question should be interpreted as a manifestation of major social and political changes in the late twentieth century, and specifically the redefinition of the state. This process can be seen clearly at the level of the British state, which has undergone a major re-orientation towards its European partners and faced significant challenges from its constituent nations. The Scottish question becomes a question of the new world order.

Guide to Further Reading

1 Scottish Politics, 1707–1995

There are many histories of Scottish politics over the period since the Union. Some of the more accessible are by Smout (1970, 1986), Lenman (1977, 1981), S. and O. Checkland (1984), Fry (1987, 1992), Hutchison (1986), Harvie (1977, 1981b), Campbell (1985) and Marr (1992).

Analysis of Scottish elections (local, Westminster and European) back to the late 1970s can be found in *Scottish Affairs* and the *Scottish Government Yearbook* of the appropriate dates. The electoral events of 1992–7 are covered by Bennie *et al.* (1997) on the 1992 general election, Edwards (1997) and Denver (1997) on the 1997 general election in Scotland, Butler and Kavanagh (1997) on the UK general election, Jones (1997a) on the decision to hold a referendum on home rule, and Jones (1997b) and Pattie *et al.* (1998) on the outcome of the referendum.

2 Politics, State and Society

This chapter draws on four connected sets of literature. In the first place, there is a growing debate about the future of the 'nation-state'. Poggi (1978 and 1990) gives a theoretical grounding in the development of the state in the West, while Held (1992) provides a useful overview. Beetham (1974 and 1984) sets out the reasons why the nation-state has lost its autonomy, while Mann (1993) argues that it is diversifying, not dying. His previous collection *The Rise and Decline of the Nation-State* (1990) includes Mommsen's review which sets out the varieties of 'nation-state'. Giddens (1985, 1991) outlines the global implications of social change.

The second set of literature relates to nations and nationalism, and the key texts used here are Smith (1991), B. Anderson (1983), Gellner (1983), Nairn (1977), and Hobsbawm (1990). Smith argues that the nation is a pre-industrial formation, while Gellner and Anderson associate it with the rise of capitalism and industrialism. Anderson is critical of Gellner's account of the nation as a cultural and political fabrication, while Nairn focuses on the break-up of Britain as a state.

More generally, the chapter draws on a third literature on social change in which Stuart Hall (1992) provides a useful and accessible review in the context of social identity, while Bauman (1992a, b) and Giddens (1991) discuss the cultural and social implications of globalisation.

Finally, the distinction between state and nation in the British context is becoming a focus for interdisciplinary study, with Colley (1992) setting out how the British state was 'forged', and Marquand (1988, 1993) and Nairn (1977) focusing on its constitutional contradictions.

3 Politics and the Scottish Constitution

This chapter draws on the theory outlined in Chapter 2, and also on Hinsley (1966) and Geertz (1983) for sovereignty, Beetham (1991) for legitimacy, Bobbio (1988) and Vajda (1988) for civil society, and Livingston (1952, 1956), Bulpitt (1983), Duchacek (1986), Keating (1988) and Moreno (1993) for the territorial dimension of constitutions. The general argument in the chapter is dealt with more fully by L. Paterson (1994).

Eighteenth-century and nineteenth-century Scottish government is covered by the texts mentioned in the guide to reading for Chapter 1, and also by Hanham (1969b), Whetstone (1981), and Levitt (1988a and b). The political aspects of eighteenth-century and nineteenth-century Scottish identity are discussed by Kidd (1993), Morris (1990) and Morton (1994). The constitutional and political significance of religion is covered by C. G. Brown (1987, 1989, 1992, 1993), C. G. Brown and Stephenson (1992), S. J. Brown and Fry (1993) and Sher (1985). Philanthropy is the subject of the book by Checkland (1980). Popular politics is covered by Fraser (1989) and Breitenbach (1993). The example of education policy is traced by R. D. Anderson (1983, 1995), Bain (1978) and Myers (1972), and commercial law is discussed by Rodger (1992).

For the comparative sections of the chapter relating to the nineteenth century, see: for Finland, Klinge (1979, 1988), Andrén (1964), Engman and Kirby (1987) and Jutikkala and Pirinen (1979); for Bohemia, Korbel (1977), Bradley (1971), Garver (1978), Wandycz (1992), Kann and David (1984) and Morison (1992); and for Ireland, Lyons (1973), Foster (1988) and O. D. Edwards (1992).

The nature of the twentieth-century state – and particularly the nature of technocracy – can be found in the works by Bell (1976), T. Johnson (1972), Kumar (1978), McIntosh (1984), Middlemas (1979), Poggi (1978, 1990), Rimlinger (1971), Steward and Wield (1984), and Wilson (1985). These also provide critiques of technocracy, but for further political discussion of the problems of that kind of government, see Hayek (1960) from the political right and Rowbotham, Segal and Wainwright (1979) and the London Edinburgh Weekend Return Group (1979) from the left.

The development of the twentieth-century UK state is traced by Addison (1975). The Scottish Office is discussed by Hanham (1965, 1969a), Harvie (1981a and b, 1992), Levitt (1994, 1998), Midwinter, Keating and Mitchell (1991), Kellas (1989b), and Moore and Booth (1989). The special treatment of Scottish legislation is described by J. Burns (1960) and G. E. Edwards (1972). Scottish educational policy is dealt with by Gray, McPherson and Raffe (1983), McPherson and Raab (1988), Hutchison (1992) and

McPherson (1990). The delicate balance between unionism and nationalism is discussed by Finlay (1997).

For the comparative examples in the twentieth century, see: for Germany, Blair (1991), N. Johnson (1991), Forsyth (1991), Klatt (1991), Leonardy (1991) and Watts (1991); for Canada, Bothwell, Drummond and English (1989), Burgess (1993), Smiley (1977a, b and c), Mallory (1977), R. M. Burns (1977), Gallant (1977) and Heard (1991); and for the USA, Hodder-Williams (1987), McSweeney (1987), Pritchett (1984) and Vile (1961). There are good general essays on the regional dimension of several European states in the volumn edited by Wagstaff (1994).

The pressure for constitutional reform in the UK is described by Kellas (1989a, 1990, 1992) and by Hutton (1995). Popular attitudes towards constitutional reform are discussed in a special issue of *Scottish Affairs* entitled *Understanding Constitutional Change* (1998). The technical aspects of implementing reform were the subject of much attention between 1992 and 1997, notably by the Constitution Unit (for example, 1996). The last thirty years of the history of the debate about a Scottish Parliament can be traced in the documents collected by L. Paterson (1998), and *Scottish Affairs* has carried a series of articles since 1995 on the likely effects of a Parliament.

4   The Scottish Economy

We have discussed several debates surrounding the performance of the Scottish economy in this chapter, paying particular attention to underdevelopment/dependency (Smout, 1980; Wallerstein, 1980); branch-plant economy status (Rosie, 1991; Aitken, 1992); de-industrialisation (Aitken, 1992; Keegan, 1984), the north–south divide (Ashcroft, 1988), women in the economy (Engender, 1993, 1994 and 1995), the European dimension (A. Scott, 1991; G. McCrone, 1993; L. Paterson, 1994), and finally the impact of constitutional change on the economy (Bell and Dow, 1995; Heald and Geaughan, 1995; Hood, 1995; and Stevens, 1995). A discussion of the so-called tartan tax is available in Heald and Geaughan (1997) and a review of the financial arrangements for UK devolution can be found in Heald, Geaughan and Robb (1998). The business guide to devolution published by the Scottish Council Foundtion (1997) also provides another perspective on the Labour Party's plans for home rule.

For a more general discussion of the characteristics and trends in the Scottish economy we have cited the work of the journalist Keith Aitken (1992). His chapter provides an accessible overview for the non-economist. Aspects of Scotland's economy are also discussed by D. McCrone (1992), L. Paterson (1994) and J. Scott (1983) and its history by Lee (1997).

For key statistics on Scotland's economy, the Scottish Office publishes various relevant documents including *Scotland: An Economic Profile*, *Regional Trends* and *Scottish Abstract of Statistics*. Additonal data and discussion papers are to be found in the publication from the Fraser of Allander Institute at Strathclyde Business School, the *Quarterly Economic Commentary*. The unemployment data which have been used in this chapter were drawn in the main from Department of Employment statistics. The Unemployment Unit provides alternative figures based on the method of calculation before the numerous changes made by the government after 1979.

5 Policy-Making in Scotland

This chapter draws on debates on policy-making before identifying texts which are of direct relevance to Scotland. For our discussion of pluralism we have used the work of Jordan and Richardson (1987), especially their concepts of policy community and policy arena, and Grant and Sargent (1987) and Lively (1978) for a development of the 'arena' theory. Grant (1985), Grant and Sargent (1987) and Williamson (1989) have been used for assessments of corporatism, while Middlemas (1979) provides a historic perspective. The development of the idea of 'dualism' is to be found in the work of Goldthorpe (1984). Critiques of corporatism and incorporation are available by Coates (1989) and Panitch (1976, 1986). Kerry Schott (1984) summarises the main Marxist theories of the state and their application to the policy-making process. Implementation by Hogwood and Gunn (1984)

With regard to policy-making in Scotland, Moore and Booth's (1989) work is particularly useful and the authors develop the theme of 'negotiated order'. David McCrone's (1992) chapter on 'Who runs Scotland?' provides a civil society answer to the question, while Midwinter, Keating and Mitchell (1991) outline and discuss the key institutions involved in the process. L. Paterson (1994) sets the question of policy-making in the context of debates about the Union. The relative exclusion of women from the economic policy-making process is discussed by Anne Phillips (1983).

The journal *Scottish Affairs* (published from 1992 onwards) and the *Scottish Government Yearbook* (which appeared between 1977 and 1992) are valuable sources of articles on different aspects of policy in Scotland. Education policy has been extensively analysed, and has proved an instructive case study of the whole system of policy-making; examples of the writing on this are McPherson and Raab (1988), Hills (1990), Humes (1986 and 1995), Marker (1994), A. Brown and Fairley (1989), Fairley and Lloyd (1995) and Paterson (1997).

6 Party Politics in Scotland

There are several good general histories of Scotland which have useful political material. These include Smout's social histories (1970, 1986), and Sidney and Olive Checkland's industrial-political one (1984). Histories which focus on politics more centrally include Fry (1987) which has the benefit – compared with the more usual political orientation of Scottish writers – of taking a more critical right-of-centre stance, and covering Scottish politics from 1832 to the 1980s. Hutchison's account (1986) brings together scholarly work for the period 1832 to 1924, and Marr's more popular book *The Battle for Scotland* (1992) provides a useful complement to both. James Kellas's books include *The Scottish Political System* (1989b) which has gone into four editions, and his earlier *Modern Scotland* (1980); together these give a historical and institutional analysis of Scottish politics.

As regards the parties themselves, there are few analytical histories apart from Richard Finlay's excellent account (1994) of the early years (1918–45) of the Home Rule movement and the SNP. Neither the Labour Party nor the Liberals in Scotland have good political histories, although Red Clydeside has attracted a lively debate about its causes and consequences (see McLean, 1983, for a critical account, and Melling's and Damer's (both in 1980) for a more sympathetic one). The decline of the Conservative Party in Scotland has attracted academic interest including Mitchell (1990) and D. McCrone (1992), while Kellas has written a useful review (1994). The growing divergence between Scotland and England as regards voting behaviour has also attracted academic study (Miller, 1981; Kendrick and McCrone, 1989).

7   Electoral Change and Political Attitudes

The data used in this chapter comes from the *Scottish Election Surveys* and *British Election Surveys*, from the *British Social Attitudes Surveys* (access to which can be obtained from the Data Archive at Essex University) and from polling organisations (access to which is directly from the organisations themselves). Specific tables have been adapted from Curtice (1988, 1992) and from Butler and Kavanagh (1992). Most of the works mentioned under Chapter 1 above provide information on electoral trends.

8   Women and Scottish Politics

Very little has been published about the participation of women in contemporary politics in Scotland. This chapter, therefore, draws on some of the general literature on women's participation in politics in Britain and elsewhere, in addition to articles published on women in Scotland in *Scottish Affairs* and the *Scottish Government Yearbook*. An overview of the role of women in party politics is available in the edited collection by Lovenduski and Norris (1993). This comparative study includes a discussion of the claims made by women on political systems and the response of political parties. Norris and Lovenduski (1995) also provide a comprehensive guide to political recruitment in Britain with relation to gender, race and class. The authors consider who selects and how, who gets selected and why, and ask does the social bias in Parliament matter?

Esther Breitenbach (1993) gives a valuable account of the history of women in Scottish politics, an assessment of the impact of Thatcherism on women in Scotland (1989), and an examination of the women's movement in Scotland (1990). The campaigns by women for improved representation in Scotland and in a Scottish Parliament are explored by Catriona Levy (1991,

1992). The book published by the Woman's Claim of Right Group (1991) records the role played by the group before the 1992 general election and includes chapters on the role of women in Scottish society.

The *Gender Audits*, published by the women's group Engender (1993, 1994, 1995, 1996, 1997), are a valuable source of general information on the position of women in Scottish society. The Audits contain a comprehensive account of the representation of women in different institutions and organisations as well as information on the education, training and labour market position of women, women's poverty, women's health, the quality of women's housing and other issues including childcare and domestic violence. For example, they include details of the Zero Tolerance Campaign initiated by Edinburgh District Council and an assesment of the impact of local government reorganisation on women. A review of the research work conducted on women in Scotland is provided in an EOC funded report (Brown, Breitenbach and Myers, 1993). This publication was updated in 1997 (Myers and Brown, 1997).

Due to the absence of published texts on the role of women in Scottish politics, this chapter has relied on the results of a research study being carried out by one of the authors. Alice Brown acknowledges the financial assistance provided by the Leverhulme Trust and the Economic and Social Research Council (Award number R000234894) in supporting her project. She has carried out interviews with women in the political parties, trade unions and local government, in addition to women in women's groups and other organisations. She has been particularly concerned to trace the role of women in the campaigns for constitutional change. Brown (1995a) provides a discussion of the low participation rate of women in Scottish politics and the part played by them in plans for a Scottish Parliament; Brown (1995b) gives details of the Electoral Contract between women in the Scottish Labour Party and the Scottish Liberal Democrats. Three Waverley Papers, published by the Department of Politics at the University of Edinburgh, offer a more comprehensive discussion of recent political developments: Breitenbach (1995), Brown (1995c) and Mackay (1995). In addition some comparisons with the position of women in Irish politics are drawn by Brown and Galligan (1993 and 1995). A historical account of the role of women in Scottish society is provided by Breitenbach and Gordon (1992), and of women's work in the nineteenth and early twentieth centuries by Gordon and Breitenbach (1990).

9 Ethnicity, Culture and Identity

Only in the last decade or so has the issue of political and other forms of identity become the subject of academic study. Mackenzie's *Political Identity* (1978) remains a key text written by a political scientist who thought the concept too long neglected. Interest has been aroused among sociologists and social anthropologists who tend to have focused on social and cultural rather than political forms (see Hall, 1992, for an excellent and perceptive overview). Anthropologists such as Fredrick Barth (1969) have explored the highly constructed nature of ethnicity generally, and more recently Eriksen (1993) has written a good review of ethnicity and nationalism. Inconsistencies in the literature include a lack of connection between 'race' and political identity, although Hall's review is a rare example, and Rutherford's edited collection (1990) is valuable. There is a useful and growing literary analysis of nationalism and identity, of which Bhabha's (1990) collection is central. Storrar's review (1990) of Scottish identities from a historical and ecclesiastical viewpoint is also useful. Howson (1993) links the debates about national identity with those about gender. Crick (1993) discusses the decline of 'Britishness'.

Surveys and opinion polls are beginning to include questions on identity as it becomes more problematic and less taken-for-granted. These include the *Scottish Election Survey* for 1992 which used the question devised by Luis Moreno (1988) and which has been replicated in polls for *The Scotsman* newspaper. There is little contemporary literature on the extent to which 'British' and 'English' identities are not seen to be in conflict. *British Social Attitudes Surveys* contain much useful material on social and political attitudes, and these data are available from the Economic and Social Research Council Data Archive at Essex University, as are the British and Scottish election surveys.

References

Addison, P. (1975), *The Road to 1945*, London: Quartet.

Adonis, A. (1990), *Parliament Today*, Manchester: Manchester University Press.

Aitken, K. (1992), 'The Economy', in Linklater, M. and Denniston, R. (eds), *The Anatomy of Scotland*, Edinburgh: W. & R. Chambers.

Anderson, B. (1983), *Imagined Communities: Reflections on the Origin and Spread of Nationalism*, London: Verso.

Anderson, R. D. (1983), *Education and Opportunity in Victorian Scotland*, Edinburgh: Edinburgh University Press.

Anderson, R. D. (1995), *Education and the Scottish People, 1750–1918*, Oxford University Press.

Andrén, N. (1964), *Government and Politics in the Nordic Countries*, Stockholm: Almquist & Wiksell.

Ascherson, N. (1988), *Games with Shadows*, London: Hutchinson Radius.

Ashcroft, B. (1988), 'Scottish Economic Performance and Government Policy: A North–South Divide?', *Scottish Government Yearbook 1988*, Edinburgh: The Unit for the Study of Government in Scotland.

Bain, W. (1978), ' "Attacking the citadel": James Moncrieff's proposals to reform Scottish education, 1851–1869', *Scottish Educational Review*, 10, pp. 5–14.

Barth, F. (1969), *Ethnic Groups and Boundaries*, Bergen: Scandinavian University Books.

Bauman, Z. (1992a), *Intimations of Post Modernity*, London: Routledge.

Bauman, Z. (1992b), 'Soil, Blood and Identity', *Sociological Review*, 40 (4), pp. 675–701.

Beetham, D. (1984), 'The Future of the Nation State', in McLennan, G. Held, D. and Hall, S. (eds), *The Idea of the Modern State*, Milton Keynes: Open University Press, pp. 208–22.

Beetham, D. (1991), *Max Weber and the Theory of Modern Politics*, London: Allen & Unwin.

Beetham, D. (1991), *The Legitimation of Power*, London: Macmillan.

Bell, D. (1976), *The Coming of Post-Industrial Society*, Harmondsworth: Penguin.

Bell, D. and Dow, S. (1995), 'Economic Policy Options for a Scottish Parliament', *Scottish Affairs*, 13, pp. 42–67.

Bennie, L., Brand, J. and Mitchell, J. (1997), *How Scotland Votes*, Manchester: Manchester University Press.

Bhabha, H. (ed.) (1990), *Narrating the Nation*, London: Routledge.

Billig, M. (1995), *Banal Nationalism*, London: Sage.

Blair, P. (1991), 'Federalism, Legalism and Political Reality: The Record of the Federal Constitutional Court', in Jeffrey, C. and Savigear, P. (eds),

German Federalism Today, Leicester: Leicester University Press, pp. 63–83.

Bobbio, N. (1988), 'Gramsci and the Concept of Civil Society', in Keane, J. (ed.), *Civil Society and the State*, London: Verso, pp. 73–99.

Bogdanor, V. (1994), *Local Government and the Constitution*, Isle of Wight: Society of Local Authority Chief Executives.

Bothwell, R., Drummond, I. and English, J. (1989), *Canada since 1945: Power, Politics, and Provincialism*, Toronto: University of Toronto Press.

Bradley, J. F. N. (1971), *Czechoslovakia: A Short History*, Edinburgh: Edinburgh University Press.

Breitenbach, E. (1989), 'The Impact of Thatcherism on Women in Scotland', in Brown, A. and McCrone, D. (eds), *The Scottish Government Yearbook 1989*, Edinburgh: The Unit for the Study of Government in Scotland.

Breitenbach, E. (1990), ' "Sisters are Doing it for Themselves": The Women's Movement in Scotland', in Brown, A. and Parry, R. (eds), *The Scottish Government Yearbook 1990*, Edinburgh: The Unit for the Study of Government in Scotland.

Breitenbach, E. (1993), 'Out of Sight, Out of Mind? The History of Women in Scottish Politics', *Scottish Affairs*, 2, pp. 58–70.

Breitenbach, E. (1995), 'The women's movement in Scotland in the 1990s', New Waverley Papers, Politics Series 95–4, University of Edinburgh.

Breitenbach, E. (1997), ' "Curiously rare?" Scottish women of interest', *Scottish Affairs*, 13, pp. 82–94

Breitenbach, E., Brown, A. and Myers, F. (1998), 'Understanding women in Scotland'. *Feminist Review*, forthcoming.

Breitenbach, E. and Gordon, E. (1992), *Women in Scottish Society 1800–1945*, Edinburgh: Edinburgh University Press.

Brown, A. (1989), 'The Context of Change: the Scottish Economy and Public Policy', in Brown, A. and Fairley, J. (eds), *The Manpower Services Commission in Scotland*: Edinburgh: Edinburgh University Press.

Brown, A. (1991), 'Thatcher's Legacy for Women', *Radical Scotland*, 50, April/May, pp. 10–12.

Brown, A. (1995a), 'Legislative Recruitment in Scotland: The Implications for Women of a New Parliament', Paper for ECPR Joint Workshops, Bordeaux, 27 April–2 May.

Brown, A. (1995b), 'The Scotswoman's Parliament', *Parliamentary Brief*, April.

Brown, A. (1995c), 'Plans for a Scottish parliment: did women make a difference?', New Waverley Papers, Politics Series 95–2, University of Edinburgh.

Brown, A., Breitenbach, E. and Myers, F. (1993), *Equality Issues in Scotland: A Research Review*, EOC Research Discussion Series, 7, Manchester: EOC.

Brown, A., Breitenbach, E. and Myers, F. (1994), 'Researching women in Scotland: problems and opportunities', *Scottish Affairs*, 8, pp. 71–85.

Brown, A. and Fairley, J. (eds) (1989), *The Manpower Services Commission in Scotland*, Edinburgh: Edinburgh University Press.

Brown, A. and Galligan, Y. (1993), 'Changing the Political Agenda for Women in the Republic of Ireland and in Scotland', *West European Politics*, (2), pp. 165–89.

Brown, A. and Galligan, Y. (1995), 'Why So Few Seats in the House for Irish and Scottish Women?: Women's Views from the Periphery of Europe', paper presented to Women and Politics in Ireland Conference, Dublin, 25 March.

Brown, S. and McIntyre, D. (1993), *Making Sense of Teaching*, Buckingham: Open University Press.

Brown, C. G. (1987), *The Social History of Religion in Scotland, 1780–1914*, London: Methuen.

Brown, C. G. (1989), 'Religion and Social Change', in Devine, T. M. and Mitchison, R. L. (eds), *People and Society in Scotland, vol. I, 1760–1830*, Edinburgh: John Donald, pp. 143–62.

Brown, C. G. (1992), 'Religion and secularism', in Dickson, A. and Treble, J. H. (eds), *People and Society in Scotland, vol. III, 1914–1990*, Edinburgh: John Donald, pp. 48–79.

Brown, C. G. (1993), *The People in the Pews: Religion and Society in Scotland since 1780*, Glasgow: The Economic and Social History Society of Scotland.

Brown, C. G. and Stephenson, J. D. (1992), '"Sprouting wings"?: Women and religion in Scotland, c.1890–1950', in Breitenbach, E. and Gordon, E. (eds), *Out of Bounds: Women in Scottish Society, 1800–1945*, Edinburgh: Edinburgh University Press, pp. 95–120.

Brown, S. J. and Fry, M. (1993), *Scotland in the Age of the Disruption*, Edinburgh: Edinburgh University Press.

Brubaker, R. (1992) *Citizenship and Nationhood in France and Germany*, Cambridge, Mass: Harvard University Press.

Bryant, C. 'Social Self-Organisation, Civility, and Sociology: A Comment on Kumar's "Civil Society"', *British Journal of Sociology*, 44 (3) pp. 397–401.

Bryson, V. (1992), *Feminist Political Theory: An Introduction*, London: Macmillan.

Bulpitt, J. (1983), *Territory and Power in the United Kingdom*, Manchester: Manchester University Press.

Burgess, M. (1993), 'Constitutional Reform in Canada and the 1992 Referendum', *Parliamentary Affairs*, 46, pp. 363–79.

Burns, J. (1960), 'The Scottish Committees of the House of Commons, 1948–1959', *Political Studies*, 8, 272–96.

Burns, R. M. (1977), 'Second Chambers: German Experience and Canadian Needs', in Meekison, J. P. (ed.), *Canadian Federalism: Myth or Reality*, Toronto: Methuen, pp. 188–214.

Butler, D. and Kavanagh, D. (1992), *The British General Election of 1992*, London: Macmillan.

Butler, D. and Kavanagh, D. (1997), *The British General Election of 1997*, London: Macmillan.

Campbell, R. H. (1985), *Scotland since 1707: The Rise of an Industrial Society*, Edinburgh: John Donald.

Checkland, O. (1980), *Philanthropy in Victorian Scotland: Social Welfare and the Voluntary Principle*, Edinburgh: John Donald.

Checkland, S. and O. (1984), *Industry and Ethos: Scotland 1832–1914*, London: Edward Arnold.

Christianson, A. (1996), 'Imagined corners to debatable lands: passable boundaries', *Scottish Affairs*, 17, pp. 120–34.

Coates, D. (1989), *The Crisis of Labour*, Oxford: Philip Allan.

Cohen, A. P. (1994), *Self-Consciousness: An Alternative Anthropology of Identity*, London: Routledge.

Colley, L. (1992), *Britons: Forging the Nation, 1707–1837*, New Haven, Conn: Yale University Press.

Commision of the Future of the Voluntary Sector in Scotland (1997), *Head and Heart*, Edinburgh: Scottish Council for Voluntary Organisations.

Constitution Unit (1996), *Scotland's Parliament: Fundamentals for a New Scotland Act*, London: Constitution Unit, University College.

Craig, F. W. S. (1989), *British Electoral Facts 1832–1987*, Chichester: Parliamentary Research Services.

Crewe, I., Sarlvik, B. and Alt, J. (1977), 'Partisan Dealignment in Britain, 1964–1974', *British Journal of Political Science*, 7, pp. 129–90.

Crick, B. (1989), 'An Englishman considers his passport', in Evans N. (ed.), *National Identity in the British Isles*, Coleg Harlech occasional papers in Welsh studies, no. 3.

Crick, B. (1993), 'Essay on Britishness', in *Scottish Affairs*, 2, pp. 71–83.

Crick, B. and Millar, D. (1991), *To Make the Parliament of Scotland a Model for Democracy*, Edinburgh: John Wheatley Centre.

Curtice, J. (1988), 'One nation?', in Jowell, R., Witherspoon, S. and Brook, L. (eds), *British Social Attitudes: The Fifth Report*, Aldershot: Gower, pp. 127–54.

Curtice, J. (1992), 'The North-South Divide', *British Social Attitudes Survey*, 9, pp. 71–88.

Curtice, J. (1996), 'One nation again?', in Jowell, R., Curtice, J., Park, A., Brook, L. and Thomson, K. (eds), *British Social Attitudes: the 13th Report*, Aldershot: Gower, pp. 1–17.

Damer, S. (1980), 'State, Class and Housing: Glasgow, 1885–1919', in Melling, J. (ed.), *Housing, Social Policy and the State*, London: Croom Helm.

Danson, M., Fairley, J., Lloyd, M. G., and Newlands, D. (1990), 'Scottish Enterprise: An Evolving Approach to Integrating Economic Development in Scotland', in Brown, A. and Parry, R. (eds), *Scottish Government Yearbook 1990*, Edinburgh, The Unit for the Study of Government in Scotland.

Denver, D. (1997), 'The 1997 general election in Scotland: an analysis of the results', *Scottish Affairs*, 20, pp. 17–35.

Dey, I. and Fraser, N. (1982), 'Scotland at Sea – the Government, the Recession and Scottish Unemployment', *Scottish Government Yearbook 1982*, Edinburgh: The Unit for the Study of Government in Scotland.

Dicey, A. V. (1950), *Introduction to the Study of the Law of the Constitution*, London: Macmillan.

Duchacek, I. D. (1986), *The Territorial Dimension of Politics: Within, Among, and Across Nations*, Colombo: Westview.

Edwards, G. E. (1972), 'The Scottish Grand Committee, 1958–1970', *Parliamentary Affairs*, 25, pp. 303–25.

Edwards, O. D. (1992), 'Who Invented Devolution?', in Paterson and McCrone (eds), *The Scottish Government Yearbook 1992*, Edinburgh: The Unit for the Study of Government in Scotland, pp. 36–49.

Edwards, O. D. (1997), 'The strange death of unionist Scotland and Wales: an Irish perspective', *Scottish Affairs*, 20, pp. 1–16.

Elliot, W. (1927), *Toryism and the Twentieth Century*, Oxford: Philip Allan & Co.

Engender (1993), *Gender Audit*, Edinburgh: Engender.

Engender (1994), *Gender Audit*, Edinburgh: Engender.

Engender (1995), *Gender Audit*, Edinburgh: Engender.

Engender (1996), *Gender Audit*, Edinburgh: Engender.

Engender (1997), *Gender Audit*, Edinburgh: Engender.

Engman, M. and Kirby, D. (1987), *Finland: People, Nation, State*, London: Hurst.

Eriksen, T. H. (1993), *Ethnicity and Nationalism: Anthropological Perspectives*, London: Pluto Press.

Fairley, J. (1989), in Brown, A. and Fairley, J. (eds), *The Manpower Services Commission in Scotland*, Edinburgh: Edinburgh University Press.

Fairley, J. (1995), 'The Changing Politics of Local Government in Scotland', *Scottish Affairs*, 10 (Winter), pp. 35–46.

Fairley, J. (1996), 'Scotland's new local authorities and economic development', *Scottish Affairs*, 15, pp. 101–22.

Fairley, J. and Lloyd, M. G. (1995), 'Economic Development and Training: the Roles of Scottish Enterprise, Highlands and Islands Enterprise and the Local Enterprise Companies', *Scottish Affairs*, no. 12 (summer), pp. 52–72.

Fairley, J. and Paterson, L. (1991), 'The Reform of Vocational Education and Training in Scotland', *Scottish Educational Review*, 23, pp. 68–77.

Finlay, R. (1994), *Independent and Free: Scottish Politics and the Origin of the Scottish National Party, 1918–1945*, Edinburgh: John Donald.

Finlay, R. J. (1997), *A Partnership for Good? Scottish Politics and the Union Since 1880*, Edinburgh: John Donald.

Firn, J. (1975), 'External Control and Regional Policy', in Brown, G. (ed.), *The Red Paper on Scotland*, Edinburgh: Edinburgh University Students' Publication Board.

Forsyth, M. (1991), 'Introduction', in Jeffrey, C. and Savigear, P. L. (eds), *German Federalism Today*, Leicester: Leicester University Press, pp. vii–ix.

Foster, R. F. (1988), *Modern Ireland, 1600–1972*, Harmondsworth: Penguin.

Fraser, W. H. (1989), 'Patterns of Protest', in Devine, T. M. and Mitchison, R. L. (eds), *People and Society in Scotland, vol I, 1760–1830*, Edinburgh: John Donald, pp. 268–91.

Fry, M. (1987), *Patronage and Principle: A Political History of Modern Scotland*, Aberdeen: Aberdeen University Press.

244   *References*

Fry, M. (1992), *The Dundas Despotism*, Edinburgh: Edinburgh University Press.
Gallant, E. (1977), 'The Machinery of Federal-Provincial Relations', in Meekison, J. P. (ed.), *Canadian Federalism: Myth or Reality*, Toronto: Methuen, pp. 216–28.
Gamble, A. (1988), *The Free Economy and the Strong State*, London: Macmillan.
Garver, B. M. (1978), *The Young Czech Party, 1874–1901, and the Emergence of a Multi-Party System*, New Haven, Conn: Yale University Press.
Geertz, C. (1983), 'Centers, Kings, and Charisma: Reflections on the Symbolics of Power', in Geertz, *Local Knowledge: Further Essays in Interpretative Anthropology*, New York: Basic Books, pp. 121–46.
Gellner, E. (1983), *Nations and Nationalism*, Oxford: Blackwell.
Giddens, A. (1985), *The Nation-State and Violence*, London: Polity Press.
Giddens, A. (1991), *Modernity and Self-Identity*, London: Polity Press.
Goffman, E. (1973), *The Presentation of Self in Everyday Life*, New York: Overview Press.
Goldthorpe, J. (1984), *Order and Conflict in Contemporary Capitalism*, Oxford: Oxford University Press.
Gordon, E. and Breitenbach, E. (1990), *The World is Ill-Divided*, Edinburgh: Edinburgh University Press.
Grant, W. (ed.) (1985), *The Political Economy of Corporatism*, London: Macmillan.
Grant, W. and Sargent, J. (1987), *Business and Politics in Britain*, London: Macmillan.
Gray, J., McPherson, A. and Raffe, D. (1983), *Reconstructions of Secondary Education: Theory, Myth and Practice since the War*, London: Routledge.
Hall, S. (1992), 'The Question of Cultural Identity', in Hall, S. (ed.), *Modernity and Its Futures*, Cambridge: Polity Press, pp. 273–316.
Hanham, H. J. (1965), 'The creation of the Scottish Office', *Juridical Review*, 10, pp. 205–44.
Hanham, H. J. (1969a), 'The development of the Scottish Office', in Wolfe, J. N. (ed.), *Government and Nationalism in Scotland*, Edinburgh: Edinburgh University Press, pp. 51–70.
Hanham, H. J. (ed.) (1969b), *The Nineteenth Century Constitution, 1815–1914*, Cambridge: Cambridge University Press.
Harvie, C. (1977), *Scotland and Nationalism: Scottish Society and Politics, 1707–1977*. London: Allen & Unwin.
Harvie, C. (1981a), 'Labour and Scottish government: the age of Tom Johnson', *Bulletin of Scottish Politics*, 2, pp. 1–20.
Harvie, C. (1981b), *No Gods and Precious Few Heroes*, London: Edward Arnold.
Harvie, C. (1992), 'Scottish Politics', in Dickson, A. and Treble, J. H. (eds), *People and Society in Scotland, vol. III, 1914–1990*, Edinburgh: John Donald, pp. 241–60.
Hayek, F. (1960), *The Constitution of Liberty*, London: Routledge & Kegan Paul.

Heald, D. and Geaughan, N. (1995), 'Financing a Scottish Parliament', paper presented to John Wheatley Conference, Edinburgh, April.

Heald, D. and Geaughan, N. (1997), 'The tartan tax: devolved variation in income tax', *British Tax Review*, 5 (forthcoming).

Heald, D., Geaughan, N. and Robb, C. (1998), 'Financial arrangements for UK devolution', *Regional and Federal Studies* (forthcoming)

Heard, A. (1991), *Canadian Constitutional Conventions*, Oxford: Oxford University Press.

Held, D. (1992), 'The Development of the Modern State', in Hall, S. and Gieben, B. (eds), *Formations of Modernity*, London: Polity Press.

Hills, L. (1990), 'The Senga Syndrome: Reflections on 21 years in Education', in Paterson, F. M. S. and Fewell, J. (eds), *Girls in their Prime*, Edinburgh: Scottish Academic Press, pp. 148–66.

Hinsley, F. H. (1966), *Sovereignty*, London: Watts.

Hobsbawm, E. (1990), *Nations and Nationalism since 1780*, Cambridge: Cambridge University Press.

Hodder-Williams, R. (1987), 'Making the Constitution's Meaning Fit for the 1980s', in Smith, J. (ed.), *The American Constitution: The First 200 Years*, Exeter: University of Exeter Press, pp. 97–110.

Hogwood, B. W. and Gunn, L. A. (1984), *Policy Analysis for the Real World*, Oxford University Press

Hood, N. (1995), 'Inward Investment and Scottish Devolution: Towards a Balanced View', working paper, Glasgow: Strathclyde International Business Unit.

Howson, A. (1993), 'No Gods and Precious Few Women: Gender and Cultural Identity in Scotland', *Scottish Affairs*, 2, (Winter), pp. 37–49.

Hughes, J. (1994), 'Employment in Scotland: A Preliminary Note', unpublished paper, October.

Humes, W. (1986), *The Leadership Class in Scottish Education*, Edinburgh: John Donald.

Humes, W. (1995), 'The Significance of Michael Forsyth in Scottish Education', *Scottish Affairs*, 11, pp. 112–30.

Hutchison, I. (1986), *A Political History of Scotland 1832–1924: Parties, Elections and Issues*, Edinburgh: John Donald.

Hutchison, I. G. C. (1992), 'The Scottish Office and the Scottish universities', in Carter, J. and Withrington, D. (eds), *Scottish Universities: Distinctiveness and Diversity*, Edinburgh: John Donald, pp. 56–66.

Hutton, W. (1995), *The State We're In*, London: Jonathan Cape.

Ignatieff, M. (1994), *Blood and Belonging*, London: Vintage.

Inter-parlimentary Union (1997), *Men and Women in Politics: Democracy Still in the Making: a World Comparative Study*, Geneva.

Johnson, N. (1991), 'Territory and power: some historical developments', in Jeffrey, C. and Savigear, P. (eds), *German Federalism Today*, Leicester: Leicester University Press, pp. 8–22.

Johnson, T. (1972), *Professions and Power*, London: Macmillan.

Johnston, R., Pattie, C. J. and Allsopp, J. G. (1988), *A Nation Dividing? The Electoral Map of Great Britain, 1979–87*, Harlow: Longman.

Jones, P. (1997a) 'Labour's referendum plan: sell-out or act of faith?', *Scottish Affairs*, 18, pp. 1–17.

Jones, P. (1997b), 'A start to a new song: the 1997 devolution referendum campaign', *Scottish Affairs*, 21, pp. 1–16.

Jordan, A. G. and Richardson, J. J. (1987), *British Politics and the Policy Process*, London: Allen & Unwin.

Jutikkala, E. and Pirinen, K. (1979), *A History of Finland*, London: Heinemann.

Kann, R. A. and David, Z. V. (1984), *The Peoples of the Eastern Habsburg Lands, 1526–1918*, Seattle: University of Washington Press.

Keating, M. (1988), *State and Regional Nationalism*, Brighton: Wheatsheaf.

Keating, M. (1995), 'Scotland in the UK: A Dissolving Union?', paper presented to ECPR Workshop, Bordeaux, April.

Keegan, W. (1984), *Mrs. Thatcher's Economic Experiment*, Harmondsworth: Penguin.

Kellas, J. (1980), *Modern Scotland* (rev. edn), London: Allen & Unwin.

Kellas, J. (1989a), 'Prospects for a New Scottish Political System', *Parliamentary Affairs*, 42, pp. 519–32.

Kellas, J. (1989b), *The Scottish Political System* (4th edn), Cambridge: Cambridge University Press.

Kellas, J. (1990), 'Constitutional options for Scotland', *Parliamentary Affairs*, 43, pp. 426–34.

Kellas, J. (1992), 'The Scottish Constitutional Convention', in Paterson, L. and McCrone, D. (eds), *Scottish Government Yearbook 1992*, Edinburgh: The Unit for the Study of Government in Scotland, pp. 50–8.

Kellas, J. (1994), 'The Party in Scotland', in Seldon, A. and Ball, S. (eds), *Conservative Century: The Conservative Party since 1900*, Oxford: Oxford University Press.

Kendrick, S. and McCrone, D. (1989), 'Politics in a Cold Climate: The Conservative Decline in Scotland', *Political Studies*, 37, pp. 589–603.

Kidd, C. (1993), *Subverting Scotland's Past: Scottish Whig Historians and the Creation of an Anglo-Scottish Identity, 1689–c.1830*, Cambridge: Cambridge University Press.

Klatt, H. (1991), 'Centralising Trends in the Federal Republic: The Record of the Kohl Chancellorship', in Jeffrey and Savigear (eds), *German Federalism Today*, Leicester: Leicester University Press, pp. 120–37.

Klinge, M. (1979), 'The Growth of Finnish National Consciousness in the Age of the Enlightenment – the Economic, Social and Cultural Factors', in Dyrvik, S., Mykland, K. and Oldervoll, J. (eds), *The Satellite State in the Seventeenth and Eighteenth Centuries*, Bergen: Universitetforlaget, pp. 174–84.

Klinge, M. (1988), *A Brief History of Finland*, Helsinki: Otava.

Korbel, J. (1977), *Twentieth Century Czechoslovakia*, New York: Columbia University Press.

Kumar, K. (1978), *Prophecy and Progress: the Sociology of Industrial and Post-Industrial Society*, Harmondsworth: Penguin.

Kumar, K. (1993), 'Civil society: An Inquiry into the Usefulness of an Historical Term', *British Journal of Sociology*, 44 (3) pp. 375–95.

Lapsley, I., Llewellyn, S. and Grant, J. (1997), *GP Fundholders: Agents of Change*, Edinburgh: Institute of Chartered Accountants of Scotland,

Lee, C. H. (1995), *Scotland and the United Kingdom*, Manchester: Manchester University Press.

Leijenaar, M. and Mahon, E. (1992), 'Power: To What End? The Extent and Impact of the Feminization of Power', paper presented to the Gender and Power workshop at the ECPR, University of Limerick.

Lenman, B. (1977), *An Economic History of Modern Scotland*, London: Batsford.

Lenman, B. (1981), *Integration, Enlightenment and Industrialisation: Scotland 1746–1832*, London: Edward Arnold.

Leonardy, U. (1991), 'The Three-Levels-System: Working Structures of German Federalism', paper presented to the International Political Science Association, Buenos Aires, 21–25 July.

Levitt, I. (1988a), *Government and Social Conditions in Scotland, 1845–1919*, Edinburgh: Scottish History Society.

Levitt, I. (1988b), *Poverty and Welfare in Scotland, 1890–1948*, Edinburgh: Edinburgh University Press.

Levitt, I. (1994), *The Scottish Office: Depression and Reconstruction, 1919–1959*, Edinburgh: Scottish History Society.

Levitt, I. (1998), 'Britain, the Scottish covenant movement and devolution, 1946–50', *Scottish Affairs*, 22, pp. 33–57.

Levy, C. (1991), 'Counting Women In', in Brown, A. (ed.), *Women in Scottish Politics*, Edinburgh: The Unit for the Study of Government in Scotland.

Levy, C. (1992), 'A Woman's Place? The Future Scottish Parliament', in Paterson, L. and McCrone, D., *The Scottish Government Yearbook 1992*, Edinburgh: The Unit for the Study of Government in Scotland.

Lieberman, S. (1989), 'Women's Committees in Scotland', in Brown, A. and McCrone, D. (eds), *The Scottish Government Yearbook 1989*, Edinburgh: The Unit for the Study of Government in Scotland.

Lively, J. (1978), 'Pluralism and Consensus', in Birnbaum, P., Lively, J. and Parry, G., *Democracy, Consensus and Social Contract*, London: Sage.

Livingston, W. S. (1952), 'A Note on the Nature of Federalism', *Political Science Quarterly*, 67, pp. 81–95.

Livingston, W. S. (1956), *Federalism and Constitutional Change*, Oxford: Clarendon Press.

London Edinburgh Weekend Return Group (1979), *In and Against the State*, London: Pluto Press.

Lovenduski, J. (1997), 'Gender Politics: a breakthrough for women', *Parliamentary Affairs*, 50 (4) pp. 708–19.

Lovenduski, J. and Norris, P. (eds) (1993), *Gender and Party Politics*, London: Sage.

Lovenduski, J. and Norris, P. (eds) (1996), *Women in Politics*, Oxford: Oxford University Press.

Lovenduski, J. and Randall, V. (1993), *Contemporary Feminist Politics*, Oxford: Oxford University Press.

Lyons, F. S. L. (1973), *Ireland since the Famine*, London: Fontana.

MacCormick, N. (1995), 'Sovereignty: Myth and Reality', *Scottish Affairs*, 11, pp. 1–13.

Mackay, F. (1995), 'The casse of zero tolerance: women's politics in action?', New Waverley Papers, Politics Series 95–1, University of Edinburgh.

Mackenzie, W. (1978), *Political Identity*, Harmondsworth: Penguin.

Mallory, J. R. (1977), 'The Five Faces of Federalism', in Meekison, J. P. (ed.), *Canadian Federalism: Myth or Reality*, Toronto: Methuen, pp. 19–30.

Mann, M. (1990), *The Rise and Decline of the Nation State*, Oxford: Blackwell.

Mann, M. (1993), 'Nation-States in Europe and other Continents: Diversifying, Developing, not Dying', *Daedalus*, 122 (3) pp. 115–40.

Marker, W. (1994), *The Spider's Web? Policy-Making in Teacher Education in Scotland, 1959–81*, Glasgow: Sales and Publications Unit, University of Strathclyde.

Marquand, D. (1988), *The Unprincipled Society: New Demands and Old Politics*, London: Fontana.

Marquand, D. (1993), 'The Twilight of the British State? Henry Dubb versus Sceptred Awe', *Political Quarterly*, 64 (2) pp. 210–21.

Marr, A. (1992), *The Battle for Scotland*, Harmondsworth: Penguin.

Maxwell, S. (1987), 'The Politics of Poverty in Scotland', in McCrone, D. (ed.), *Scottish Government Yearbook*, Edinburgh: Unit for the Study of Government in Scotland, pp. 81–98.

McAllister, I. and Rose, R. (1984), *The Nationwide Competition for Votes*, London: Francis Pinter.

McConnell, A. and Pyper, R. (1994), 'A committee again: the first year of the revived select committee on Scottish affairs', *Scottish Affairs*, 7, pp. 15–31.

McCrone, D. (1992), *Understanding Scotland: The Sociology of a Stateless Nation*, London: Routledge.

McCrone, D. and Elliott, B. (1989), *Property and Power in a City: The Sociological Significance of Landlordism*, London: Macmillan.

McCrone, D., Paterson, L. and Brown, A. (1993), 'Reforming Local Government in Scotland', *Local Government Studies*, 19, (1) pp. 9–15.

McCrone, G. (1985), 'The Role of Government', in Saville, R. (ed.), *The Economic Development of Modern Scotland, 1950–1980*, Edinburgh: John Donald, pp. 195–213.

McCrone, G. (1993), 'The Scottish Economy and European Integration', *Scottish Affairs*, 4 (Summer) pp. 5–22.

McIntosh, M. (1984), 'The Family, Regulation, and the Public Sphere', in McLennan, G., Held D. and Hall, S. (eds), *The Idea of the Modern State*, Milton Keynes: Open University Press, pp. 204–40.

McLean, I. (1983), *The Legend of Red Clydeside*, Edinburgh: John Donald.

McPherson, A. (1990), 'How Good is Scottish Education, and how Good is the Case for Change?', in Brown, A. and Parry, R. (eds), *Scottish Government Yearbook 1990*, Edinburgh: Unit for the Study of Government in Scotland, pp. 153, 67.

McPherson, A. and Raab, C. D. (1988), *Governing Education*, Edinburgh: Edinburgh University Press.

McSweeney, D. (1987), 'Political Parties and the Constitution in the Twentieth Century', in Smith, J. (ed.), *The American Constitution: the First 200 Years*, Exeter: University of Exeter Press, pp. 83–96.

Meehan, E. (1993), 'Citizenship and the European Community', *Political Quarterly*, 64 (2) pp. 172–86.

Mercer, K. (1990), 'Welcome to the Jungle: Identity and Diversity in Post-Modern Politics', in J. Rutherford (ed.), *Identity; Community, Culture and Difference*, London: Lawrence & Wishart, pp. 43–71.

Middlemas, K. (1979), *Politics in Industrial Society: The Experience of the British System since 1911*, London: Deutsch.

Midwinter, A., Keating, M. and Mitchell, J. (1991), *Politics and Public Policy in Scotland*, London: Macmillan.

Miller, W. (1981), *The End of British Politics? Scots and English Political Behaviour in the Seventies*, Oxford: Clarendon Press.

Mitchell, J. (1990), *Conservatives and the Union*, Edinburgh: Edinburgh University Press.

Mommsen, W. (1990), 'The Varieties of the Nation-State in Modern History', in Mann, M. (ed.), *the Rise and Decline of the Nation-State*, Oxford: Blackwell, pp. 210–26.

Moore, C. and Booth, S. (1989), *Managing Competition: Meso-Corporatism, Pluralism, and the Negotiated Order in Scotland*, Oxford: Oxford University Press.

Moreno, L. (1988), 'Scotland and Catalonia: The Path to Home Rule', in McCrone, D. and Brown, A. (eds), *The Scottish Government Yearbook*, Edinburgh: The Unit for the Study of Government in Scotland.

Moreno, L. (1993), 'Ethnoterritorial Concurrence and Imperfect Federalism in Spain', paper presented at the Joint Conference of the International Association of Centres for Federal Studies and the International Political Science Association on 'Federalism: A Contemporary Perspective', Centre for Constitutional Analysis, Kwae Maritane, South African Republic, 1–6 August.

Moreno, L. (1995), 'Multiple Ethnoterritorial Concurrence in Spain', in *Nationalism and Ethnic Politics*, 1 (1) pp. 11–32.

Morison, J. (ed.) (1992), *The Czech and Slovak Experience*. London: Macmillan.

Morris, R. J. (1990), 'Scotland: 1830–1914: The Making of a Nation within a Nation', in Fraser, W. H. and Morris, R. J. (eds), *People and Society in Scotland, vol. II, 1830–1914*, Edinburgh: John Donald, pp. 1–7.

Morton, G. (1994), 'Unionist Nationalism: The Historical Construction of Scottish National Identity, Edinburgh, 1830–1860', PhD thesis, Edinburgh University.

Myers, F. and Brown, A. (1997), *Gender and Equality in Scotland: A Research Review Update*, Research Discussion Series No.19, Manchester: EOC

Myers, J. D. (1972), 'Scottish Nationalism and the Antecedents of the 1872 Education Act', *Scottish Educational Studies*, 4, pp. 73–92.

Nairn, T. (1977), *The Break-Up of Britain*, London: Verso.

Norris, P. and Lovenduski, J. (1995), *Political Recruitment: Gender, Race and Class in the British Parliament*, Cambridge: Cambridge University Press.

Panitch, L. (1976), *Social Democracy and Industrial Militancy*, Cambridge: Cambridge University Press.

Panitch, L. (1986), *Working Class Politics in Crisis*, London: Verso.

Parliamentary Affairs (1995), *The Quango Debate*, special issue, April.

Parry, R. (1981), 'Scotland as a Laboratory for Public Administration', Paper presented to the Political Studies Association UK Politics Group Conference, Glasgow, September.

Parry, R. (1988), *Scottish Political Facts*, Edinburgh: T & T Clark.

Paterson, L. (1994), *The Autonomy of Modern Scotland*, Edinburgh University Press.

Paterson, L. (1997), 'Policy making in Scottish education: a case of pragmatic nationalism', in Munn, P. and Clark, M. (eds), *Education in Scotland*, London: Routledge, pp. 138–55.

Paterson, L. (1998), *A Diverse Assembly: the Debate about a Scottish Parliament*, Edinburgh: Edinburgh University Press, forthcoming.

Paterson, W. (1994), 'Britain and the European Union Revisited: Some Unanswered Questions', *Scottish Affairs*, 9 (Autumn) pp. 1–12.

Pattie, C., Denver, D., Mitchell, J. and Bochel, H. (1998), 'The 1997 Scottish referendum: an analysis of the results', *Scottish Affairs*, 22, pp. 1–15.

Phillips, A. (1983), *Hidden Hands: Women and Economic Policies*, London: Pluto.

Pi-Sunyer, O. (1985), 'Catalan Nationalism: Some Theoretical and Historical Considerations', in Tiryakian, E. and Rogowski, R. (eds), *New Nationalisms of the Developed West*, London: Allen & Unwin, pp. 254–76.

Poggi, G. (1978), *The Development of the Modern State*, London: Hutchinson.

Poggi, G. (1990), *The State: Its Nature, Development and Prospects*, Cambridge: Polity.

Pritchett, C. H. (1984), *Constitutional Law of the Federal System*, Englewood Cliffs, NJ: Prentice-Hall.

Rasmussen, J. (1983), 'The Electoral Costs of Being a Woman in the 1979 British General Election', *Comparative Politics*, 18, pp. 460–75.

Rimlinger, G. V. (1971), *Welfare Policy and Industrialisation in Europe, America, and Russia*, New York: Wiley.

Rodger, A. (1992), 'The Codification of Commercial Law in Victorian Britain', *The Law Quarterly Review*, 109, pp. 570–90.

Rosie, G. (1991), 'How Scotland is Losing the Heid', *The Scotsman*, 29 November.

Rowbotham, S., Segal, L. and Wainwright, H. (1979), *Beyond the Fragments*, London: Merlin.

Rutherford, J. (1990), *Identity: Community, Culture and Difference*, London: Lawrence & Wishart.

Said, E. (1993), *Culture and Imperialism*, London: Chatto & Windus.

Schlesinger, P. (1991), 'Media, the Political Order, and National Identity', *Media, Culture and Society*, 13, pp. 297–308.

Schott, K. (1984), *Policy, Power and Order*, New Haven and London: Yale University Press.

Scott, A. (1991), 'Scotland and the Internal Market', *Scottish Government Yearbook 1991*, Edinburgh: The Unit for the Study of Government in Scotland, pp. 31–43.

Scott, J. (1983), 'Declining Autonomy: Recent Trends in the Scottish Economy', *Scottish Government Yearbook 1983*, Edinburgh: The Unit for the Study of Government in Scotland.

Scottish Constitutional Commission (1994), *Further Steps: Towards a Scheme for Scotland's Parliament*, Edinburgh: Cosla.

Scottish Constitutional Convention (1990), *Towards Scotland's Parliament*, Edinburgh: Cosla.

Scottish Council for Voluntary Organisations (SCVO) (1997), *Head and Heart*, Edinburgh: SCVO.

Scottish Council Foundation (1997), *Scotland's Parliament: a Business Guide to Devolution*, Edinburgh: Scottish Council Foundation.

Scottish Office (1991), *Scotland: An Economic Profile*, Edinburgh: Scottish Office.

Sher, R. B. (1985), *Church and University in the Scottish Enlightenment*, Edinburgh: Edinburgh University Press.

Siltanen, J. and Stanworth, M. (1984), 'The Politics of Private Woman and Public Man', in Siltanen, J. and Stanworth, M. L. (eds), *Women and the Public Sphere: A Critique of Sociology and Politics*, London: Hutchinson, pp. 185–208.

Smiley, D. V. (1977a), 'Federal-Provincial Conflict in Canada', in Meekison, J. P. (ed.), *Canadian Federalism: Myth or Reality*, Toronto: Methuen, pp. 2–18.

Smiley, D. V. (1977b), 'Cooperative Federalism: An Evaluation', in Meekison, J. P. (ed.), *Canadian Federalism: Myth or Reality*, Toronto: Methuen, pp. 259–77.

Smiley, D. V. (1977c), 'Federalism and the Public Policy Process', in Meekison, J. P. (ed.), *Canadian Federalism: Myth or Reality*, Toronto: Methuen, pp. 366–74.

Smith, A. (1991), *National Identity*, Harmondsworth: Penguin.

Smith, J. (1984), 'Labour Tradition in Glasgow and Liverpool', *History Workshop Journal*, 17, pp. 32–56.

Smout, T. C. (1970), *A History of the Scottish People, 1560–1830*, Glasgow: Collins.

Smout, T. C. (1980), 'Scotland and England: Is Dependency a Symptom or a Cause of Underdevelopment?', *Review*, 3 (4) pp. 601–30.

Smout, T. C. (1986), *A Century of the Scottish People, 1830–1950*, London: Collins.

Stevens, J. (1995), 'The Scottish Public Finances in 1992/93', *Quarterly Economic Commentary*, 20 (3) pp. 74–7.

Steward, F. and Wield, D. (1984), 'Science, Planning and the State', in McLennan, G., Held, D. and Hall, S. (eds), *State and Society in Contemporary Britain*, Cambridge: Polity, pp. 176–203.

Storrar, W. (1990), *Scottish Identity: A Christian Vision*, Edinburgh: Handsel Press.

STUC (1994), *Towards the Next Century*, Glasgow: STUC.

Surridge, P., Paterson, L., Brown, A. and McCrone, D. (1998), 'The Scottish electorate and the Scottish parliament', in Paterson, L. (ed.), *Understanding Constitutional Change*, special issue of *Scottish Affairs*, pp. 40–63.

Swann, J. and Brown, S. (1997), 'The implementation of a national curriculum and teachers' classroom thinking', *Research Papers in Education*, 12 (1) pp. 91–114.

Tamir, Y. (1993), *Liberal Nationalism*, Princeton University Press.

Touraine, A. (1981), 'Une sociologie sans société', *Revue Française de Sociologie*, 22 (1) pp. 3–13.

Vajda, M. (1988), 'East-Central European perspectives', in Keane, J. (ed.), *Civil Society and the State*, London: Verso, pp. 333–60.

Vallance, E. (1979), *Women in the House: A Study of Women Members of Parliament*, London: Athlone Press.

Vile, M. J. C. (1961), *The Structure of American Federalism*, Oxford: Oxford University Press.

Wagstaff, P. (ed.) (1994), 'Regionalism in Europe', *Europa*, 1 (2/3) pp. 1–120.

Wallerstein, I. (1980), 'One Man's Meat: The Scottish Great Leap Forward', *Review*, 3 (4) pp. 631–40.

Wandycz, P. S. (1992), *The Price of Freedom: A History of East-Central Europe from the Middle Ages to the Present*, London: Routledge.

Watts, R. L. (1991), 'West German Federalism: Comparative Perspectives', in Jeffrey, C. and Savigear, P. (eds), *German Federalism Today*, Leicester: Leicester University Press, pp. 23–39.

Whetstone, A. E. (1981), *Scottish County Government in the Eighteenth and Nineteenth Centuries*, Edinburgh: John Donald.

Williamson, P. (1989), *Corporatism in Perspective*, London: Sage.

Wilson, J. Q. (1985), 'The Rise of the Bureaucratic State', in Rourke, F. E. (ed.), *Bureaucratic Power in National Policy Making*, Boston, Mass: Little, Brown, pp. 125–48.

Woman's Claim of Right Group (eds) (1991), *A Woman's Claim of Right in Scotland*, Edinburgh: Polygon.

Worsley, P. (1984), *The Three Worlds: Culture and World Development*, London: Weidenfeld & Nicolson.

Young, S. (1984), 'The Foreign-Owned Manufacturing Sector', in Hood, N. and Young, S. (eds), *Industry, Policy and the Scottish Economy*, Edinburgh: Edinburgh University Press.

Index